Texts in developmental psychology

Series Editor:
Peter Smith
Goldsmiths College, University of London

ALSO IN THE *TEXTS IN DEVELOPMENTAL PSYCHOLOGY* SERIES:

CHILD DEVELOPMENT: THINKING ABOUT THEORIES
Phillip T. Slee and Rosalyn H. Shute
0 340 80818 7

CHILDREN'S LITERACY DEVELOPMENT
Catherine McBride-Chang
0 340 80800 4

THE CHILD AT SCHOOL
Peter Blatchford and Anthony Pellegrini
0 340 73182 6

ATTACHMENT AND DEVELOPMENT
Susan Goldberg
0 340 73171 0

FRIENDS AND ENEMIES
Barry H. Schneider
0 340 73209 1

Ageing and Development:
Theories and Research

Peter G. Coleman MA, PhD, FBPsS, AcSS
Professor of Psychogerontology, The Schools of Psychology and Medicine, University of Southampton

Ann O'Hanlon MSc, PhD
Health and Lifespan Developmental Psychologist, Department of Psychology, Royal College of Surgeons in Ireland, Dublin

First published in Great Britain in 2004 by
Arnold, a member of the Hodder Headline Group,
338 Euston Road, London NW1 3BH

http://www.arnoldpublishers.com

Distributed in the United States of America by
Oxford University Press Inc.
198 Madison Avenue, New York, NY 10016

British Library Cataloguing in Publication Data
A catalogue record for this book is available from the British Library

Library of Congress Cataloging-in-Publication Data
A catalog record for this book is available from the Library of Congress
ISBN 13: 978-0-340-75894-6

1 2 3 4 5 6 7 8 9 10

What do you think about this book? Or any other Arnold title?
Please send your comments to feedback.arnold@hodder.co.uk

To the memory of Joep Munnichs and Jan-Erik Ruth,
pioneers in psychogerontology

Contents

List of figures and tables

Figures

Tables

Picture credits

The authors and publishers would like to thank the following for permission to reproduce material in this book:

Figure 2.1, Titian, *An Allegory of Prudence*, *c.*1565 © National Gallery, London; Table 2.1, adapted with permission from Erikson, Erikson and Kivnick (1986) and Kivnick (1991); Figure 2.2, reproduced with permission from Levinson *et al.* (1978) Copyright © 1978 Daniel J. Levinson; Figure 3.1, reproduced with permission from McAdams and de St Aubin (1992); Table 3.1, adapted from Baltes and Smith (1990); Figure 3.2, reproduced with permission from Kramer (1990); Figure 3.3, after Staudinger *et al.* (1997); Figure 4.1, adapted with permission from Heckhausen, Dixon and Baltes (1989); Figure 4.2, reproduced with permission from Patricia M. Crittenden © 2002 Patricia M. Crittenden; Figure 6.1, reproduced with permission from Poon *et al.* (2005)

Every effort has been made to obtain necessary permission with reference to copyright material. The publishers apologise if inadvertently any sources remain unacknowledged and will be glad to make the necessary arrangements at the earliest opportunity.

Preface

This volume in the Texts in Developmental Psychology series owes its origin to the inspiration of Jan-Erik Ruth who, before his untimely death in 1997, had invited me to join him in writing a textbook on psychogerontology. His work has a direct connection with this volume since some of the material he shared with me forms the basis for the present Chapter 2. Jan-Erik sought to re-evaluate the mature years of life as a time of continued growth and development. Theory construction and its evaluation are essential to this process. Although this book is different in many respects from the one he had in mind, it does share with Jan-Erik a fundamentally positive view of human ageing. The years referred to variously as 'the second part of life', 'old age' and 'late' or 'later life' are not only quantitatively an important part of the life-span, they are and have always been an essential and meaningful part. It is not necessary for everyone to reach this stage of life, but it has probably been important for the stability and vitality of human culture that a significant minority of society did so in every period of history.

Now increasing proportions of the world's population live to experience old age, and for them, as for previous generations, it is important to use the opportunity this gives both to reflect on the life they have experienced so far and to give witness to lasting values. Later life can be a time for continued achievement and for fresh understanding, but above all it is a time for celebrating and for being 'in life', even as the conditions that sustain life become more precarious.

Since I had long wished to write a textbook on the developmental psychology of ageing, I was very pleased to be invited to contribute to this series, and would like to thank Peter Smith for this invitation, as well as for his continuing support through the completion of the project. Hopefully in the future this series, or other like-minded series, will contain a variety of developmental books on ageing. For the present it is sufficient that a developmental perspective on ageing is at least recognised as important to the study of developmental psychology.

Jan-Erik's definition of psychogerontology, as expressed in his contribution to Jim Birren's *Encyclopedia of Gerontology*, is 'a scientific field of inquiry focused on psychological development and aging' (Ruth, 1996: 281). This is the definition that Ann O'Hanlon and I have adopted as well, and our emphasis in this book is on development, adjustment and survival of the human spirit, despite the decrements of time. I would also like to thank Jim

Birren for the encouragement he has shown me, as well as so many other scholars and researchers working in the field of ageing studies.

I am especially grateful to Ann for joining me in writing this book. Her input reflects the contribution of a new generation of psychogerontologists, concerned to give more scientific weight to the subject, employing detailed theoretical reflection and rigorous empirical research methods. Theory and research are the twin themes of this book. We have judged it appropriate for a postgraduate text to show research in action. We have therefore selected illustrations of important work carried out in the last decade or so, and tried to express our critical appreciation of it, drawing attention to methodological features to be considered in evaluating research studies. At the same time we have given equal importance to theory. Jim Birren, some years back, noted the weakness of gerontology as a subject that had become 'data rich, but theory poor'. Theory needs research for its validation, but research also needs theory if it is to move in purposeful directions. We consider that psychogerontology now has a sufficiently rich theoretical basis for this also to be the subject of scrutiny in its own right.

The selection of material, both theories and research studies, reflects in large part our own interests. Naturally we think the subjects we have chosen are important ones – others may have different views – but, since the subjects of our own interests are more or less interrelated, we hope on this basis to have produced a more coherent and integrated account than would otherwise have been the case. The developmental psychology of ageing is potentially a very large subject. Ours is only one perspective. We look forward to future postgraduate texts in this field that will improve on our work.

This book is dedicated to the memory of Jan-Erik Ruth and also to that of Joep Munnichs who, like Jan-Erik, was a pioneer in establishing a constructive approach to human ageing, less dominated by concerns about biological degeneration, more about the potentialities of the human spirit. Joep acted as a mentor in my own life in the very best sense of that word. As a young researcher he validated my own interest in gerontology, introduced me to international and cross-cultural perspectives on ageing, confirmed the value of the subject despite the lack of public interest, and became and remained a close friend.

Peter G. Coleman
Southampton
July 2003

Introduction

1 Theory and research on ageing, continued development and adaptation to change

This book is concerned with theory and research about ageing, a phenomenon with which we tend to consider ourselves well acquainted, at least from the point of view of an observer, even if we have not experienced its effects at first hand. The danger, however, is that much of what we think we know about ageing is really only hearsay, received opinion that reflects the stereotyped and exaggerated attitudes about decline and fall that are so common in western culture. Because ageing is such a widespread and common phenomenon we need to look at it with fresh eyes, and preferably with a vision widened by experience that is not restricted to our own culture. Even though it can be defined precisely in biological terms, ageing is also from another perspective an entirely social construction. How we perceive age varies from culture to culture and from one historical period to another.

A principal value of theory, certainly in psychology and the other social sciences, is that it provides new perspectives on human phenomena that, because they are part of common social discourse, we think we already understand. Of course, we do have a basic understanding of human life just by being part of it, but we are always in need of new insights. Despite subsequent criticism of the details of his theory, Sigmund Freud's emphasis on the early origins of human emotional difficulties has made us see childhood in a way that is different to those of previous historical periods. As a result we are more ready than our predecessors to accept the importance of sensitive periods in people's lives. Yet theory can at the same time also be a hindrance to fresh thought. An overdeterministic view of the consequences of childhood trauma and deprivation for the rest of the life course may have made people overly pessimistic about the possibilities for therapy and positive interventions in adulthood. Even after the substantial research endeavours of Michael Rutter and others, outlining the redemptive effects of positive relationships in adolescence and young adulthood for those abused in childhood, the pessimistic legacy of childhood determinism still looms large in psychology and in society generally.

Theory, then, is a double-edged sword. It points in new directions while at the same time barring the way along alternative paths. It is for this reason that we are always in need of new theoretical input. Scientific understanding is always provisional – the best approximation until the next more comprehensive system is developed. A little humility is appropriate therefore when considering any one theory, and safety is better in numbers: keeping company with multiple theories, appreciating their strengths, recognising their weaknesses, observing how they get on together, and taking others on board as one can, is the best recipe for continued growth and development. Also, since we want to understand better the psychology of the individual person, we benefit from a wide range of perspectives. No one theory is likely to satisfy our curiosity about the complexities of human behaviour and experience.

Theory and research share an intimate relationship. Theory is the starting point for research. Research can also produce new theory, but without at least some interpretative framework it is impossible to make coherent observations. We need to take a stand on some basic assumptions. In psychology, for example, careful observation of one individual can provide ideas that form the assumptions for subsequent larger-scale investigations. It is often assumed that quality of research methodology is the main test of useful research. The choice of theoretical ideas to test, their origin and rationale, are seen as less controversial. But ideas, too, have their history and require nurture in conscientious and open observation of phenomena, with a self-conscious recognition of the many biases operating, which are often necessary for our own welfare, but which can sometimes serve to prevent important new insights emerging.

As part of a developmental psychology series, this book is concerned to emphasise the developmental aspects of ageing, thus its themes centre on continued development and adaptation to change. It is not primarily a book about the psychological decrements of ageing. These can be studied elsewhere, in reviews of the experimental psychology of later life and of cognitive ageing. Most of the early work in the psychology of ageing was of this character – for example, in the performance comparisons between different age groups pioneered by Sir Francis Galton. Their subsequent dominance of the field has made it almost natural to associate the psychology of ageing with the psychology of decline. But ageing is also about development.

There is often some confusion in terminology in this area, which requires clarification. Sometimes the term ageing is used to imply decline, as when we talk about a machine that ages, or when we refer to biological ageing. But psychological ageing is more ambiguous. Processes of loss and gain take place, often in interaction, throughout the life cycle. The child's naive approach to artistic representation, which we find so charming, along with a spontaneous response to self and others, often disappear as intellectual and social developments proceed. These are also forms of ageing, but we accept them more readily. If the losses of later life impress us more than the gains, it could be because we do not value the gains sufficiently and deplore the losses overmuch. Yet this is not necessarily so. Other cultures have perceived better the spiritual developments that physical decline makes possible. We need to become sensitised to cultivating more positive attitudes towards ageing, even towards its more extreme manifestations, which at present we find very hard to appreciate.

Even though this book focuses only on developmental issues, it must also be selective. The literature in this field is expanding fast and we cannot do justice to all current theoretical ideas, let alone all significant research findings. The book has been deliberately constructed in three main parts, each containing a theory chapter and a research chapter. The latter examine studies selected to represent research carried out on particular theoretical themes referred to in the previous chapter.

Part 1 (Chapters 2 and 3) considers normative developmental theories of ageing. This includes what have now become classic accounts of ageing written by such psychodynamic theorists as Carl Jung and Erik Erikson, as well as influential frameworks based on systematic observation such as Daniel Levinson's adult life structure, and recent developmental hypotheses, including Lars Tornstam's theory of gerotranscendence. It is possible to regard such theories as ideal models of adult development and ageing, thus not necessarily normative accounts of average trends with age, but descriptions of what is possible and also what is desirable in advanced age. Such theorising is presently not popular, since it seems too prescriptive to contemporary postmodern societies that prefer to leave value choices to the individual, but it contains important notions that continue to have resonance in research findings.

All these theories can be considered in historical terms as reactions to the denigration of age, which had become a habitual thought pattern by the early twentieth century. In their distinct ways Jung, Erikson and their successors as theorists of adult development have sought to provide guidance on the latter parts of the life course to modern humans. Interestingly, many such thinkers have found inspiration in studies of traditional cultures outside of the western mainstream.

As examples of research investigation we include three distinct areas of current research. The first is 'generativity', Erik Erikson's concept of midlife development, initially neglected by researchers, but in recent years the subject of some major studies carried out by the US personality theorist Dan McAdams and others. The second is wisdom, perhaps the most developmental of all concepts traditionally associated with age. Wisdom, however, as traditional culture also tells us, is not a necessary product of experience. Nevertheless that there should be a connection is suggested by the sense of dismay inherent in the adage 'there is no fool like an old fool'.

The final topic we have chosen to highlight is reminiscence, probably the most practical product so far of normative developmental theory, influenced by Erikson's late-life concept of 'integrity', but even more so by Robert Butler's theory of the 'life review'. This reflects another powerful traditional myth: the replaying of life's key scenes in the mind's eye preceding death. Empirical investigation, however, suggests that reminiscence has various other functions too, and that life review itself is not a universal phenomenon. Much of our discussion of reminiscence focuses on the conceptual clarification that often has to take place before research can progress.

In this pair of chapters we critically examine first theories and then empirical research. We draw attention to problems with the theoretical formulation, but emphasise also the creative power of theory – the way it can bring new questions into focus and stimulate interest in phenomena previously ignored or taken for granted. As regards the empirical studies, we have selected for the most part studies we admire, and have drawn attention to methodological points of interest, strengths as well as weaknesses in the research design.

Part 2 of the book (Chapters 4 and 5) considers approaches to development and ageing that have become more popular since the 1970s. These are mainly attributable to the rise of a dominant school of life-span developmental psychology, associated especially with the work of Paul Baltes, who has worked both in his native Germany and the United States. This group of researchers has come to eschew what it would regard as oversimplistic normative developmental theory in favour of a more plastic view of adult development. It has followed Erikson, though, in showing a preference for an interdisciplinary view of human development, in which social, historical and cultural influences have a key influence. These external influences, however, act not just to support or inhibit intrinsic psychological strivings and potential, but determine in a more direct way the structure and goals of life by establishing societal life patterns that guide development.

This is not necessarily a more deterministic view of ageing. Theorists working in this field stress human plasticity right until advanced age, as well as the possibilities for adaptation to change that exist both at the individual and the social level. Generalisation is difficult, though, except at the more abstract level of defining the limits of human competence and adaptability. Interesting questions arise about the different trajectories people can follow through life. Differentiation, not standardisation, is the norm and becomes greater with age. Thus there is no one path to 'successful ageing', rather different styles of living, managing change and surviving. The previously popular concept of 'adjustment' has been superseded by less value-laden concepts such as adaptation and coping. However, we have kept a link with developmental theory by including consideration of attachment styles as important influences upon adaptation to ageing.

We illustrate research in this area likewise with three distinct topic areas.

The first is attitudes to ageing on the part of older people themselves. This is a surprisingly neglected area of research, but one to which we have made recent contributions. It seems to us of great importance to future developments in the study of ageing that we pay more attention to the factors that influence people's prospective views on their own ageing process. The second is the protective role of personal relationships, crucial to an older person's sense of identity and continuing place in the world. The third topic is meaning and spirituality, also a relatively new but rapidly expanding area of research activity. As many novels that revolve around the theme of ageing demonstrate, questions of meaning, of one's own life but also of life in general, become critical in the later years.

Part 3 of the book (Chapters 6 and 7) may seem a surprising inclusion, since it is about advanced old age. This is the period of life that has come to be called the 'fourth age', when the optimal conditions for self-determination that distinguish the 'third age' begin to be seriously diminished by the biological limitations of ageing. This is not typically thought of as a time of development, but in fact very late life provides some of the most remarkable illustrations of adaptation, and of successful coping with very taxing life situations. Perhaps because we find it more difficult to identify with those facing massive loss of control and energy at this stage of life, we do not appreciate as we should the sometimes dramatic behaviour changes that older people display in the face of these challenges.

As Paul Baltes has emphasised, extreme old age, in its present pervasive character and duration, is a relatively new stage of life, and we do not yet have adequate conceptual frameworks with which to understand it. For example, it could not easily be conceptualised within the first two parts of this book. The classic developmental theories have typically not included consideration of the fourth age. Interestingly, Erik Erikson, as we know from the accounts of his widow Joan Erikson, had realised that his original eight-stage theory did not do justice to this new stage of life. Erikson himself lived to 92 and spent his last period in a nursing home. An extended life in some form of care situation is what awaits increasing numbers of us.

Similarly, the models of coping we have available for understanding other periods of life seem less than adequate when applied to the fourth age. We need to observe and reflect more on the psychological implications of this apparently expanding period of life. As theory in this area is scarce, in Chapter 6 we examine rather more what is known about the facts of this stage of life, and the concepts that have been put forward to understand it better. This is a field of work that needs much more attention. By the middle of this century the numbers of the very old – over 85 years – will have greatly increased. In the more wealthy parts of the world they may well exceed those aged under five years. We urgently need better conceptual frameworks for understanding the issues we are all likely to face either as caregivers or those receiving care, or as both in turn. Particular attention is given in this chapter to the study of dementia, but the understandable concerns about mental infirmity should not minimise more generalised issues about psychological adaptation to physical frailty.

In Chapter 7 we survey three developmental topics relating to advanced old age on which some significant research studies have been conducted in recent years: whether there are distinct developments to the self in advanced old age; the conditions for optimal living in institutional care; the application of attachment theory to improving quality of life for those with dementia. This last topic is an interesting example of how developmental theory from early life has been used to throw light on previously little understood phenomena at the other end of the life-span.

To conclude the book, in Chapter 8 we try to draw some brief lessons from this limited survey of theories and research on developmental aspects of ageing. We indicate some of the characteristics that we think are important for those wishing to work in this field. We also give some advice on further reading in developmental psychogerontology.

1

Normative developmental models of ageing

Wisdom is detached concern with life itself, in the face of death itself …
(Erikson *et al.*, 1986)

2 Theories of adult development: mid-life to old age

The last 30 years have seen an impressive growth in interest in the study of ageing. Enthusiasm has been kindled across the whole range of academic disciplines, particularly in biology, sociology and psychology but increasingly also in geography, anthropology and economics, and especially within the humanities (Cole *et al.*, 1992). This broadening of interest has led to new questions. We can see better now that the experience of ageing is the product not only of inevitable biological and psychological processes, nor even of the individual's particular life history and present circumstances, but also of the attitudes, expectations, prejudices and ideals of the societies and cultures in which people develop and grow old. Some present-day investigators have been led to explore how certain images, models and assumptions about the nature of ageing lie behind everyday speech, and how the very language we use may restrict and inhibit older people, and even promote their decline (Coupland and Coupland, 2003).

It is important therefore to begin this account of theories and ideas on development in later life with a reflection on the importance of attitudes towards ageing. Not so long ago it would have been thought paradoxical to say the least to include a chapter on 'development' in a book about ageing, let alone publish a whole book on the subject. A simplistic picture of the life-span as 'rise and fall' is deeply embedded within western culture. It is most graphically depicted in the medieval representations of the ages of man, in which the path of later life is one of remorseless decline (Burrow, 1986; Cole, 1992). The idealisation of young adulthood has been attributed by some to an 'iconic triphasic illusion', a gestalt of rise, peak and fall, which western culture tends to impose on life experience, as in the familiar domestic mantelpiece with the prized object placed at the top in the centre (Pruyser, 1975). It is important to bear in mind, however, that such taken-for-granted assumptions about the course of life may be very different in other cultures. For example, Hindu culture traditionally speaks of stages of life not in terms of rise and fall but of a forward cyclical movement (Ram-Prasad, 1995; Tilak, 1989).

Figure 2.1 The three ages of man: Titian's *An Allegory of Prudence*

   As a consequence of the social changes brought about in the historical period we call the Enlightenment, with its emphasis on reason rather than tradition, and the subsequent industrial and technological revolutions, attitudes to older people seem to have become more disrespectful (Fischer, 1978). Their expertise was seen as based on outmoded ways of behaviour and therefore as less relevant to a fast-changing society. It is not surprising, then, that when the first attempts were made in the nineteenth century to study scientifically the behaviour and performance of people of different ages, it was natural to adopt a pessimistic stance. Even a thinker as imaginative as Freud conformed to this pattern, viewing people above the age of 50 as too inflexible to be able to benefit from the practice of psychoanalysis (Biggs, 2005). Such thinking about age is so ingrained in our culture that we are hardly conscious of what we say. It lies behind many of our casual comments about age, such as 'being over the top' and 'past it', and the overwhelmingly unflattering depictions on birthday cards designated for older people. All such forms of 'ageism', the unjustified attribution of character-istics to a person on the basis of their chronological age, need to be com-bated firmly and resolutely, and with a skill commensurate to the very considerable forces of prejudice that lie behind them.

The encouragement of positive and constructive attitudes to older people is one of the main themes of this book. We now have the evidence that older people are capable of much more than we sometimes imagine, and that they can be flexible and learn new things. What often holds them back are the negative expectations of others and, perhaps even more importantly, of themselves. But we must also avoid going to the opposite extreme, by almost demanding new qualities from individuals regardless of their cir-cumstances and particular experience of life. As the distinguished French historian of old age Minois (1989) has commented, some of the societies cruellest to the old have been those in which the highest standards of wis-dom, serenity and maturity were expected of them. The questions sur-rounding growth and decline, change and development throughout life are very complex.

In this chapter we shall consider some of the theories and models pro-posed in the last century about ideal patterns of psychological development in later life. We will begin with changes from mid-life onwards and the evocative stage theories of adult life put forward by the psychoanalysts Carl Jung and Erik Erikson. The later theories of psychologists such as Daniel Levinson, David Gutmann and Lars Tornstam, which build on the ideas of Jung and Erikson but in addition reflect findings from empirical investiga-tions, will then be discussed. The following chapter will examine in more depth recent and current research on the particular aspects of these devel-opmental theories, namely the development of concern for subsequent gen-erations, the meaning of wisdom and its age-related character, and the functions and purposes of reminiscence.

Psychodynamic theories

Modern psychological theorising about human development, both in con-nection with cognition and personality, began in central Europe in the late nineteenth century. Whatever one may think of the detail of his theories, Sigmund Freud (1856–1939) revolutionised thinking about human behav-iour by proposing a dynamic model for human motivation, and opened up interest in much broader fields of psychology than cognitive performance alone. He stressed that people did not always act in rational ways, nor were they necessarily aware of the bases of their actions. Freud and his immedi-ate followers were not, strictly speaking, psychologists but clinicians involved in the treatment of mentally disturbed people, but in a short period of time at the turn of the century they produced a wealth of ideas about human motivation, often conflicting and so broad ranging that they have not yet been properly examined.

Freud himself was not particularly interested in ageing, or even in adult development, and his description of developmental stages is limited to the very early periods of life. His one-time colleague Carl Jung (1875–1961), however, who broke away from Freud to establish a rival school of psychoanalysis, did give much greater importance to what he called the second half of life. For him mid-life was a crucial turning point when the individual was provided with opportunities for new developments. These were less to do with involvement in the outside world but more interior processes that he referred to using the term 'individuation'. A person could achieve a new balance in personality – a man accepting his 'feminine' as well as 'masculine' aspects, for example. Jung placed great stress on the value of symbolic and religious experience in creating a state of harmony between the individual and the world around, and derived evidence for his theories from his wide-ranging knowledge of other cultures and societies.

Another of Freud's associates, Alfred Adler (1870–1937), also came to stress different aspects of human motivation. Disagreeing with Freud's emphasis on the overriding importance of sexuality he proposed that the prime motivating force in all people's lives is a feeling of inferiority. All individuals have this feeling to some extent because of the inferior position they once occupied as children, when power and privilege were exerted by adults. Some feel this more strongly than others – for example, as a result of physical defects or heavy-handed parenting. Adler saw subsequent developments of an individual's lifestyle as a means of compensating for feelings of inferiority. In extreme examples this could take the positive form of remarkable achievements by people with handicaps, but could also be expressed negatively in excessively self-assertive behaviour. Adler himself saw the most successful resolution of problems of inferiority to be in involvement with others, in the development of 'social interest'.

The particular relevance to psychogerontology of Adler's thinking lies in the fact that feelings of inferiority and loss of self-esteem can become major issues in late life (which we shall explore more in Chapter 6), as a result of physical decline, loss of status, physical beauty and mental capacities. At the same time, the possibilities for friendship and close relationships may appear diminished. In Adlerian terms rigid, rejecting attitudes on the part of older people and even disengagement can be seen as problems resulting from a fear of inferiority. The perspective of an Adlerian approach to therapy is essentially constructive. Inferiority feelings and neurotic lifestyles can be overcome by helping the individual to develop a wider interest in others and cultivate a sense of belonging.

Although the early psychoanalytic theorists contributed interesting ideas on personality development, these have proved difficult to investigate in practice. As clinicians they cited their own observations on patients, but these are open to the criticism that they are not independently verifiable observations and refer in any case to a biased sample of people not necessarily representative of the general population.

The establishment of acceptable methods of research has remained a major problem for the study of adult development. Although the observations and interpretations of the psychoanalysts can be criticised for their unrepresentative nature, the standard methods of experimental psychology – laboratory-based research on randomly selected individuals – also do not provide a suitable basis because of the artificiality of the situations that can be studied in this way. In the last 25 years, ethology (a branch of zoology dealing with the study of animal behaviour by means of observation in its natural setting) has had a growing impact on the study of human psychology. The challenge is to develop naturalistic methods of observation and systematic recording of human thought, feeling and behaviour. Psychologists have also been learning from the methods of anthropologists, who are experienced in recording activities and customs in different societies.

Jung: the mid-life transition

Of all the early psychodynamic theories, Jung's ideas have been the most influential in the field of ageing. Jung lived and worked in Switzerland, and trained there as a psychiatrist. He was strongly influenced at first by Freud's theories, but a mental breakdown which he suffered in mid-life led him to give more importance than did Freud to adult developments. Jung lived to a great age and wrote a lot. Much of his work has been assembled by editors after his death. Jung has many suggestive ideas about ageing, although they are often opaquely expressed.

According to Jung, the life course can be divided into four main parts: childhood, youth, middle age and old age. In Jung's thinking the child is guided by instincts, the unconscious processes in the psyche, while youth and middle age are gradually guided more by will – the conscious processes. In old age, and especially in late old age, more room should be given again for the unconscious. Too rational a life or too much unlived life leads eventually to psychological problems. The prevalence of depressive and neurotic reactions when approaching mid-life may have its origins in giving the rational will too much space, while suppressing more irrational and emotional urges. There is a danger for the mid-life-aged persona to grow increasingly rigid and eventually become intolerant and fanatic around the age of 50. In an oft-quoted passage Jung writes,

> We cannot live the afternoon of life according to the program of life's morning, for what in the morning was true will at evening be a lie. Whoever carries into the afternoon the law of the morning ... must pay with damage to his soul.
>
> (1972: 396)

There is, and should be, less emphasis on external activity and more on the internal developmental tasks to which Jung gave the name 'individuation', a process of becoming more fully integrated, more truly oneself.

Change and transition in mid-life is possible if the individual gives attention to his or her inner wishes and strivings. The result is increasing diversification and at the same time greater 'wholeness'. Thus, if you are a man, you can give increased space to your feminine features, and to your masculine features if you are a woman. Persons also can become increasingly familiar with their 'shadow' – that is, they can recognise better both the bad and the immoral aspects of themselves as well the good and moral aspects. Therefore, Jung advises an ageing person to show some serious attention to him or herself, to withdraw and spend more time in contemplation in order to get a deeper understanding of the self. He argues that the long period of human ageing must have a meaning of its own and not be simply a continuation of the developmental trends of earlier periods of life.

Jung criticises the tendency of the old to continue competing with the young and not to develop visions and knowledge of their own, which reflect the wisdom they have acquired through life experiences. In traditional culture, older adults are the guardians of group heritage and the mysteries of the tribe, which gives them a special position in their societies. Thus old age should consist of natural preparation for death, but in modern western societies many older adults seem so preoccupied with the realisation of what has been unlived that there is little room for developing a personal outlook on life and death. In Jung's view, too, the resistance of many people towards religion or the numinous can hamper their search for a soul, and hence produce difficulties in attaining wisdom. We have become too well educated and too rational, and have lost the 'art' of living and dying. For the sake of 'mental hygiene' it is necessary for an ageing person to discover death as a goal towards which he or she is striving. The shying away from this insight – previously learned through religious teachings – robs the second half of life of its purpose.

Jung agreed with Freud that there were two basic structures in the psyche: the conscious and the unconscious. He especially stresses the importance of the unconscious, since many of our reasons for acting are not necessarily known to us. We do not typically analyse the unconscious motives for our actions. Some of our fears (or phobias), as well as our compulsive behaviour (or neuroses), are derived from stressful life events or trauma, and they might not become visible to us if we do not actively engage in psychoanalysis. However, Jung differs from Freud in his presupposition that two different unconscious processes exist: the 'personal unconscious' and the 'collective unconscious'. The latter concept is Jung's alone and reflects his interest in myths, mysticism and religious issues.

He postulates that the collective unconscious is not something personally acquired, but something inherent in the human psyche, in much the same way as instincts or drives constitute general features of all humans and animals. These phenomena are 'patterns' of the human mind, which we have not acquired but have inherited from past generations. These unconscious processes become visualised in 'picture language', in the symbols shared by all cultures. He gives the term 'archetypes' to these mythological motives and basic images. The archetypes are visualisations projected into mythology, legends and fairy tales. Jung also sees religious stories as reflections of the collective unconscious. Some of them, like those relating the birth of a great prophet or redeemer, can be found in many different religious belief systems. Everyday experiences shared by all, such as the daily course of the sun and the regular alternations of day and night have imprinted themselves on the psyche, and become the basis of human thought. There are countless stories and beliefs connected to these regular fluctuations of nature in all cultures, and, according to Jung, the creative processes involved emanate largely from this part of the unconscious.

Jung stresses the importance of the mid-life crisis for establishing a new pattern of development for the second half of life. Mid-life is also a period of 'de-illusionment'. A person may have to admit that some of their earlier-life structures were not built upon realistic goals, and that some of their cherished relationships or activities have not turned out to be rewarding in the end. Some things that he or she hoped for did not turn out as wished, but it is not too late to create new dreams, to change life's path, to take up new interests, friendships and love relationships. The danger is of stagnation, or regression in this last passage of life, to become stuck in the present restricting life structure, and to give up hope.

The search for meaning in life may also lead to a wish to leave something behind. This has both positive and negative aspects. The creative pole can be seen in a person's wish to achieve or make something for which he or she can be recognised. The destructive pole might be seen in that one can recognise the negative and evil in one's life and in those that are close to one, and be unable to accept them. One has done harm to others and others have hindered one's own development. This is all part of the de-illusionment of this period of life. To tolerate the ambivalence that one both loves and detests aspects of one's self and one's life, including, for example, one's next of kin, also fosters the process of individuation.

Some of Jung's ideas now appear somewhat outdated. We no longer conceive the period of 'youth' as extended from puberty to mid-life. Adolescence has become an important stage of life in itself, and one with expanding boundaries. Present-day conceptions of ageing would also dispute the tendency to withdraw from society and productive work too early in order to contemplate the life that has already been lived and to prepare for death. The active newly retired of the early twenty-first century and those wishing to continue working into their seventies and beyond cannot adequately be described by these ideas alone. Moreover, the concept of a collective unconscious reflecting inherited human wisdom and influencing individual development has remained a speculative idea. Nevertheless many of Jung's ideas continue to provide food for thought to those concerned with developing new theories on adult life. The notion of the individuation process in mid-life has influenced the work of several contemporary developmental psychologists, including Roger Gould and Daniel Levinson who will be discussed later. Jung's greatest value to ageing studies is perhaps that he directed attention to the importance of the mature adult's transition to a different life perspective, and that the second half of life should not be judged by standards more appropriate to the first half.

Erikson: developmental tasks of later adulthood

Even more influential to the study of ageing has been the work of a psychodynamic theorist of the next generation – Erik Erikson. Like Jung, Erikson's primary focus was not on old age *per se*, but he argued that all stages of development, including early life, could not be studied without reference to the whole life-span. One of his main contributions to developmental psychology is his recognition that child development could not be understood outside the context of the child's social environment, and that this was peopled by adults who were confronted by their own developmental tasks. In his book *Childhood and Society* (first published, 1950; revised edition, 1963) Erikson provided a framework for the study of the life-span in terms of a series of psychosocial tasks to be fulfilled. Thus Jung describes the child's, or rather baby's, first psychological task in life as developing a sense of trust rather than a sense of mistrust. The ensuing childhood stages are characterised in terms of 'autonomy', 'initiative' and 'industry'. In adolescence the issue is the development of 'ego identity' versus 'identity diffusion' – Erikson is probably best known for his formulation of the concept of 'identity crisis' as something particularly characteristic of modern man – and in early adulthood the development of 'intimacy' versus a sense of 'isolation'.

In middle age the issue becomes one of 'generativity', a term coined by Erikson himself. He describes it as 'primarily the interest in establishing and guiding the next generation'. This can mean a focus on one's own family, but it can also include broader interests and concerns in the society in which one lives. The opposite state Erikson calls 'stagnation', for which he offers a succinct illustration: 'individuals, then, often begin to indulge themselves as if they were their own – or one another's – one and only child' (1963: 259). The task of the last stage of life is to attain 'ego integrity', an assured sense of meaning and order in one's life and in the universe, as against despair and disgust. This involves 'acceptance of one's one and only life cycle as something that had to be and that, by necessity, permitted of no substitutions' (Erikson, 1963: 260). Despair may be expressed in a feeling that one has failed and does not have the time to attempt another life or an alternative road to integrity, and also in a disgust with other people, especially the young.

Table 2.1 Erikson's eight psychosocial themes

Stage of emergence	Developmental task	Consequent life strengths
Infancy	Trust vs mistrust	Hope & faith
Early childhood	Autonomy vs shame, doubt	Wilfulness, independence & control
Play age	Initiative vs guilt	Purposefulness, pleasure & imagination
School age	Industry vs inferiority	Competence & hard work
Adolescence	Identity vs identity confusion	Values & sense of self
Young adulthood	Intimacy vs isolation	Love & friendship
Middle adulthood	Generativity vs stagnation	Care & productivity
Old age	Integrity vs despair	Wisdom & perspective

Erikson himself was born of Danish parents but brought up by a German-Jewish stepfather, so he became conscious of being different from the community in which he grew up. Like many other psychologists from continental Europe, he emigrated to the United States following the rise of Nazism, where he and others created a flourishing interest in developmental psychology. In Britain, too, notable contributions were made in this area by psychiatrists and psychoanalysts, especially by John Bowlby who demonstrated the negative consequences of maternal deprivation in early life for personality development, and whose theory of attachment we will refer to in following chapters for its implications for ageing (Bowlby, 1969). However, Erikson has been one of the few developmental theorists who, despite his primary interest in child and adolescent development, also took an explicit interest in late life. It is no wonder, then, that his statements about old age are so often quoted.

Erikson calls his stage theory 'epigenetic', using a term paediatricians of that time coined to describe the genetic plan, the step-by-step growth of the foetus. Behind Erikson's epigenetic principle we can see the idea of critical time periods, during which certain adaptive strengths of the ego develop. It seems that Erikson also got this epigenetic metaphor from the development of the organs of the foetus in the womb. In referring to the psychosocial crises development passes through, he uses the Greek word 'crisis' in its original meaning as challenge or turning point, as the driving force for development. When describing his developmental scheme, 'The

Eight Ages of Man', he writes,

> if the chart, for example, lists a series of conflicts or crises, we do not consider all development a series of crises: we claim only that psychosocial development proceeds by critical steps – critical being a characteristic of turning points, of moments of decision between progress and regression, integration and retardation.
>
> (Erikson, 1963: 270–1)

When the individual faces a developmental crisis, there is a conflict between a harmonious ('syntonic', as Erikson calls it) and a disruptive ('dystonic') element. Thus there are basically two paths for the individual to follow in resolving the conflict, one leading to progression and growth and the other to stagnation or regression. When the conflict is solved positively the individual reaches a new, qualitatively different stage of development. From the start Erikson stresses the necessity for experiencing both positive and negative emotional states as a prerequisite for personal growth. He was alarmed that some of his colleagues tended to gloss over the negative experiences in life, focusing only on the positive, and wanted to build something like an 'achievement scale' out of his harmonious (syntonic) psychological elements. Thus, when describing development in the first critical period of life, of the stage of 'trust' versus 'mistrust', he comments:

> they blithely omit all the 'negative' senses (basic mistrust, etc.) which are and remain the dynamic counterpart of the 'positive' ones through life. ... The personality is engaged with the hazards of existence continuously, even as the body metabolism copes with decay.
>
> (Erikson, 1963: 274)

In Erikson's theory the developmental stages are conceived as hierarchically arranged, the next stages presupposing the development of the previous stage. But even if the next stage is built upon the previous stage it does not replace that earlier stage. So when a person's development through the life cycle is coming to completion in old age, that stage represents all earlier stages added together, as well as all the psychological strengths (or drawbacks) that have evolved earlier. Throughout life the developmental phases come together to create a whole. They arise in turn, each part having its time of special ascendancy, until all parts have risen to form a functional whole. In the end, a person may reach the highest stage of ego integrity, gaining wisdom through pondering upon the life that has been lived and pulling the various parts of life's puzzle together, or at the opposite pole, experience despair at what life did not bring. Although he argues for a universal genetic blueprint, Erikson acknowledges that individuals can proceed through the stages in varying tempo and intensity.

Erikson also acknowledges the impact of socio-cultural factors. When drawing up his developmental chart for the first time – a chart he later modified somewhat, but never changed fundamentally – he wrote:

> the underlying assumptions for such a charting are:
> 1) that the human personality in principle develops according to steps predetermined in the growing person's readiness to be drawn toward and act with a widening social radius;
> 2) that society, in principle, tends to be so constituted as to meet and invite this succession of potentialities for interaction.
>
> (Erikson, 1963: 270)

The emergence of adaptive strengths is a sign of successful completion of each developmental stage or crisis. According to Erikson (1950; 1963) and Erikson *et al.* (1986), these strengths are:

- 'hope' when a sense of trust is developed in infancy
- 'will' that grows out of autonomy in early childhood
- 'purpose' resulting from seizing initiative in play age
- 'competence' that comes from industriousness in school age
- 'fidelity' growing out of attaining an identity cohesion in adolescence
- 'love' resulting from experiences of intimacy in young adulthood
- 'care' fostered by generativity in adulthood, and finally
- 'wisdom' as a result of attaining ego integrity in old age.

It is important to understand that there is ongoing process also in the final stage (Rosel, 1988). There is a balance to be achieved between integration and despair, which although it is in favour of the former, maintains the tension between them. It is in this state that the strength of wisdom develops. 'Wisdom is detached concern with life itself, in the face of death itself. It maintains and learns to convey the integrity of experience, in spite of the decline of bodily and mental function' (Erikson *et al.*, 1968: 37–8). The emotional and cognitive integration that wisdom is built upon results from vital involvement in diverging social spheres in earlier periods of life, such as politics, religion, economy, technology, the arts and the sciences. Wisdom is gaining the insight that a single individual is just one member of the family of man that shares characteristics in different generations and cultures.

> Each individual, to become a mature adult, must to a sufficient degree develop all ego-qualities mentioned, so that a wise Indian, a true gentleman and a mature peasant share and recognise in one another the final stage of integrity.
>
> (Erikson, 1963: 269)

In reflecting upon the life lived and the predicament of being human a heightened awareness or an existential identity develops. Wisdom, Erikson stresses, is 'truly involved disinvolvement'; the last stage is not only a continuation of the productivity and procreativity of the previous stage, it is a new way of being, 'which must remain loyal to a defined and planned role for old age within an order of wisdom' (Erikson *et al.*, 1986: 51).

Achieving ego integrity does not only involve reflecting on one's own life. It also implies an acceptance of the society that will continue after one's own death. Ill-health and the other stresses of later life may lead to self-absorption with one's own problems unless interest in the world outside can be maintained. Yet if society is to be so different from the one known, if it appears likely to overthrow, or indeed has already overthrown, the values that were so important in guiding one's own life, it can be harder to die. It needs courage and imagination to see through the different manifestations of human interests and activities, and to perceive an underlying constancy. Erikson refers to 'the comradeship with the ordering ways of distant times and different pursuits' and the 'relativity of all the various life styles which have given meaning to human striving' (1963: 260).

Acceptance of death is also central to this stage of life. In fact, Erikson brings his account of the life cycle full circle with the closing statement: 'it seems possible to further paraphrase the relation of adult integrity and infantile trust by saying that healthy children will not fear life if their elders have integrity enough not to fear death' (1963: 261). However, surprisingly few gerontologists have taken up this point. Butler's (1963) concept of the life review, which is triggered by awareness of the approaching end of life, is one example we will discuss in the following chapter. Disengagement theory – which we consider later in this chapter – also explicitly acknowledges death in arguing that older people prepare society for their eventual demise by disengaging first from key roles. Much gerontological writing, though, has almost given the impression that death is an avoidable rather than inevitable conclusion to old age. Joep Munnichs, more than any other psychogerontologist, continued to stress throughout his career that the growing awareness and acceptance of death and finitude are major developmental tasks of adulthood and a crucial part of the dynamic of ageing (Munnichs, 1966; 1992). There does appear now at last to be a growing interest in the relationship between ageing and death (see Neijmeyer and Werth, 2005).

Erikson's theory of development over the life-span has been highly influential, but also much criticised. Erikson never offered any clear time limits for when one developmental period ends and another begins. He is not particularly exact in describing developmental crises or the strengths that result after the successful completion of a developmental stage. He has also been seen as paying insufficient attention to negative developments – for example, the 'bad products' of human life, how a person can become a mentor of evil, ensuring that the next generation carries on with destruction as the previous one (Kotre, 1984).

We would argue, however, that the generality of Erikson's developmental scheme is one of its basic strengths, reflecting a high level of creativity. The more general the solution, the more it can be utilised in different fields.

Erikson's theory has been (and still is) an inspiration in many professional fields. For example, Helen Kivnick and others have employed it in care settings to develop assessment of 'life strengths' (Kivnick, 1991; Pomeroy *et al.*, 1997), thus teaching care staff to recognise the adaptive strengths elderly persons have developed over a long life, and to consolidate and build on them. Erikson's developmental scheme sprang also from narrative case studies of clients, as well as life histories of well-known persons such as Luther and Ghandi. These kinds of data are seldom exact, but are important stepping stones to theory construction.

Contrary to Freud, Erikson describes not only biological development and its consequences for the psyche but also the psychological development of the individual in the social system of which the individual is a part. It is rather paradoxical that in spite of Erikson's readiness to accept the impact of culture and historical period on development, one can criticise the theory for being so period and culture bound. The theory clearly reflects norms and values from the 1950s. The timing of life events, rights, obligations and roles tied to different ages – the social construction of the life-span – has changed since then. The claim of universality for the theory, meaning it would also fit other time periods and other cultures without modification, does not hold.

As he grew older, Erikson seems to have become more and more aware of the shortcomings in earlier descriptions of late life. In his last book, *Vital Involvement in Old Age. The Experience of Old Age in Our Time*, written together with his wife and Helen Kivnick, he raised the question of the need to add further stages to his scheme, but refrained from doing so in the end:

> Actually, we have already faced the question of whether a universal old age of significantly greater duration suggests the addition to our cycle of a ninth stage of development with its own quality of experience, including, perhaps, some sense or premonition of immortality.
> (Erikson *et al.*, 1986: 336)

Since her husband's death Joan Erikson has continued to ponder on the need for changing the theory. In a letter to social gerontologist Lars Tornstam, to whose gerotranscendence theory we shall refer later, she wrote after becoming acquainted with the theory:

> When I got to 91 myself, I became aware of the inadequacy of the words 'wisdom' and 'integrity', feeling that they in no way represent[ed] what I was experiencing as an elder. ... So boldly I revised the eight stages ... including a ninth and tenth stage, which even attempt to deal with 'gerotranscendence'.
> (Cited in Tornstam, 1996a: 48)

We shall return in Chapter 6 to the issues of a distinct psychology of advanced old age.

Does this mean that those researchers and professionals who find developmental schemas useful should feel free to change and modify Erikson's system? To make a chart based on the norms and values of the period, and the surrounding socio-cultural systems would actually be in line with Erikson's basic thinking. So far no one has dared do that, however, and this influential system still stands as it appeared when it was first created in 1950. One of its lasting achievements is to have brought to the forefront of gerontological concern questions to do with the psychological and social conditions necessary for later life to flourish.

Theories based on empirical investigation

The theories we have considered so far have been based on clinical and other experience, as well as considerable personal reflection, but were not developed in the context of empirical enquiry. The opportunity for the large-scale research required to validate adult developmental theory, including the necessary academic infrastructure of institutional support for such investigation, did not begin to be put in place until the 1950s. One of the first centres to emerge in the field of ageing studies was established by the Committee for Human Development at the University of Chicago, a collaborating group of scholars that included both sociologists and psychologists. The theories that developed from their pioneering work came to provide more precise ideas on developmental patterns of ageing in the 1950s and 1960s (Cumming and Henry, 1961; Havighurst and Albrecht, 1953; Neugarten, 1964). However, we begin this survey of research-based theory with the somewhat later work of the life-span psychologist Daniel Levinson, working at Yale University, whose ideas are based more explicitly on those of Jung and Erikson. Levinson is probably the best known of a number of a psychologists working in the 1960s and 1970s investigating Jung's concept of the mid-life transition (Levinson, 1977). Levinson placed this work within an ambitious conceptual framework that covered the whole adult life-span.

Levinson: the mid-life transition in men's lives

In the final publication derived from the initial project, *The Seasons of a Man's Life* (1978), Levinson *et al.* (1978) presented the distillation of ideas developed from in-depth interviews with 40 American men (aged 35–45), followed over two years (thus a relatively small group of men studied over a short period of adult life). These were a group of workers in industry, academic biologists, business executives and novelists. In-depth biographical interviews lasting a total of 10–12 hours per person were conducted on issues such as education, work, marriage, friendships, leisure, and political and religious activities. Levinson adopted a 'non-directive' method of interviewing. Although covering an overall framework of topics, the interviewers were consciously sensitive to the feelings these men expressed as they spoke, and attempted to follow themes that had obvious meaning for them. For each person a biography was later reconstructed based on these interviews. In order to create some hypotheses Levinson also used a more diversified data set drawn from descriptions of men's lives found in biographies, autobiographies, poetry and novels, as well as key works in the western literary canon written by authors such as Dante and Shakespeare. In this book Levinson also gave credit to the psychological theoreticians who had inspired him, notably Freud, Jung and Erikson.

Like Erikson, Levinson identified developmental periods, but larger in number and more delineated in character. He divided these developmental phases into 'eras', and into 'periods' within these eras. He also distinguished between stable and turbulent periods in development, the main transitions constituting turning points between eras. The developmental periods thus vary in dynamism. Some have to do with finding one's way in a totally new era, whereas others refer to a more calm settling-down in an already established era of life. The stable periods ordinarily last about six to eight years, and the transitional periods four to five. The anatomy of the life cycle is given by the eras and there are four eras lasting about 25 years each: childhood and adolescence (age 0–22), early adulthood (17–45), middle age (40–65) and late adulthood (60-plus). In an earlier paper Levinson (1977) also mentioned a fifth era, 'Late, late adulthood' (80-plus), but he seems never to have elaborated upon this. The first study he conducted allowed him to describe in detail two of these eras, early and middle adulthood, and to each he ascribed four periods. In what follows we will describe the characteristics of Levinson's middle adulthood, but first it is important to understand something more about his core constructs.

The most important concept in Levinson's theory is the life structure. This is the basic pattern, the design, the fabric of a person's life at a given time, within which both the self and society are interwoven. How the self is engaged in the world can be analysed by looking at the life structure. The individual and his socio-cultural environment have to be approached concomitantly, because they both define each other and both, in a way, are each other ('like a fish is in the water, and the water is in the fish', comments Levinson).

The life structure consists of three elements: the socio-cultural world and its impact on the individual, the self, and the self's participation in the world. In emphasising the socio-cultural world, Levinson stresses that we have to examine how the individual is affected and modified by factors such as class, religion, ethnicity, family, political system and occupation. Likewise in studying the self we have to ask which aspects of the personality are openly expressed, and which are inhibited. The self consists of 'complex patterns of wishes, conflicts, anxieties and ways of resolving and controlling

Figure 2.2 Developmental periods in early and middle adulthood (Levinson *et al.*, 1978)

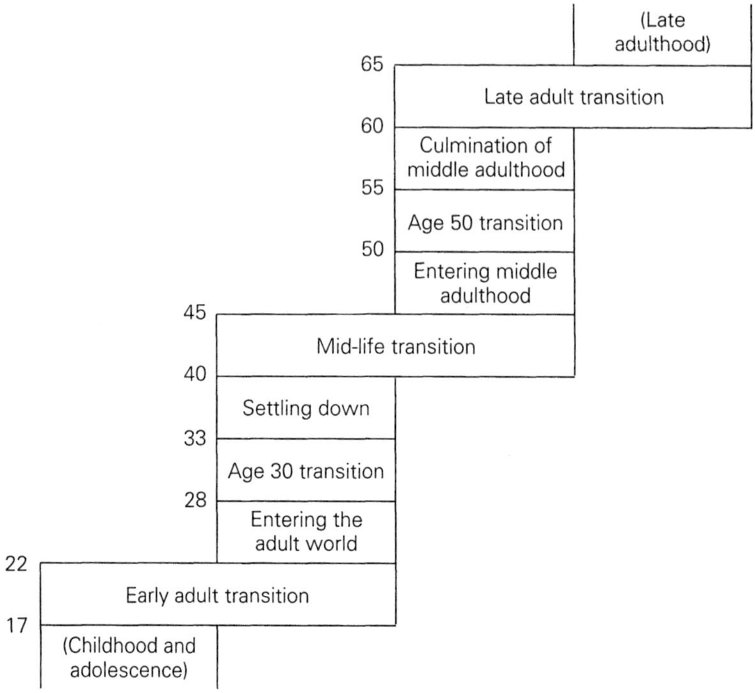

them' (Levinson *et al.*, 1978: 42). Some of these patterns are conscious, some unconscious. Some have their origin in earlier developmental periods, some are tied to the present or to the future that has to be faced and challenged.

The external world also offers both possibilities and obstacles for development, but a person has to choose which activities to take up, and in which social arenas to become involved:

> A man selectively uses and is used by his world, through his evolving relationships and roles as a citizen, lover, worker, boss, friend, husband, father, member of diverse groups and enterprises ... [they] take obvious forms, but subtle meaning and feelings play an important part in them.
>
> (Levinson *et al.*, 1978: 43)

According to Levinson, both involvement and commitment are two central forces in development. The self has to be engaged, and has to invest time and energy in the world. A man must also let the world have an impact on him, learning from it, enduring it or even being corrupted by it. Development is built upon engagement and mutual involvement that carries a person's life forward.

Levinson and his co-workers several times express their astonishment at finding such a delineated and fixed developmental scheme in the various evolving lives they studied. They had not set out such hypotheses prior to the research, nor did the developmental literature suggest them. But when comprehensive life histories were developed for each participant and the life structures compared, a striking congruence appeared. The timing and the phases of the developmental tasks that faced individuals were very similar. There seemed to be a typical age for onset of every developmental period, as well as a fixed time for its closure. The periods did not vary more than two to three years between individuals. Thus the developments in this theory are closely linked to chronological time, in contrast to Erikson's model. Levinson's model only allows for relatively slight variation according to the diverging impact of the biological, psychological and social conditions in a man's life.

Moreover the periods seem to occur in a rather fixed sequence. Persons may navigate their lives in different ways, but the order of the developmental periods is given. There might be blockages, impairment and decline for a while, some of it having to do with disappointments in the past, but developmental progress shows the same basic structure for all. Levinson also maintains that his system is not hierarchical as Erikson's is, but simply sequential. 'One period is not higher or better than the preceding ones. ... Each season plays its essential part in the unfolding of the life cycle, and the sequences follow a prescribed route' (Levinson *et al.*, 1978: 319). However, each period demands a successful completion of the previous one before the developmental sequence can continue.

Transition from one period (or era) to another is made possible by engagement in a process of evaluation of how well the person has met the developmental task of the preceding period. Through reappraisal a man comes to an understanding of when the life structure has become too limiting or dysfunctional, and whether there is a need for setting new goals, making new commitments and finding new ways of forming a satisfactory life structure. Once the questioning and exploring of the transitional phase has lost its urgency, the new choices and options that have been made must be woven into a new life structure, which is given new meaning. In this process questions still arise about how satisfactory the new life structure is, how much leeway there is for inner dreams, fantasies and wishes, and how viable it is for the society the person lives within.

However, even if the transition forward in the life cycle demands leaving behind earlier relationships, roles and commitments, the separation is partial rather than total. The individual is likely to have continuing contact with central elements from the former life structure, but this relationship has changed in many ways, and been given new meaning. An example is the relationship a man has to his parents, or to a former mentor or protégé. The relationship continues, but its character changes over the life cycle, as does the meaning it has for the person.

The mid-life transition can pass by rather smoothly, or even hardly be noticeable for some, but for the majority of the participants in Levinson's study (80 per cent) it was a period of turmoil and life crises. The doubting and searching is quite normal, Levinson points out, even if a crisis always includes irrational and emotional elements. The man approaching middle adulthood is typically between 40 and 45 years old, according to Levinson's model, and at this point many existential questions may challenge the present life structure and demand a change. He may ask the following questions. What do I give and what do I get in return from my wife and children? Is my present job recognising my talents and does it fulfil my life-dream? Is my involvement in community affairs and personal friendships fruitful? What are my real values, and does the present life structure allow them to be realised? A person in mid-life transition is listening to internal voices:

> He hears the voice of an identity prematurely rejected; of a love lost or not pursued; of a valued interest or relationship given up in acquiescence to parental or other authority; of an internal figure who wants to be an athlete or nomad or artist, to marry for love or remain a bachelor, to get rich or enter the clergy or live a sensual carefree life – possibilities set aside earlier to become what he now is. During the Mid-life Transition, he must learn to listen more attentively to these voices and, in the end, to decide what part he will give them in his life.
>
> (Levinson, 1977: 108)

It is in this period that the process of individuation begins in earnest. This was also Jung's view. It is a time for the termination of dysfunctional involvements and for the initiation of new goals and commitments. To reflect on the existential questions in life leads to confrontation with and reintegration of the four polarities that constitute the challenge of the mid-life transition: youth/age, destruction/creation, masculinity/femininity, and attachment/separateness. Both sides of these polarities co-exist within the whole life cycle, but become especially urgent at this stage of life. For example, 'youth' depicts joy, innocence, initiative, excitement, possibility and energy, but also fragility and imperfection. 'Age' is an archetypal symbol for maturity, stability, competence and wisdom, but also authoritarianism and impotency.

Levinson also follows Jung in considering a shift in the masculine/feminine balance in middle age. Levinson's thinking is as follows. In his earlier years a man was drawing quite heavily on the central cultural stereotype of what a man should be. But in this middle stage of life both the sexual drive and the macho script start to lose their pressing influence. It is now time to allow room for nurturing and caring, not just achieving and doing. Also the body may give signals that the days of machismo are over and the developmental task is now to explore the area of 'feeling', not only the area of 'thinking'. In this phase of life a man might change his relationship to his wife, as well as to his mother. He gets a deeper understanding of their world-views and behaviour. He might also gain an insight, that the tenderness and nurturance that he earlier considered only female features also reside within himself; and he may form his first non-sexual intimate relationship with a woman, as a friend. Mentorship can grow out of this, mostly acting as mentor for another man, but in some cases, also as a mentor for a woman.

For the individuation process to advance there is also an increased need for separateness in mid-life. The man needs more time to pursue his most valued tasks, to create a product of the highest standard, to leave a true mark of his own in his field. Persons with a profession traditionally considered as creative, such as an artist or a writer, typically need substantial periods of self-selected solitude in order to be truly creative. But the same applies to most jobs and areas within which one would create something substantially new and original. Now is the time for separateness, for reducing the workload as a whole and concentrating on the most important tasks, loosening involvement in the external world and becoming more engaged in the internal one:

> In this period the archetypal self takes a greater definition and vitality ... the self is the 'I' a man has in mind when he asks 'What do I really want? How do I feel about my life? How shall I live in the future?'
>
> (Levinson *et al.*, 1978: 241)

According to Levinson a man at this stage enjoys solitude more and puts less emphasis on outer signs of success such as possessions, rewards and social approval. He is becoming more critical of trends in society, and he may decide not to associate with some of these. 'He forms a more universal view of good and evil, and a more tragic sense of their coexistence in himself and in all humanity' (Levinson *et al.*, 1978: 242). It is a major developmental task in this season of a man's life to attain a better balance between the needs of the self and the needs of society.

Levinson's theory of adult development contains a number of powerful concepts that others have built on, such as the 'dream' and the 'mentor'. For Levinson, a person's dream should be lifelong. It begins in youth as a sense of how the self will be in the adult world. It gives excitement and vitality to life. Levinson stresses how important it is for people's lifelong development that they hang on to that dream. It may require modification, but a continuing coherence of desired goals and ends is the engine of growth. His point about mentoring also seems a valid one. People gain greatly by having a mentor, a senior role model who supports the person in his or her dream and gives entrée into the adult world. A sad thing about modern society, comments Levinson, is that relatively few people have effective mentors.

There have been major criticisms of Levinson's work. It seems to claim universality on the basis of a limited study of a few American men in select occupations. In defence, Levinson does acknowledge that his study is exploratory. That he was able to construct such a rich theory on the basis of a relatively small study is a tribute to his methods of research. The fact that his initial focus was on men only also caused controversy. Some of the conclusions also appear very chauvinistic. This is particularly evident in regard to the importance of the dream. The ideal relationship for fostering a man's development is one where the woman is able to support and animate his dream, if necessary allowing him to project onto her his own feminine side. However, Levinson does go on to make the point that the couple can only form a lasting relationship if it furthers the woman's development as well as the man's. He notes that if the woman's dream involves an identity more distinct than one based on the roles of wife and mother, then to build a life structure that contains both persons' dreams is a heroic task – and he adds ominously, 'one for which evolution and history have ill prepared us' (Levinson *et al.*, 1978: 110).

Levinson: the mid-life transition in women's lives

Levinson was sensitive to the criticism that his first major study concentrated solely on men, and just before his death he completed a similar major enterprise on women's lives (Levinson, 1996). The study was based on women of the same age as those in the men's study, 35 to 45. There were 45 women involved, both homemakers and career women (from the corporate-financial and academic sector). The study employed a new scheme of intensive biographical interviewing developed by Levinson's wife Judy. The interviews lasted for about half an hour to two hours per session, and eight to ten such sessions were conducted with each person. The researchers sought to construct a detailed life story for each participant, from which they reconstructed the core elements.

Levinson's resulting chart for women's life-span follows exactly the same eras and periods as for the men, but there are many differences between the genders in terms of the contents and dynamism in the life structures within this scheme (Levinson, 1996). One thing that stands out is that the women displayed much more ambivalence and distress about their life structures. There were many goals and commitments that clashed, the main one being the career woman's dream of having a family and being a good mother as well as being a successful professional person. For the homemakers the dream of having an ideal family and being an ideal mother had to be reappraised in the mid-life transition when the realities of the empty nest and a possible dysfunctional marriage had to be accepted. To understand these results better, Levinson introduces the term gender-splitting. By this he means the fact that men's and women's worlds are built up very differently on many levels. There is the splitting of the domestic and the public sphere. The man is supposed to take an active and visible role in the public sphere, while much of the domestic sphere is reserved for women. In the traditional marriage there is also the split between the man as provider and the woman as homemaker. Both on the job market and at home there is the split between a man's work and a woman's work. Finally, within the individual sense of self, there is a split between the masculine and the feminine.

There are also different mythical scenarios on which persons within each gender build up their life structures. If you choose the 'traditional marriage enterprise', you build it up, not solely on love, but more substantially on how you can each support one other in realising the life dreams of both partners. A woman opting for the traditional marriage enterprise is centring her life structure on caring: giving care to others, receiving care as well as taking care of herself. She gives care by

> nurturing her children and husband, being chiefly responsible for the household, being a good daughter to parents and in-laws, maintaining her own and her husband's extended families, being helpful to friends and a wider social network, dealing with crises stemming from illness, death, change in family fortunes, geographical moves, aging parents – ultimately, assuming [responsibility for] the survival of the family.
>
> (Levinson, 1996: 43)

There are many rewards, as there are many frustrations, in this kind of relationship. Among the rewards are the bonding the mother has with her infant(s), the possibility she has to 're-mother' herself by being the ideal kind of mother that she herself once longed for, and the care she gets from her husband through his financial support, his social position or access to the social group she otherwise would not have access to.

Many factors, however, had led to a change in the way the women in Levinson's study experienced this role. One factor is increased longevity, which means that a woman will live many decades with an 'empty nest', when she might want to benefit from the greater independence resulting from a job or other activities that foster her development as a person. Another is the development of the welfare state, with child care offered out of the home setting and meals offered at school as well as at work. This has led to a decreased demand for women's contribution to family care. A third factor is the increased incidence of divorce. A woman can no longer take for granted that the family will last for a lifetime, and that there will be always be a provider for her. She therefore needs to consider developing labour skills of her own.

The gender revolution has produced a quite different anti-traditional woman figure. She wants greater freedom and equal opportunities for development, thus more room for personal dreams, goals and commitments outside the home that override traditional role restrictions. This anti-traditional figure may want to participate in the male world, sharing men's long-term career goals, without jeopardising her femininity. She may also want to have a family and children, and therefore dream of equal job-sharing of care-taking duties within the home. But the latter is still a dream that few women can yet realise. Even if there is more sharing within modern relationships, there still is considerable gender-splitting of roles. A career woman often has to carry the heavier load of caring.

For many women within Levinson's homemaker sample, the mid-life transition was a time of questioning agreements and commitments made earlier, bringing the earlier life structure to an end, and forming a new one. These women wanted a more carefree future life, not a life tied to the needs of others. The bargain made at the beginning of their marriage, to be a homemaker within the traditional marriage enterprise, had to be changed. The homemaker at this stage in her life felt cheated. She had sacrificed her early adulthood at great cost and now felt that she had not got back the love and care she had given to others. She wanted more space to satisfy her own needs and wants in life. The homemakers' husbands were not usually sufficiently involved with them or with their children or with the whole issue of homemaking, so the homemaker women had come to feel isolated. In some of the marriages there was little psychological or physical love expressed. Many a homemaker felt trapped in the role of cook and cleaning woman. They were not valued either as women or as individuals. The children generally did not need the homemaker mother's services much any more, having created a more independent life for themselves. In some cases, however, the women were burdened by grown-up children still clinging to the care and services they had been used to when they were younger.

Even if there were many reasons for discontentment with the present marriage, most homemakers did not consider divorce an alternative. There was clearly a need, however, for restructuring the marriage and redistributing care duties. The woman had become too much of a domestic servant, and needed both more assistance and more spare time for personal involvements outside the home. Some women managed to create a more equal and personally satisfying relationship with their spouses. Others, however, just stayed on in a troubled and unsatisfying marriage, feeling increasingly resentful at having to pursue the domestic duties that, earlier, had come so easily to them. A few realised that their marriage had already passed through a 'psychological divorce' long ago, with their spouses living completely separate lives, and finally filed for a legal divorce.

By contrast, the career women were often struggling with the dream of becoming successful at this stage of life. Now in their forties, some of them could clearly see that this dream would remain an illusion and never become reality. Most of them held jobs at a middle-management level. The mythic scenario of the heroic woman who by arduous effort would 'have it all' – a thriving career, a happy marriage, close family ties and an active leisure life – had been seriously challenged. After much resentment and inner conflict most of these career women realised that they had to make a choice. Should they devote more of their time to marriage and family or to their career? They were asking the basic existential questions 'Who am I?', 'What do I want for myself?', 'Is the marriage/job worth the effort?' About half of these women had sought therapy, not because they had serious mental problems, but because they felt they needed a sounding board for these questions and psychological support in finding a new way forward. A few had left a full-time career for motherhood earlier in life. Several decided that they would be better off as divorced working mothers. Of the latter, some remarried and built up a new life structure with their new partner.

Women with a successful career, as the men in Levinson's earlier study, had begun to think about the legacy of their life and their responsibilities for mentoring younger persons who were starting their careers. They wanted to enjoy professional relationships more deeply and in a more relaxed atmosphere. The women who had not found fulfilment in their jobs but nevertheless stayed on, had a feeling of emptiness and aimlessness that was damaging to their sense of self. 'Psychological retirement' – giving little and receiving little – was one solution. Burnout, alcoholism and absenteeism were other ways of expressing dissatisfaction. A few of the successful career women did get the promotion they were wishing for around the time of the mid-life transition. But, because of gender discrimination in the labour market, many others who earlier had been considered promising were now considered too old to occupy higher managerial positions and were moved, or themselves asked for a move, elsewhere in the organisation, sometimes to an even less demanding position. For the women in academia the absence of good female role models had been a handicap, and they often felt the presence of a 'glass ceiling' preventing opportunities for promotion.

In summary, the career women Levinson studied at the time of the mid-life transition were struggling with many ambivalent feelings and felt strongly the need to restructure the most important sectors of their life: family, marriage and career. Equal access to jobs, more independence within the family sphere, mutuality in love relationships were all important aspirations for women at this stage of life. Of course it is important to bear in mind that the women Levinson studied were a pioneering generation in breaking the mould of women's lives in the USA. The development of the self that came so hard to these women has become, thanks to their efforts, a more legitimate developmental task for subsequent generations.

Other social developmental theories of the second half of life

Daniel Levinson's writings constitute probably the most delineated theoretical description of the main developmental issues concerning adulthood – in particular the mid-life crisis and the early stages of later life – that can be found in the literature. But it is important to acknowledge other theorists, some of whom Levinson draws on himself. One example of earlier theorising that Levinson incorporates in his thinking is Robert Havighurst's (1972) notion of developmental task. This concept is somewhat more fluid than Levinson's 'period'. Developmental tasks consist of the major social-psychological accomplishments expected of a person in early, middle and late adulthood, but the task for any given developmental period is only loosely connected to time. For example, in middle age (35–60 years) the developmental tasks consist of:

- achieving adult responsibilities within the personal and social sector
- maintaining economic standards of living
- relating to one's spouse as an individual
- guiding one's teenage children to become independent and responsible persons
- establishing adult leisure-time activities
- accepting the changes of one's middle-aged body
- adjusting to one's ageing parents.

In contrast, the developmental tasks of later life (beyond 60 years) are, according to Havighurst (1972):

- meeting civic and social obligations and preparing for retirement
- adjusting to reduced income in retirement
- arranging for satisfactory living arrangements
- making an explicit affiliation with one's age group
- adjusting to one's declining physical strength
- adjusting to the death of one's spouse.

It can be seen that Levinson has revised Havighurst's concepts according to his own findings.

In the same year as Levinson's theory was published in book form, Roger Gould (1978) published his detailed study of the experience of middle age, based on his research at the University of California at Los Angeles. Gould's picture of the need for change in mid-life reconfirms some of the findings, as well as some of the concepts, of Levinson. But his distinct focus is on the false assumptions people have in different phases of the life-span that hinder their development. There are four illusions about security and safety that the younger adult clings to:

1. that we will always live with our parents and be their child
2. that they will always be there to help when we cannot do something on our own
3. that their simplified version of our complicated and changing world will always be correct
4. that there is no real death or evil in the world.

Although we gradually come to accept the loss of these illusions, this is often by means of their transformation into alternative illusions that serve similar functions, which then have to be confronted again in mid-life.

Thus the first component transforms itself into the assumption that the illusion of safety can last forever. Disillusion in mid-life involves realising that we are losing our impact on our children and that they might soon move away, whether we like it or not. Our relation to our spouse may well change when this happens. Similarly our illusions about death disappear as our parents die, or our spouse or good friend develops a serious medical condition. This leads to greater reflection on life and death, and possibly a slowing down and decrease in our workload. Women's assumptions about the impossibility of living without a protector may be challenged by experiences after the empty nest of reforming roles, going out to work and other forms of self-development. Career women start feeling more independent at this time, realising that they do not need a protector, that they have most masculine and feminine features within themselves. A questioning of marriage may arise as well as renegotiations of sexual relationships within marriage. Finally mid-life is a time to recognise our darker, mysterious centre, and a shift from a more childhood to a more adult consciousness. 'We can afford to know what we feel, because, and only because, we now have the mental strength to control our desires. We can contain a passion without acting on it' (Gould, 1978: 295). At the end of mid-life, the culmination of the separation-individuation process results in the victory of inner-directedness: 'I own myself' (Gould, 1978: 309).

Gould's as well as Levinson's theory has been criticised for the 'soft' method used, which makes replication difficult, and for not giving exact markers as to how development shifts from one era to another. But these are features to be expected from studies within the hermeneutical tradition. What the hermeneutical researcher looks for is new phenomena not described before, and correspondingly new concepts or models to understand these phenomena. He or she is not studying the phenomena in an 'objective' and 'standardised' way but is attempting to reproduce a 'subjective' picture where the meaning given to phenomena by the informants is the focus of interest. Moreover the aim is not to produce a very exact and finalised picture of what is studied, but to make important phenomena visible.

While Erikson's developmental stages have been criticised for being inexact, Levinson's and Gould's developmental periods have also been criticised for being tied too tightly to chronological time, thus creating the opposite problem (see Sugarman, 2001). The diversity in human development, it is argued, is obscured in this system, and average features become normative. Shall a man or woman who is a loner and does not live in formal family relationships be considered as failing one of his or her main adult developmental tasks? Should persons not terminating their jobs and taking up grandparent and leisure roles in their sixties be considered abnormal?

Perhaps such a person is a forerunner of a new life structure. Indeed neither of these scenarios seem so abnormal today as they did 25 years ago when Levinson's and Gould's works were first published. A theory such as Levinson's appears too closed a system that does not give sufficient attention to the influence of socio-cultural change. Theories have to reflect the fact that development in adulthood is more fluid and less fixed a structure than development in childhood.

Other theorists of the adult life-span have taken more note of the impermanence of social structures. Bernice Neugarten, for example, has pointed out that time is a factor that has a profound impact on how the life cycle is organised and experienced. In her earlier writings she concentrated on the impact of 'the social clock' – that is, those underlying norms and behaviour expectations that tell us when 'the best time' is for different things in life, such as getting a job, bearing a child, or taking retirement (Neugarten, 1968). But in her later writings, Neugarten placed greater emphasis on how the social clock has seemed to lose more and more of its impact in modern (or postmodern) society. Thus, in contrast to Levinson, she advocates that the time borders between developmental periods in life are changing. Puberty, for instance, comes earlier today (at 12 to 14 years) than some generations ago (at 14 to 16). Retirement, too, in many countries, comes earlier than it used to, although there is growing economic pressure now to postpone it.

Moreover time limits are not experienced as so pressing as in earlier generations. The life cycle has become more fluid, and various parts of it are being reorganised (Neugarten and Neugarten, 1987). Whereas childhood and the teenage years formerly meant education, early adulthood and middle age work, and old age leisure, this does not always hold true today. Many teenagers take a year out – a 'sabbatical' – to travel and gain experience before they either continue with their studies or make a commitment to a job. Many middle-aged persons do the same, either voluntarily in order to rest, to re-educate themselves, or because they become unemployed for a period of time. Older people might take up adult educational classes or work part-time or as a volunteer for some periods of their retirement. Neugarten has referred to the coming of an 'age-irrelevant society' where other factors such as education or ability have more impact on opportunities than a person's age.

Perhaps we will increasingly see a menu of roles and behavioural possibilities offered to people regardless of their age. Other social gerontologists who have been writing about these issues include Matilda White Riley, who considers the concept of 'cohort' to be the most important one (Riley, 1973; Riley et al., 1999). Every ageing cohort has its different developmental conditions, depending on the developmental trends of the society, culture and era in which they age. What we mistakenly take for factors reflecting development and ageing might to a great extent be reflections of generational differences produced by socio-historical change. These reflections are clearly contrary to any time-linked, fixed developmental scheme that would be the same in the 1960s–1970s when Levinson studied his men and the 1980s–1990s when his interviews with women were conducted.

Disengagement, re-engagement and gerotranscendence

Both Neugarten and Havighurst started their careers in gerontology as members of the Committee of Human Development at the University of Chicago. Besides extending interest in the psychology of ageing to include personality as well as cognitive change (Neugarten, 1964), this group formulated the first major psychosocial theory of ageing, the so-called 'Disengagement Theory'. This was the product of a large-scale cross-sectional study of different age groups carried out in Kansas City in the late 1950s (Cumming and Henry, 1961). It was both a psychological theory of the individual's decreasing involvement with the world around and a sociological theory in that it explained these changes as functional to society. The individual withdrew from the major roles of life, while society concomitantly ceased to depend on the individual for the performance of those roles.

Disengagement Theory aroused immediate controversy. An opposing 'Activity Theory' was established and much research effort over more than ten years was focused on the question of which was the most valid perspective. Studies showed that disengagement was not always as voluntary as Cumming and Henry has suggested, but often forced on people by events, and those who remained engaged were often the happiest. Even more damning were claims for the theory's insidious effects on social policy, buttressing custodial forms of treatment in institutions, for example. The reaction against the idea of disengagement was so great that it came to be cited as an example of the type of general theorising that gerontology should not indulge in (Achenbaum and Bengtson, 1994).

However, the original theory of disengagement needs to be seen in the context Cumming and Henry themselves described. It was set up consciously as a reaction to the implicit 'theory' of ageing current in American society at the time, that becoming old was intrinsically deteriorative and that successful ageing consisted in being as much like a middle-aged person as possible. A healthy old age was seen as a contradiction in terms; anyone who was old was, by definition, unhealthy. Cumming and Henry challenged this view. The behaviour of an average five year old is different from that of a ten year old, and so is that of a 20 and 40 year old; yet they are all regarded as normal for that age group. Why do we not treat the average behaviour of a 70 and 80 year old in the same way? Cumming and Henry argued for a re-evaluation of the changes in behaviour that characterise old people, that they should not be casually labelled pathological, but regarded as normal and healthy.

Typical of these changes, they claimed, was the process of social disengagement. This was so important for them that they gave its name to the whole theory. But they also attempted to characterise other features of normal ageing. For example, one neglected part of the original conception is that society at the same time as releasing older people from social obligations allows them a new kind of licence. Therefore ageing can also bring liberation. Perhaps for the first time in their lives, older people are free to say what they think about anything and everything. The picture of the old person as a 'free spirit' is clearly a positive element in the original theory, which has been neglected by subsequent research. Yet it can be seen reflected in some of the more 'positive stereotypes' we have about old age in our society.

Cumming and Henry failed in their attempt to gain acceptance for the disengagement view of ageing. The implicit theory of ageing continues to dominate ordinary thinking. Growing old is still seen to be intrinsically negative. People resist using the term 'old' to describe themselves for as long as possible (Thompson *et al.*, 1990). This may be a healthy reaction on older people's part, but it also shows that our concepts for late life require redefinition. One theorist who has expressed a vigorous demand for a re-evaluation of old age is David Gutmann. He has set out an ambitious developmental theory of ageing, which is the culmination of many years' work in diverse societies around the world (Gutmann, 1987; 1997). It is significant that he was one of the researchers on the original Kansas City study, part of the team of psychologists directed by Bernice Neugarten. Her own edited collection of this work (Neugarten, 1964), which came out a few years after Cumming and Henry's book, was relatively neglected in comparison with theirs. In this period Gutmann developed the use of Henry Murray's 'Thematic Apperception Test' (Murray, 1938; 1943) to investigate personality change. He demonstrated striking age and gender differences. Older men in particular reacted as if they were less oriented towards coping with stress by producing changes in the situation itself, and more oriented towards accommodating themselves to the environment. As a result adjustment appears to be increasingly achieved through changes in perceptions of the self in relation to the environment.

In his subsequent work Gutmann used similar techniques to study older people in a variety of traditional societies around the world. Most impressively, he has been able in some cases to carry out longitudinal studies by tracing the same individuals he interviewed in earlier years. He claims that the psychological potentials that develop in later life enable older people to play important roles in traditional societies. The term he adopts is that of 'emeritus parents'. While women become more assertive and powerful within the realm of the extended family, older men do appear to 'disengage' from the world of pragmatic action, but in order to become the tenders of the values of their culture. Their detachment from ordinary affairs frees them to make this advance so that they represent the abstract but vital elements underlying their culture. They do this by engaging closely with the moral values and religious practices that underlie their culture. In so doing they gain new meaning in their own eyes and in the eyes of others. In the last 200 years or more, Gutmann suggests, western societies have increasingly failed to provide the circumstances for older people in general to develop their potentials. It is vital for the health of the whole of society that we find ways of recovering these potentials. In this endeavour he has made common cause with the 'Grey Panthers' movement in the USA.

The link with the previous disengagement theory view of development in late life is intriguing. Gutmann argues that Cumming and Henry too readily associated functional withdrawal from society with the emergence of more accommodative states, and presents examples to show that the two can be quite dissociated. In the case of the Druze of Syria, Lebanon and Israel, the greater passivity of the older man is a central component of his greater association with social norms, religious traditions and moral values: 'Instead of being the center of enterprise, he becomes the bridge between the community and the productive, life-sustaining potencies of Allah' (Gutmann, 1987: 225). As previous anthropologists have noted, elders in various societies often become the interpreters and administrators of the moral sector of society. Disengagement from social action is not the end state. Rather, it is only the first step in a total process of transition and re-engagement, a process that is interrupted or aborted in a secular society.

The reaction to Gutmann's ideas has been surprisingly muted. Some have acknowledged their imaginative scope, others have queried his methods (particularly the use of projective tests), but there has been little attempt either to integrate his ideas into current gerontological thinking or to be openly critical. Although regularly invited to express his views at leading conferences, such as those of the Gerontological Society of America, he has attracted few followers attempting like him to apply lessons from traditional societies to modern American society. However, the recovery of a cultural role for older people has also been stressed by other writers. For example, the social historian Peter Laslett has urged older people to re-engage within the cultural and educational sphere, seeing them as standard bearers for cultural values that may be neglected in the second age (Laslett, 1989). Cross-cultural and historical study does seem to be important to further advance in developing ideal models of ageing. We can learn much from examining the emergence of different ideas about ageing. The disengagement idea itself is not new. It is clearly expressed for instance in early Hindu writings. Tilak (1989) demonstrates how deeply troubled as well as interested Indian tradition has been concerning ageing. Disengagement is a central theme in the solutions provided. Again, as with Gutmann's formulation, this is not disengagement for its own sake, but to unloose possibilities for greater self-realisation which is also to the benefit of society as a whole.

The most recent theory of ageing that presupposes a qualitative shift in the development of later life is Lars Tornstam's theory of gerotranscendence (Tornstam, 1994; 1996a; 1996b; 1997; 1999a). According to this theory, the gerotranscendent individual experiences a redefinition of time, space, life and death, and the self. 'Simply put, gerotranscendence is a shift in meta-perspective, from a materialistic and pragmatic view of the world to a more cosmic and transcendent one' (Tornstam, 1997: 17). The theory draws upon many earlier formulations, such as Erikson's concept of ego integrity, Cumming and Henry's disengagement theory, as well as Gutmann's ideas, but is a creative reformulation of them. According to Tornstam, the debate on the limitations of disengagement theory might have been led astray by mistakenly projecting mid-life patterns and values into old age. Tornstam also draws upon the life philosophy of Zen Buddhists, whereby the developmental tasks of later life would be with-drawal into spiritual meditation reaching a stage of cosmic transcendence over time where past, present and future become one. Tornstam further refers to Jung's concept of the collective unconscious where the individual reaches affinity with universal psychological structures that have charac-terised man in different cultures. He suggests that there is an intrinsic and culture-free transcendence process in old age that is the product of normal living. He explicitly rejects a conceptualisation in terms of a defence mech-anism for the ageing ego.

The different signs of gerotranscendence that Tornstam describes, as well as the echoes they find in other developmental theorists, can be summarised as follows.

- An increased feeling of communion with the 'spirit of the universe': Tornstam refers to a feeling of flow of energy coursing through the uni-verse and making the person feel in communion with nature, expressed, for example, in the oceans and the starry night.
- A redefinition of the perception of time, space and objects: the borders of past, present and future are blurred and an affinity with earlier times and other cultures develops in the ageing person. The borders between the self and others also become diffuse and may lead to a decreased self-centredness and the development of a more cosmic self.
- A redefinition of life and death, and a decreased fear of death: as a result of the above processes, it is not the individual life, but the general flow of human life that becomes important.
- An increased feeling of affinity with past and coming generations: this corresponds to Erikson's conceptualisation that the older person experi-ences an increased feeling of affinity with the past and coming genera-tions, and becomes more accepting of death.
- A decrease in interest in superfluous social interaction: the individual loses his or her interest in establishing new acquaintances. For a young person a broad social network means access to multiple areas of

information. But for an ageing person whose needs and preferences are more clearly delineated, selective social interaction is more desirable – for example, with those old friends and/or relatives that confirm the identity of the person. This accords with the theory of age-related socio-emotional selectivity (see Chapter 4).

- A decrease in interest in material things: older persons realise that material goods do not necessarily open up the yellow brick road to happiness. It is not uncommon for older people to give away personal goods such as sets of silverware, books or larger heirlooms, and money or assets to their younger relatives or for some charitable purpose.
- A decrease in self-centredness: developmental theory indicates that narcissistic personality features are common in early stages of life, but decrease with maturity. Maturation in middle age leads to generativity towards younger individuals and a greater insight into the selfish and unselfish aspects of the self.
- An increase in the time spent in meditation: pondering on life and on self as a part of the psychosocial processes of old age is also considered a sign of gerotranscendence. This accords with a conception of life review as itself a healing process in later life (see Chapter 3), with Gutmann's findings that passive mastery of life is typical of old age in traditional societies (Gutmann, 1987), and also with Neugarten's emphasis on increased 'interiority' in old age (Neugarten, 1964).

In the theory of gerotranscendence ageing has again come to be seen as a normative process of disengagement. Gerotranscendence describes an altered state of consciousness in old age, but one that has been obstructed by the changes inherent in the development of modern western civilisation, particularly its secular and individualistic features (Ahmadi Lewin, 2001). As in Erikson's and Gutmann's theories, cultural factors appear crucial to development in later life. However, Tornstam also proposes that the inner dispositions in combination with the process of living one's life come eventually to elicit gerotranscendence. Age per se is not a crucial factor. Even a younger individual will develop gerotranscendence if he or she encounters a major life crisis such as a serious illness that confronts the individual with death. Tornstam has produced some support for this theory from large-scale surveys of the Swedish population between 20 and 85 years (Tornstam, 1997). He has also shown a clear differentiation between his conception of gerotranscendence and depression, i.e. gerotranscendence is not withdrawal in a pathological sense. Far more replication is required, however, before an adequate perspective can be gained on the value of this theory. Interest in Tornstam's concept, though, does reflect the recent growth of research on ageing and spirituality (see Chapter 5).

Tornstam (1996a) has described the dimensions of gerotranscendence on three levels: cosmic, self, and relationships. At the cosmic level, changes in the definitions of time and space develop. The transcendence of the borders between past and present is an example of this. A greater connection is felt with earlier generations. The fear of death diminishes and a new comprehension of life and death results. From great events to more subtle happenings in life, joy is regularly experienced. At the level of the self, hidden aspects, both good and bad, are discovered. The self ceases to be seen as the centre of the universe, and there is a loss of concern with the ageing body, along with a general shift from egoism to altruism. The individual experiences a return to and transfiguration of childhood, and accepts himself or herself as he/she is and the life lived as it has been unfolding. There is also a changed meaning given to relating. The individual becomes more selective and less interested in superficial relations, exhibiting an increasing need for solitude. The difference between self and role is acknowledged, with a tendency to abandon roles. Roles are viewed from a comforting distance. A transfiguration of experience towards experiencing a new innocence enhances maturity. An understanding of the deadening weight of wealth and the freedom of 'asceticism' develops. Withholding from judging and from giving advice is discerned and transcendence of the right/wrong duality ensues.

A further sign of gerotranscendence concerns the transcendence of the right/wrong duality, leading to a more broad-minded understanding of others (Tornstam, 1996a). Such changes have been described before in the psychological literature as signs of the maturation of moral thinking. Also typical is the tendency to transcend the self and one's body image. The signs of gerotranscendence can be seen when a more universal, cosmic self is developed, instead of the earlier more self-centred one. The importance of the body is also reduced and the individual becomes what Tornstam calls 'body-transcendent'. Peck (1968) earlier described a similar change in ageing businessmen. According to Peck the increased awareness of ageing and death elicits these changes. It is a sign of maturity in old age not to put one's own self or the body in focus. Even if the body as well as the self is changing, the awareness of these changes does not become obsessive.

Tornstam (1996a) gives some examples, based on the work of Chinen (1989), of the development of wisdom in old age by referring to biographical analysis of some outstanding scientists and philosophers. For instance, Ludwig Wittgenstein changed his philosophical attitude from a rather rigid and self-assured logical positivism to a more pragmatic stance in mid-life, ending up with a transcendent outlook in later life. Similar changes have been described for the life cycle of Albert Einstein. The increased awareness of moral issues led Einstein into becoming a political activist, opposing nuclear weapons and warfare in his mature days. Within psychogerontology an excellent example is provided by James Birren. He started his career in experimental psychology by studying the reaction times of mice of different ages while they were swimming in water-filled mazes in a laboratory setting.

In mid-life, while still interested in issues of 'ageing, brain and behaviour', he also initiated guided autobiography classes at the universities in Southern California. In his seventies and eighties he has been collaborating in studies based on phenomenological criteria in an effort to capture 'ageing from within' (Ruth *et al.*, 1996), published to show how biographical approaches can be used both as research and practice methods (Birren and Deutchman, 1991; Birren *et al.*, 1996), and has set up a special programme for research based on narrative methods and reminiscence processes.

Gerotranscendence theory has had growing impact, especially in Tornstam's native Sweden. Criticism is increasing, too, also within Sweden (Jonson and Magnusson, 2001). The empirical evidence for the main theoretical propositions remains weak and the hypothesised obstructive influence of society is perhaps used to explain overmuch. It is also possible to question Tornstam's sharp distinction between gerotranscendence as a developmental rather than a coping process. In coping with serious life distress, a reorganisation of values and behaviour can often be seen after the stress period is over. This constitutes a qualitative shift, or a change in 'meta-theoretical framework' in Tornstam's terms. Coping cognitively using either defence strategies or reappraisal of the nature and importance of the life event are well-known processes within the coping literature (Ruth and Coleman, 1996). The process of gerotranscendence may be inhibited by caregivers – or even gerontologists! – who are constantly striving to keep an old person active. This may obstruct the integration of personality necessary at the end of life. Having the time, and energy, available to meditate may be a prerequisite for growth in very late life.

Tornstam has also set up an Internet site at the University of Uppsala on the theory of gerotranscendence, which includes various papers and theses, as well as critical and favourable reviews of the theory. It is interesting to see how a classic developmental theory is being promoted with the help of modern technology. Strikingly, Tornstam has also been interested in the possibilities of applying the theory in gerontological practice among professional caregivers such as nurses. The results showed that a significant minority of them reported that the theory had positively affected their outlook on old age and on their own ageing, and that the effect was stronger among the better-educated professional caregivers (such as registered nurses). Almost every second interviewee reported that the theory gave them new understanding of the care receivers. The care receivers' need for solitude was recognised, and a clearer view was given of the difference between the value systems of the caregivers and the care receivers (i.e. concerning the 'need' for activation). These insights helped in giving higher priority to the desires of the care recipients. The theory also functioned as a stress-releaser for guilt feelings among the staff for not being engaged enough in activating their clients (Tornstam, 1996b).

These effects were most clear in settings outside retirement homes and other institutional settings. This has led Tornstam (1996b) to consider that the theory might describe 'normal ageing' better than 'ageing as disease'. It stands to reason that older individuals suffering from severe illnesses such as dementia do not have either the cognitive capacity or sufficient energy to ponder issues of life and death, or to meditate in isolation. As we pointed out at the beginning of this chapter, we have to beware of the tendency of developmental theory on ageing to be over-idealistic and, as a consequence, to neglect those older people in greatest need of support. We shall return to this subject in Chapter 6.

3 Research on developmental concepts of ageing

In this chapter we limit our attention to research on particular themes and concepts in the literature on developmental stages of ageing. We start with recent work on one of Erikson's more neglected concepts, which he employed to refer to the mid-life stage of 'generativity versus stagnation'. Within Erikson's model, generativity is defined as 'primarily the concern in establishing and guiding the next generation' (Erikson, 1963: 258). Recent work conducted on this concept demonstrates the importance of rigorous definition and operationalisation if theories are to be adequately tested and a sound empirical knowledge base constructed.

Research on wisdom is the second topic we review. Compared to 'generativity', which is a relatively modern construct, the cultural importance of wisdom and ideas on its developmental trajectory are to be found in most if not all human societies. However, although modern psychological theorists refer readily to this area of human attainment, wisdom has proved to be a difficult field of empirical investigation. Concepts of wisdom vary and conflicting definitions constitute a barrier to consolidating empirical findings into a coherent whole.

The third and final topic in this chapter is reminiscence and life review, an area of developmental theory that came to prominence in the 1970s and 1980s as a way of improving methods of caring for older people by stimulating their capacity to talk about their past lives. Reminiscence is a concept that is closely related to Erikson's last stage of integrity, but is also relevant to other developmental theories that have emphasised reconciliation between past and present. Despite its relatively long history as a live research topic in ageing, it has needed a recent injection of new thinking from outside gerontology, especially from studies on the development of autobiographical memory, to stimulate further growth.

Reminiscence research is a good example of the danger of isolating particular areas of investigation, and as a result missing opportunities for learning from related areas of enquiry. This is a problem all psychology faces as its separate fields expand and become more self-contained. In gerontology there is the particular danger of splitting from its constituent disciplines. The entry of fresh thought from parent disciplines, including the arts and humanities, as well as biological and social sciences, is always to be welcomed. We hope our discussion of these three research fields demonstrates the need for creative interaction between psychogerontology and other fields of study.

Generativity

Generativity versus stagnation is the seventh of eight successive stages in Erikson's (1950) theory of human development. It refers to the vital role adults can play in teaching, guiding and supporting the next generation. Through many decades of life, adults accumulate experience and expertise that can be used to help and guide younger generations. The prototypic generative behaviour is parenting, but generativity can also manifest itself in a wide range of ways, often involving activities such as teaching, mentoring and supporting younger generations. Generative adults can also be engaged in practical activities such as building or creating things that will benefit others. Depending on the inclinations and strengths of older adults, generativity can manifest itself socially or politically as well, in activities aimed at maintaining and improving experiences and well-being for larger groups of people. Such activities can include passing on social values and ideals to upcoming generations (Bellah *et al.*, 1991) or working to create new schools or parks for children. Generativity, however, is distinct from altruism, as the latter may not necessarily be directed towards supporting or helping the next generation.

Research on this topic is important for a wide range of reasons. Generativity challenges negative images and stereotypes of ageing because it highlights the important role that adults in mid- and later life have in supporting and caring for others. Generative activities are believed vital for the well-being of individuals and whole communities, as younger generations need the experience, advice and skills that people only accumulate with time. This is especially the case given that other sources of information often available to younger generations, such as books or the Internet, do not usually offer advice tailored to particular situations and people. Furthermore, the listening and experiential skills that older adults typically have cannot easily be found for younger people through other avenues.

Just as younger generations need older adults, so older adults need to be generative to younger generations; generativity is hypothesised to be important for the health and well-being of older adults. Each of Erikson's stages involves a conflict between two opposing factors. The favourable resolution of the conflict between generativity and stagnation is believed to be crucial for healthy adaptation. For some people the resolution may not be towards generativity, but towards a persistent sense of stagnation and personal impoverishment (Erikson, 1950). Within this model, such adults have little sense of purpose in their lives, and this in turn increases the probability of poor mental and physical heath, as well as reducing the quality of interpersonal relationships.

Recently, researchers have examined the onset and occurrence of generativity, including whether it is an issue most salient for adults in mid-life. Also queried is the nature of the relationship between health and generativity. Before discussing this research, we will examine the ways researchers in this field have sought to measure generativity. Measurement is a central issue for quantitative researchers, and the measures we use can profoundly shape the ways a given experience or entity is viewed.

Measuring generativity

McAdams and colleagues have developed a detailed conceptual and methodological framework for the scientific study of Eriksonian generativity. Although other researchers have worked on aspects of Erikson's theory (Kotre, 1984; Ochse and Plug, 1986; Vaillant and Milofsky, 1980), McAdams and colleagues were the first to put forward a model of generativity as a configuration of seven different but interrelated psychosocial features (McAdams and de St Aubin, 1992; McAdams *et al.*, 1993). Their research reflects a rigorous and systematic approach to the development of theory. The measures they have developed are widely used and have provided a valuable base for further empirical research in this area.

McAdams and colleagues have developed a model with seven features, which is shown in Figure 3.1. This suggests that inner desires for symbolic immortality and the need to be needed, alongside cultural expectations or demands, lead adults towards a concern for the next generation. These generative concerns will ideally be underpinned by a belief in the goodness or value of human beings. Generative concerns are hypothesised to then lead to generative commitments and generative actions.

Figure 3.1 Seven features of generativity (McAdams and de St Aubin, 1992)

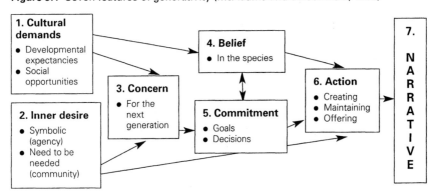

Generative commitments are recognised through the formulation of plans and goals aimed at assisting the next generation. In contrast, generative actions are defined as any actions that the individual is typically or characteristically trying to do or accomplish, which are directed towards helping, guiding or teaching the next generation. Examples of generative actions include bearing/raising children (e.g. biological or parental generativity), teaching someone a skill (e.g. technical generativity) or behaving in a particular way for the benefit of the community (e.g. cultural generative acts) (Kotre, 1984). These aspects of generativity are all believed to be underpinned by generative narration that refers to the larger life story or narrative that contributes to the individual's identity.

McAdams and de St Aubin (1992) have developed scales to measure generative concerns, generative commitments and generative actions. To measure generative concerns they developed a 20-item self-report scale, the Loyola Generativity Scale (LGS). Participants rate each item on a four-point scale from '0' (the statement item never applies) to '3' (the statement applies very often). Items included in the generative concern scale were based on earlier empirical literature; possible items were discussed and amended as a consequence of data gathered from their first study (McAdams and de St Aubin, 1992). Internal reliability scores for this scale were acceptable (alpha = .70).

To measure generative commitments, they use a sentence completion test: participants describe each of ten personal strivings, defined as things the individual 'typically or characteristically is trying to do each day'. For each striving, participants complete the sentence 'I typically try to ...'. Responses are coded and scored with reference to involvement with the next generation, providing care, help or guidance to others, and creative contribution (McAdams et al., 1993). Scores are then summed across the three coding criteria and across the ten personal strivings. The generative commitments measure is thus more open-ended; rather than focusing on any specific preconceived ideas of the researcher, participants are free to report their own plans and commitments. This gives the scale greater validity.

Finally, generative actions can be measured by a behavioural checklist of 50 items, including ten 'distracter' items, which are not related to generativity. Examples of generative behaviours within this measure include 'invented something', 'donated blood' and 'did volunteer work for a charity'. Participants are asked to rate how often they carried out each behaviour within the previous two months. Scores range from 0 (not carried out) to 2 (carried out two or more times). Although not as sophisticated as the earlier two measures, this generative action checklist was found to be correlated with the other two measures.

A strength of the work by McAdams and colleagues is the way they have grounded their complex model in the work of earlier researchers; these include Erikson (1950), Browning (1975) and Kotre (1984). In the model of McAdams and colleagues, cultural demands and inner desires are seen as being motivational sources for generative concerns, commitments and actions. In the context of culture, society places certain expectations on individuals to support, help and guide younger generations through young adulthood and into mid-life. These motivational concepts draw on Erikson's views about 'the need to be needed' and Kotre's (1984) thinking about the quest for symbolic immortality (i.e. acts and experiences that live on in others). Erikson also believed that generativity was grounded in adults' beliefs about the goodness and worthwhileness of human beings. Erikson's 'belief in the species' is also incorporated into the model, and this belief is seen to support the relationship between generative concerns, commitments and actions. By basing their model on earlier work, McAdams and colleagues have highlighted the range of components encompassed by generativity. Researchers need to distinguish carefully and define the component of generativity of interest to them. These components could include generativity as: a developmental need, an internal motive, a cultural expectation, concerns or thoughts about others, commitments or plans for others, and particular behaviours.

Erikson first drew up his life-span theory of development in the 1950s, but he did not offer any systematic way to measure or examine his theory empirically. Indeed, there were very few empirical studies in this field (for exceptions see Ryff and Heinke, 1983; Vaillant and Milofsky, 1980), and few measures that offered any complex insights into the nature, origins or consequences of this construct. Ochse and Plug (1986) sought to develop their own measure of generativity; this scale does have good internal reliability, but this measure focuses on multiple dimensions of Erikson's theory rather than giving us detailed insights about generativity itself as achieved by McAdams and colleagues. The measures McAdams and colleagues developed offer a useful extension of this early work; their measures are easy to use, grounded in theory and have good psychometric properties.

Nevertheless, one of the limitations of their work is that of defining and measuring generativity from a largely individualistic and western perspective. Although most of the research on generativity to date has been carried out in the United States, cultural differences in generativity do exist (Ochse and Plug, 1986), and the way in which generativity is being conceptualised can be different in both western and eastern cultures (Alexander *et al.*, 1991). Culture or society can play a significant role in shaping and influencing the occurrence and course of generativity in mid-life and later life. This can be because the occurrence and development of generativity will be influenced by the opportunities society offers to its members; society places expectations on adults to be generative, but the outlet for these demands and expectations will be influenced by the support offered to adults and also by the occupational and lifestyle opportunities available in our societies. (For more discussion on culture, see Chapter 5.)

Many questions remain for future studies. It is not clear, for instance, what level of generative actions are needed before an individual can be said to be behaving generatively. This is especially puzzling as people can be generative in some roles (e.g. as parents), but not in other roles or settings (e.g. in taking care of the wider social community). Researchers in this field should also examine the way the above model performs with adults in different circumstances and settings, such as non-US samples or adults in different socio-economic groups. The latter may be particularly important given that research so far on generativity has focused largely on samples that are relatively affluent and highly educated. It is also important to develop measures for other components of generativity – for example, a measure of faith in the species, or faith in the fundamental goodness or value of human beings.

Generativity as a feature of mid-life

In his eight-stage theory of life-span development Erikson placed generativity in mid-life for several reasons. He hypothesised that it was only when the individual had negotiated issues of identity in adolescence, and had established bonds of intimacy as a young adult, that he or she was ready, psychosocially, to take some responsibility for the survival and improvement of the larger community through the next generation (Erikson, 1950). He also recognised the cultural demands and expectations that he believed society does and should impose upon adults at this time. He argues that it is the 'responsibility of each generation of [mid-life] adults to bear, nurture and guide those people who will succeed them' (Erikson et al., 1986: 73). Understanding whether generativity is an issue most salient for adults in mid-life is important if we are to understand better the nature and occurrence of generativity and its consequences in a range of settings, e.g. in understanding and promoting the health and well-being of individuals and communities.

There is disagreement in the literature about the onset and course of generativity, and whether indeed it is something most salient for adults at mid-life. On the one hand, a number of researchers have found that aspects of generativity are more salient in mid-life than in young adulthood (e.g. McAdams et al., 1998; Ochse and Plug, 1986; Peterson and Stewart, 1990; Vaillant, 1993). For example, Levinson, interviewing men between the ages of 35 and 45, found that there was a shift from an emphasis on achievement towards a concern with 'the development of young adults who will soon enter the dominant generation' (Levinson, 1986: 6). Other researchers, however, have found either no relationship between generativity and chronological age (e.g. Van de Water and McAdams, 1989) or mixed evidence (e.g. McAdams et al., 1993).

There are a number of possible explanatory factors for the above discrepancies; these include the use of different socio-economic groups, the lack of clarity about which aspects of generativity are being assessed, and few attempts so far to replicate studies. Differences between cross-sectional and longitudinal research may also provide important insights: a study by Stewart, Ostrove and Helson (2001) provides a possible solution to the above discrepancy by separating developmental and historical cohort effects.

Stewart and colleagues (2001) explored the prevalence and nature of generativity in mid-life longitudinally and retrospectively from three sample groups. The first sample group, the Michigan sample, involved a random sample of 102 women graduating from the University of Michigan in 1967 (Tangri, 1972; Tangri and Jenkins, 1993). The data analysed and reported by Stewart and colleagues (2001) was gathered in 1993, when members of this sample were around 47 years of age. The second sample group, the Mills sample, was representative graduates from Mills College in 1958 and 1960. This sample was followed up in 1964, 1981 and 1989 when participants were around the ages of 27, 43 and 52 years respectively (Helson and Moane, 1987; Helson and Wink, 1992; Peterson and Klohnen, 1995). The final sample was the Smith sample. The Smith College class was studied by researchers at the University of Michigan in 1964, and then again in 1994 at their thirtieth-anniversary reunion when they were about 52 years of age. This study, then, included both longitudinal and retrospective data (Stewart et al., 2001).

Consistent with Erikson's theory, results indicated that scores on generativity increased in mid-life (when participants were in their forties) by comparison with early adulthood when participants were still in their thirties. When data was examined retrospectively in one sample, and followed up longitudinally in another, there was consistency in that generativity typically increased over time. However, generativity scores were also found to increase further from early to later middle age, i.e. when participants moved from their forties into their fifties, except for the Mills sample, where generativity was lower in their early fifties by comparison with the early forties. The authors suggest that a possible explanation for this finding may be because two items asked at age 43 ('having a wider perspective' and 'interest in things beyond my family') were not asked at age 52; alternatively, further research should examine other possible explanations for these discrepant findings such as changes in material or personal resources, or changes in family responsibilities such as caring for ageing parents.

In their analysis, Stewart and colleagues examined the potential confound of decade and historical time. This confound can be problematic because adults in particular age groups can have certain experiences (e.g. the Second World War for current generations of older people) that impact on their lives, irrespective of their current age. This would mean that what is true for one generation is not necessarily true for another. In the study by Stewart and colleagues there was a ten-year age difference between participants in the Michigan and Mills samples, yet both were assessed when they were in their forties, which was in the 1990s for the Michigan sample and the 1980s for the Mills sample. Sophisticated statistical analyses were used to investigate differences between the two samples at the same age but at a different historical time. No significant effect was found – that is, both samples reported the same feelings at the same ages although they were rating their experiences at different time points in different decades. These results provide evidence that findings were a consequence of development rather than cohort or particular generational social experiences.

One of the strengths of the Stewart *et al.* (2001) research is its attempt to analyse the onset of generativity across different sample groups. Longitudinal research offers unique opportunities to explore changes over time. Longitudinal designs also enable researchers to distinguish between factors that are best considered in terms of individual difference variables rather than variables associated with a particular time or stage in life.

Although the above results suggest that generativity increases into midlife, this should not necessarily be taken as evidence to support a stage theory of generativity. McAdams *et al.* (1998) and Stewart and Vandewater (1998) argue that generativity is too complex and multifaceted to be a discrete developmental task in the adult life-span as Erikson would suggest, and that, instead, aspects of generativity may occur at different time points throughout the life course. For instance, although young adults may have the desire for generativity, Stewart and Vandewater suggest that it is only in mid-life and later life that these desires reach accomplishment; similarly, drawing on the work of Kotre (1996), biological generativity may have an earlier conclusion than cultural generativity, particularly for women.

Future research will benefit from detailing the sub-components of generativity under investigation, and the context and conditions under which generativity occurs in its different formats. Given the limitations of using chronological age as a causal factor (Rutter, 1989), researchers might also wish to consider what other factors may influence the onset and course of generativity, such as the role of early experiences, culture or socio-economic status. The study by Stewart and colleagues is also biased towards women and towards adults with more educational and material resources; more research is, therefore, needed to examine the onset and occurrence of generativity with other sample groups, including adults with particular responsibilities (such as caregiving to frail parents), which may impact significantly on the occurrence and course of generativity.

The relationship between generativity and well-being or adjustment

Only a small number of studies have examined the consequences of generativity, particularly for health and quality of life. We will consider a study by Keyes and Ryff (1998) as an example of work in this area. They explored the relationship between generativity and health and well-being in a sample of over 3000 non-institutionalised, English-speaking adults; they also examined the relationship between these variables and social stratification. Participants ranged in age from 25 to 74 years, and were recruited in 48 US states. Adults who agreed to participate were given a computer-assisted telephone interview lasting about 30 minutes. Two questionnaires were then posted to them, whose completion took about one and a half hours. All participants were offered incentives or gifts for their involvement, including US$20, a commemorative pen, and reports of the study findings. Generativity was assessed by indicating whether they had performed typically generative acts in an average month to any of three generative targets, including children/grandchildren and people at church. Generative commitments were assessed by giving participants a list of hypothetical situations and asking them to rate the level of obligation they would feel if the situation happened to them. Generative concerns or qualities were also measured by a number of methods, including a shorter form of the Loyola Generativity Scale (McAdams and de St Aubin, 1992). A measure of generative facilitation was also included, in which participants indicated how much, on a scale from 0 (not at all) to 10 (very much), they felt they were caring, wise and knowledgeable. Higher scores were indicative of greater generative identities.

The findings showed that all the generative components – having civic obligations, generative concerns, more generative sources and more generative qualities – were related to better social and psychological well-being. There was only one exception: more primary obligations were found to be related to lower social well-being. They also found that social-structural differences have an important role in generativity and social well-being. Up to 40 per cent of the variance in the relationship between education and well-being is predicted by generativity components. The researchers argue that these findings indicate the strong role that society and social opportunities play in our lives. Such thinking is echoed by McAdams and colleagues (McAdams *et al.*, 1993), who argue that the manifestation of generativity is likely to be related to the opportunities and constraints experienced within society.

There are many strong features of this research. One strength is its inclusion of well-being, not in terms of the absence of depression or anxiety, but in terms of positive health features. These included:

- having a positive attitude towards the self, including its complex and less favourable aspects
- having trusting, satisfying and warm relations with others
- having self-determination and independence, and capable of resisting social pressures
- being competent in managing the environment and making use of surrounding opportunities
- having goals in life and a sense of direction, also having a sense of continuous development with a growing and expanding self.

Another strength of the Keyes and Ryff (1998) study is the multidimensional way in which generativity was addressed and measured, in terms of generative concerns, generative commitments and generative actions. Using multidimensional measures is vital if some components of generativity are related more strongly to later health and well-being. Generative actions may have a less strong relationship to health because the active involvement in the lives and experiences of other people can be difficult, draining and complex. In contrast, active concerns about others may not result in the same worry or anxiety people can feel when actively engaged in generative behaviours with and for other people. More research is necessary to examine the conditions and contexts under which different components of generativity impact significantly on later health and well-being, and in a variety of different contexts.

Further research should examine factors that may mediate or moderate the relationship between generativity and health. As one example, agency and communion refer to the internal motivations adults can have to be generative (de St Aubin and McAdams, 1995; Kotre, 1984; 1996). Future studies should examine whether these motivating factors have a direct effect on health, or whether their effect is mediated through other generative avenues such as though generative concerns or actions. Researchers in this field should also seek to examine negative generativity, or the negative legacies that people can leave behind them, and the ways these impact on health for individuals and others in their social or family networks.

Finally, in order to avoid biasing samples towards those adults who are more generatively inclined, researchers should consider offering participants some form of payment for their time. Unless an incentive or payment is offered, recruiting participants via posters or advertisements in public places (e.g. Ackerman *et al.*, 2000; McAdams and de St Aubin, 1992) could lead to a self-selection bias towards adults who are intrinsically more generative or altruistic.

Wisdom

Wisdom is not an easy concept to define. Arlin (1990) defines wisdom as the art of questioning, and for Meacham (1990) wisdom is defined in terms of the awareness of ignorance. Some researchers have differentiated between different types of wisdom by distinguishing between practical knowledge and a knowledge that is more spiritual or metaphysical (e.g. Orwoll and Perlmutter, 1990; Wink and Helson, 1997). We will examine different research paradigms, incorporating studies from cognitive as well as developmental psychology. Research on particular acquired expertise will be considered, as well as the general ability to make 'wise' judgements, and areas for future research will be outlined.

Research on wisdom is important for theoretical, applied and clinical reasons. Wisdom is often seen as a desired goal of development, and so a challenge and 'hoped-for antidote' to negative stereotypes about later life (Labouvie-Vief, 1990: 52). In addition, wisdom has been associated with a range of positive attributes and experiences often admired by others. The latter include: greater intelligence and maturity (Sternberg, 2000); greater ego development, autonomy and psychological mindedness (Wink and Helson, 1997); better psychological health (Ardelt, 1997; Erikson *et al.*, 1986); greater success in dealing with life challenges (Kramer, 2000); and more successful ageing (Baltes *et al.*, 1992). Wisdom may also help people deal with the inevitable losses that occur in the latter part of the life course. The judgements made in wise decisions can facilitate better quality of life and a more harmonious world.

Research on wisdom may shed light on the nature and quality of relationships adults have with others. The development of wisdom necessitates the presence of certain characteristics, including awareness and empathy with others, and greater insight into human experiences and human potentials. People who have developed such attributes, who have reflected on their experiences and who are sympathetic and compassionate with others, are likely to attract, develop and sustain warmer relationships with others. They are also more likely to be able to offer the outcomes of that experience to others, including younger generations. This has been discussed earlier, in the section on generativity. (For additional research and discussion on the under-studied area of wisdom and relationships, see Montgomery *et al.*, 2002; Staudinger and Baltes, 1996.)

The development of wisdom can have a negative side, however. Wisdom can bring with it greater responsibility, worry and danger (Csikszentmihalyi and Rathunde, 1990). It can bring greater sorrow, for experiences and relationships that might have been, and for the irresponsible or destructive actions that human beings can direct towards each other. The latter negative experiences can result in sorrow because a distinguishing and necessary condition of wisdom for many researchers and theoreticians is the direction of efforts and interests towards the common good (see Sternberg, 2000; 2001). Although 'the common good' is likely to differ between individuals, experiences and countries, this concept should involve directing efforts towards the interests and well-being of others, rather than furthering the interests and ends of the self. Consequently, sorrow can result when the interests and common good of others are impeded or harmed, whether through natural disasters or man-made challenges and errors.

Wisdom has long been a focus of interest for philosophers and theologians, but for psychologists and social scientists research on wisdom is comparatively new. A decade ago, research on wisdom was actually described as one of the 'least studied' (Sternberg, 1990: ix) and 'long neglected' (Birren and Fisher, 1990; 317) of all psychological constructs. The lack of research in this area may be due to gerontologists being more concerned with deficits and declines in late life functioning, rather than in directly examining ways to facilitate and extend boundaries in performance, development and health. In addition, however, there are many difficulties inherent in defining, measuring and capturing this complex and illusive construct. Not only do wisdom researchers address this construct from many different theoretical perspectives, but there is much discussion and debate about the relevant components that should be incorporated, and the ways these should be defined and measured.

Defining wisdom and its components

There is no standard definition of the term wisdom, but researchers in this field have sought to examine and define this concept by drawing on a range of theoretical perspectives, including philosophy and theology (Labouvie-Vief, 1990; Taranto, 1989), as well as both 'implicit' and 'explicit' theories of wisdom (Sternberg, 1985; 1990). Implicit theories and definitions of wisdom develop from informal folk ideas about wisdom and wise persons (Clayton and Birren, 1980; Heckhausen *et al.*, 1989; Sternberg, 1985; 1990), while explicit theories are theories intentionally developed by expert researchers, scientists and theoreticians (Baltes and Smith, 1990; Baltes and Staudinger, 1993). We will examine definitions of wisdom from researchers using both implicit and explicit theories.

Implicit perspectives on wisdom: folk wisdom
Early research examined the characteristics people associate with wisdom or with people typically viewed as being wise. In one such study, Holliday and Chandler (1986) asked 150 participants (age range 22–86) to generate descriptors of wise people (and also shrewd, perceptive, intelligent, spiritual and foolish people). They found that wisdom was defined in terms of learning from experience, being open-minded and knowledgeable, being of an older age, and having the ability to consider different perspectives. In another study, participants were asked to rate the extent to which these attributes were characteristic of wise people; surprisingly the only age-descriptive term (being older) was not rated as being very characteristic of wise people (we discuss the relationship between age and wisdom more on pp. 63–66).

In a separate study, Sternberg (1985) asked groups of university professors (in a range of science, business and arts fields) and lay people to list behaviours that they thought were characteristic of wise, creative and intelligent people in their respective fields (or for people in general for the lay persons). In Sternberg's first study, participants used a nine-point scale to rate the extent to which the behaviour was characteristic of a wise, creative or intelligent person. In a second study, students were asked to sort the behaviours into as many or few 'piles' as possible on the basis that these would be found together in a person. In further studies, participants were asked to rate either themselves or hypothetical individuals in terms of wisdom, creativity and intelligence. Sternberg found that people do have implicit theories about wisdom, creativity and intelligence, and that these theories are used in evaluating the self and hypothetical others. Unlike Holliday and Chandler (1986), however, Sternberg found some differences between wisdom and intelligence. This finding is important because although intellectual functioning can decline in later years, wisdom-related knowledge and insight is believed by many to continue to grow and develop (see also Ardelt, 2000b).

Sternberg's work found interesting differences between disciplinary groups in terms of the ways in which wisdom, intelligence and creativity were seen to relate to each other. Wisdom and creativity were positively correlated among arts, physics and philosophy professors, but this relationship was negative for the business professors; the business professors did not see similarities between wisdom and creativity. The meaning of wisdom, then, may differ with the population being studied.

Although there is agreement that wisdom is a complex construct with a wide range of dimensions, there is much debate about its associated components. Components identified to date include greater awareness and empathy with others, and greater insight into human experiences and human potentials. The occurrence of wisdom is also believed to necessitate an awareness of conflict and ambiguity (Sternberg, 2000; 2001), greater use of humour (Taranto, 1989), greater openness to experience (Staudinger *et al.*, 1997; Wink and Helson, 1997) and the ability to successfully regulate emotions (Ardelt, 1997; Kramer, 1990). Wise persons are also believed to reflect widely on experiences and challenges, and to generate more alternative solutions to problems (Birren and Fisher, 1990).

The above characteristics might suggest that wisdom occurs only rarely. This was disputed by Randall and Kenyon (2001), who used biographical interviews to explore wisdom as being more broadly and regularly manifested in the lives of 'ordinary' people. The types of wisdom they delineated include cognitive, practical-experimental, interpersonal, ethical-moral and spiritual-mystical. In documenting 'narrative wisdom', they argue that wisdom can be discovered in all our lives, by exploring the lives we have lived, the challenges that have been addressed and the choices that were made.

Implicit or folk theories offer a valuable approach to the study of wisdom. Implicit theories are grounded in the experiences of people themselves, and this can give them a validity and truth that can be difficult to ignore. The themes that emerge from the storytelling work of Randall and Kenyon (2001) are rich and varied; in exploring the narrative of life-as-lived, these authors engage in a rich interactive process. Depending on the questions being asked, research from this perspective can also offer insights into the ways in which wisdom manifests itself, the characteristics associated with this attribute, and the factors, such as experiences in close relationships, that might impact on its development and occurrence. But this perspective is not unproblematic; there can also be difficulties and limitations with implicit theories of wisdom. Not only can there be little insight into why people have the theories they do, but much of this research can be descriptive with little regard to the validity of ideas and insights, or the factors that can lead to the development of such views.

Explicit perspectives on wisdom

One of the most dominant and influential explicit theories on wisdom is that developed by Baltes and colleagues. These researchers have pursued several lines of enquiry: these include positive aspects of the ageing mind (Baltes and Baltes, 1990), conceptions of intelligence (Dixon and Baltes, 1986), and advanced and exceptional levels of human performance (Smith *et al.*, 1989). They have argued that wisdom should be defined in terms of a rich factual and procedural knowledge about the 'fundamental pragmatics of life' (Baltes and Staudinger, 2000: 122). This phrase essentially refers to important aspects of the human condition such as life planning and management, and the reality of death. Wise people are seen as those who have both exceptional insights into human development, and good judgement and advice about difficult life problems. Baltes and colleagues' work on wisdom is a good example of integrating multiple lines of enquiry into a single framework of theory-driven research. We will examine this theory, and its validity and usefulness.

Baltes and colleagues make distinctions between the mechanics and the pragmatics of the mind, the latter of which is most relevant to wisdom. The mechanics of cognition, which are dependent on the hardwiring (neurophysiology) of the mind, can decline or slow in later life. In contrast, pragmatic features, including culturally acquired information and knowledge, are likely to increase with age and experience at least into the seventh or eighth decade of life.

In their empirical work, Baltes and colleagues hypothesised five criteria necessary for this pragmatic acquisition of a knowledge-based state of wisdom; these criteria reflect both content and process aspects of wisdom (see Table 3.1). Content criteria include factual and procedural knowledge and are hypothesised to be fundamental to wisdom. Process criteria include lifespan contextualism, value relativism, and the recognition and management of uncertainty (Baltes *et al.*, 1995). They hypothesise a developmental shift in the onset and development of these five criteria, with the acquisition of (factual and procedural) knowledge occurring first, while the three process criteria develop later alongside greater experience of life and of others.

Despite the importance of knowledge as a criterion for wisdom, this focus is not unproblematic. Knowledge would seem to be an important criterion for wisdom, and it seems unlikely that people can make wise choices without some basic level of knowledge about a given issue or experience.

Table 3.1 Wisdom criteria according to Baltes and Smith (1990)

Knowledge criteria (content)	
Rich factual knowledge	General and specific knowledge about the conditions of life, and its values and variations
Rich procedural knowledge	General and specific knowledge about strategies of judgement and advice concerning matters of life

Meta criteria (processes)	
Life-span contextualism	Knowledge about the context of life and its temporal (developmental) characteristics
Relativism	Knowledge about differences in values, goals and priorities
Uncertainty	Knowledge about the relative indeterminacy and unpredictability of life and ways to manage

Nevertheless, some researchers have criticised this aspect of Baltes and colleagues' definition, saying that it relies too much on expertise, and narrows rather than broadens people's ideas about the nature of wisdom.

An alternative way for researchers to define and examine wisdom is not in terms of knowledge, but in terms of the integration of cognition and affect (see Ardelt, 1997; Clayton and Birren, 1980). Kramer (1990) argues that cognitive and affective development can interact in reciprocal ways to produce wisdom-related skills or processes, and that wisdom can manifest itself through advising others, engaging in spiritual reflection and the making of life decisions (see Figure 3.2).

Figure 3.2 A model of wisdom (Kramer, 1990)

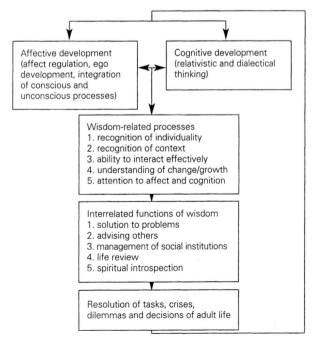

Other researchers have defined and examined wisdom in terms of reflexivity and affect alongside the cognitive components of wisdom. While the cognitive components of wisdom necessitate knowledge particularly about interpersonal experiences, reflective practices can be central to the process of knowledge accumulation. It is only by engaging in reflective thinking and by looking at experiences and phenomena from different perspectives that the cognitive and knowledge-based aspects of wisdom can occur. Through a process of reflexivity, people are more likely to see reality without the occurrence of distortions, and thus the probability of gaining true insight about people and experiences is increased.

A better understanding of others can facilitate a warmer affect between people, including feelings of sympathy and compassion. For many researchers, these characteristics are believed vital for the occurrence of wisdom (Ardelt, 2000a; 2003; Sternberg, 2001; Webster, 2003). Without the affective component, knowledge-based measures may capture intelligence or advanced cognitive functioning but not necessarily wisdom. Similarly, care can occur without wisdom, but wisdom cannot occur without care. Such views echo Sternberg's notion of the common good; in his balance theory of wisdom, significant components of wisdom are the balanced integration of cognition and affect, which are directed towards the welfare of others.

However wisdom is ultimately defined, it is important to examine the relationship between its constituent factors and their consequences for health and well-being. It is not yet clear, for instance, whether some aspects of wisdom are more important or useful than others in facilitating health, development and well-being. In addition, the findings produced so far need to be replicated with samples from other countries and cultures. In any such research, issues of measurement will feature strongly and this is the topic for the section to follow.

Measuring wisdom

We have seen that there is little agreement about the ways in which wisdom should be defined or the perspectives/components that should be addressed in such work. Nevertheless, measurement is a fundamental issue for researchers in this field. Many researchers have tended to draw upon lists of characteristics and adjectives in their work – for example, Wink and Helson (1997) used a self-report Adjective Checklist Practical Wisdom Scale. However, some recent researchers have developed questionnaire- and interview-based approaches to empirical research on wisdom. Let us look at some of these approaches next.

Questionnaire-based measures
Several quantitative or questionnaire-type measures of wisdom have been developed; we will look at two in detail.

The Self-Assessed Wisdom Scale, or SAWS, was developed by Webster (2003). This has 30 items; these were developed from theoretical insights about wisdom and the dimensions deemed typical of wise individuals. The dimensions that can be scored from these are emotional regulation, the use of humour, the occurrence of critical life experiences, reflectiveness/reminiscence and openness to ideas, and values and experiences, particularly those different from one's own; scores on these dimensions can be summed for a total wisdom score. Participants are asked to indicate their level of agreement with each item on a six-point Likert-type scale (from 1 = strongly disagree to 6 = strongly agree). In several studies of US-based adults of all ages and both genders, the psychometric prosperities for the SAWS have been found to be good; internal reliability scores ranged between .78 and .87 for the total scale. The SAWS was also found to correlate in the expected directions with other measures, including Eriksonian generativity and ego integrity, providing evidence for construct validity.

There are many questions remaining with the SAWS that warrant further research. As noted by the author, this measure needs to be tested further with adults in different socio-economic groups, in different countries, and even from different patient or health groups. Future research should also examine the relationship between the different sub-components within the SAWS; in terms of later health and well-being, it may be that some wisdom components are more important than others. By changing the phrasing of the instructions, researchers could also ask people to rate their level of agreement about items from different time points, including through earlier and later adulthood; such research could be especially useful if external raters are also recruited to validate participants' responses about the occurrence of these attributes at these different time points.

Another measure of wisdom is Ardelt's (2003) Three-Dimensional Wisdom Scale (3D-WS). In this questionnaire, she sought to develop a measure of wisdom based on quantitative and qualitative interviews carried out with adults in mid- and later life. The scale has sub-scales that measure cognitive, affective and reflective components of wisdom. While some items were developed from existing scales, others were newly developed; the final scale consists of 12–14 items for each of the three sub-scales. This measure was tested on 180 US-based adults aged 52–81 years, incorporating a range of cultural groups. The three sub-scales were found to have good psychometric properties; internal reliability scores for the three sub-scales ranged from .71 to .85, and the sub-scales were significantly correlated with each other.

The use of questionnaire-based measures of wisdom means that researchers have ways that were lacking until recently to carry out empirical research with wider groups of individuals. These measures often have good psychometric properties; however, it is important that they are tested further and with different groups of participants such as adults in different cultural, clinical or socio-economic groups. Such work can facilitate our understanding of the nature of wisdom, its origins and consequences for later health, development and relationships. However, some researchers have argued that research on wisdom is so complex and multifaceted that only interview-based methods are appropriate (Sternberg, 1990). Let us examine this approach next.

Interview-based research

Interview-based research on wisdom can range from open-ended and exploratory-type research to more focused interviews in which particular issues are being investigated. New researchers to this field need to consider the theoretical framework underpinning different qualitative frameworks and make decisions about which framework is most suitable for them (Yardley, 1997).

One framework for this is phenomenology; this approach implies using interview-based questions that seek to explore and understand the subjective and lived experience of individuals. An interesting study of this kind was carried out by Montgomery, Barber and McKee (2002). Using interviews with six older adults (aged 60–88 years), they included questions such as 'Can you describe one or more times in your life in which you believe you were wise, or acted wisely?' and 'Can you describe a wise person in your life?' The interviewer here seeks to encourage individuals to present their own experiences. The interviews were audiotaped and transcribed. Results highlighted a range of wisdom-related elements, including knowledge, experience and compassionate relationships.

The strategy used by Baltes and colleagues involves a more focused interview in which participants are given vignettes of hypothetical dilemmas which then form a focus for discussion. These vignettes typically centre on different types of experiential and relational challenges, including career and parental challenges, suicide and gender role-conflicts. One vignette involves a 14-year-old girl who wishes to move out of the family home immediately; participants are asked about what they/she should do and consider. Another vignette involves the receipt of a phone call from a good friend who indicates he/she has decided to commit suicide. After some practice and warm-up exercises in thinking aloud, participants are asked what one should do and consider for each of the vignettes (Baltes, 1987; Staudinger and Baltes, 1996). Raters following rules specified in the *Manual for the Assessment of Wisdom-Related Knowledge* (Staudinger *et al.*, 1994) rate each response for five specified criteria; these are basic factual knowledge, procedural knowledge (cost–benefit analysis and advice giving), and life-span contextualism (the extent to which the past, current and future contexts are considered and the ways these can be related to each other). Internal consistency is high (alpha scores range from .73 to .88), and inter-rater reliability scores are within an acceptable range. Correlations with standard psychometric tests in other domains found that they only accounted for 14 per cent of the variance, indicating that wisdom is a construct of value in itself and not just explained by other psychological variables or constructs (Staudinger *et al.*, 1998).

The strength of Baltes' approach to measuring wisdom is that it allows to some extent for the perspective of the individual; although the raters scoring responses have particular criteria they are searching for, participants are free to record and note whatever they wish. On the other hand, however, this approach is labour-intensive and necessitates much training. Unlike questionnaire-based measures of wisdom, sample sizes will be smaller using this technique.

Antecedents to wisdom

As the onset and development of wisdom is associated with many positive attributes and experiences (as noted in the opening section), it is important for researchers to understand the antecedents to wisdom if they are to help facilitate its occurrence among more people. This is especially the case given arguments by some researchers (e.g. Baltes, 1993; Blanchard-Fields and Norris, 1995) that wisdom is a relatively rare occurrence. Researchers have sought to examine a wide range of characteristics likely to favour the development and onset of wisdom. These include early experiences with emotionally available adults (Erikson *et al.*, 1986), the social environment, the ability of the individual him/herself to adapt to changing circumstances, and psychosocial constructs such as differences between people in terms of goals, interests and values (Sternberg, 2000), or individual traits and specific experiential factors such as experience in dealing with life problems (see Figure 3.3). In this concluding section, we examine the relationship between chronological age and wisdom.

Wisdom is placed at the latter part of the life course, because, theoretically, the development of this characteristic involves attributes and experiences that are often believed to occur only with the passing of time. Erikson placed wisdom at the end of the life course because he believed it to be an attribute that would only arise when other psychosocial experiences and issues had been addressed. Associated attributes for wisdom include openness to experience, self-reflection and self-awareness, determination (Kramer, 1990), and recognition and acceptance of the limits of knowledge for human beings (Meacham, 1990; Sternberg, 1990; Taranto, 1989). These attributes are not directly related to biological ageing and so need not necessarily decline in later life. The experience and knowledge that adults develop in the latter part of the life course can be a good source of advice for younger adults, particularly in the area of human relationships and experiences.

Wisdom is an attribute that people do associate with adults in mid- and later life. Heckhausen *et al.* (1989) carried out a study examining the

Figure 3.3 An ontogenetic model of antecedents, correlates and/or consequences of wisom-related performance (Staudinger *et al.*, 1997)

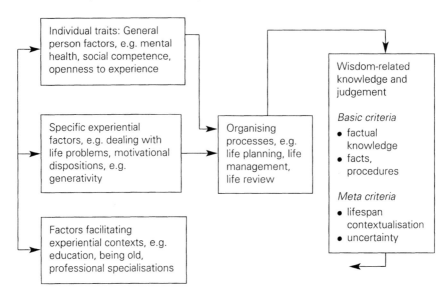

positive and negative characteristics people associated with the latter part of the life course. Participants were recruited via newspapers and grouped into three cohorts: young adults (age 20–36), mid-life adults (aged 40–55) and older adults (aged 60–85). In two separate group sessions, participants were asked to rate a number of adjectives (e.g. wise, intelligent, absent-minded, patient) in terms of their desirability ('very undesirable' to 'very desirable'), the chronological age at which the attribute was believed first likely to occur, and the age at which the attribute was believed to finish. They were also asked to rate a list of attributes in terms of their controllability and significance. The researchers found that participants in each of the three age groups generally reported similar expectations and beliefs. Although the latter part of the life course was associated with many 'undesirable changes', the attribute of wisdom was believed to begin only at around the age of 55.

Research examining the relationship between chronological age and wisdom is scarce; in part, the lack of research in this area is a consequence of the negative and ageist attitudes people had about older people and about the experience of later life. In the words of Holliday and Chandler,

> the traditional linkage between wisdom and ageing which seems to have characterised the thinking of many earlier civilisations has become something of a mockery in a technical era that finds so little utility in the elderly and has elevated the notion of planned obsolescence to previously unimagined heights.

(1986: 3)

However, recent researchers have found evidence to support a relationship between chronological age and the onset of wisdom. For instance, Wink and Helson (1997) found that practical wisdom was higher for adults in their early fifties than adults in their late twenties.

Some researchers have questioned whether wisdom is most likely to occur in later years (Holliday and Chandler, 1986; Sternberg, 1990). In examining age differences in wisdom as measured by his Self-Assessment Wisdom Scale (SAWS), Webster (2003) found no significant effect for age. Although total SAWS scores were positively correlated with age (r = .12), this did not reach significance level. Older adults were not significantly more likely to score high on SAWS by comparison with their younger counterparts. Researchers in the field of cognitive psychology have also found declines in functioning with age. Although such findings have motivated researchers to examine cognitive processes that show stability and growth with age, the conclusion for many investigators is that growth in performance is a rare occurrence (see Staudinger, 1999).

Nevertheless, this issue is far from conclusive and further research examining the relationship between age and wisdom is needed. Baltes *et al.* (1995) found that up to the age of 80, older adults performed well on many wisdom-related tasks, as did younger adults. Staudinger and Baltes (1996) also found that wisdom-related performance increased for older adults when these participants were provided with actual or 'virtual' interaction with others or when participants were asked about factors relevant to their own lives.

Additional studies need to be carried out to examine the relationship between age and wisdom among different groups of adults, including adults of different occupational or health groups. This research may be helped by the new quantitative measures being developed (Ardelt, 2003; Jason *et al.*, 2003; Webster, 2003). Studies drawing on personal histories and biographical methods can also shed light on the relationship between age and the occurrence of wisdom. Participants should include adults from a range of cultural or socio-economic backgrounds; the latter is especially urgent as most studies to date have examined wisdom in adults who are relatively well educated and affluent. Studies could also include comparison groups, such as adults in different occupational groups or at different stages of the same occupation. As an example of the relevance of occupational grouping, Staudinger *et al.* (1998) found that clinical psychologists, trained in the pragmatics of life, scored more highly on knowledge-based wisdom by comparison with their colleagues working in other areas of life. This group also scored highly on wisdom tests and did as well as adults specially nominated by others as being wise. Nevertheless, it is not clear whether such findings can be replicated when other definitions and measures of wisdom are used – for example, cognitive and affective integration (Kramer, 1990).

Future studies in this field could also examine wisdom in adults who have had different life experiences, including those who have experienced challenges and traumas that may influence the occurrence and onset of wisdom. Such studies could have additional benefits in terms of helping us to understand the ways in which people can overcome tragic life events.

When examining wisdom among adults in advanced years, care will need to be taken to control statistically for health status and intellectual functioning; measures of these other explanations for wisdom performance need to be taken and entered as co-variates when the statistical analysis is being carried out.

Reminiscence and life review

The last field of research activity we examine in this chapter is reminiscence, the process of recalling past events and experiences, and in particular the concept of life review, which is a more focused consideration of one's past life as a whole. We end with reminiscence because of its historical importance as a research field in the developmental psychology of ageing, but also because it illustrates the practical relevance of developmental theory when applied to the later stages of life. Encouraging older people to reminisce is seen as a natural activity nowadays, and very much part of care work. Some 30 years ago, however, this was not the case. Although there has also been a general cultural shift in favour of remembering the past, much of the impetus has come from gerontological theory, research and practice.

Reminiscence work owes a particular debt to Erikson's definition of integrity as 'the acceptance of one's one and only life cycle as something that had to be and that, by necessity, permitted of no substitutions' (Erikson, 1963: 260), but even more to Robert Butler's concept of 'life review' (Butler, 1963). Writing in a psychiatric journal from his experience as a practising therapist, Butler put forward the view that life review is a normative process that all people undergo as they realise that their lives are coming to an end. This article had a considerable impact, containing many literary references to illustrate its points, while being rooted in the author's own clinical observations.

The connection with the humanities is an important feature of subsequent developments in reminiscence theory and application (Disch, 1988; Kaminsky, 1984). Both Butler in his original article and Erikson in later writings (Erikson, 1978) refer with approval to Ingmar Bergmann's film *Wild Strawberries* as depicting well the late-life processes they refer to. This film depicts an egocentric professor who through a process of disturbing dreams and, later, more conscious recollections comes to appreciate his personal shortcomings and to show greater sensitivity to his family. Its positive ending indicates the healing value of the life review. However, despite the attention given to Butler's concept in the literature on reminiscence, relatively few commentators refer to the negative elements of life review he also highlighted. Where no resolution can be found for troublesome memories, feelings of despair may result. Butler cites Samuel Beckett's *Krapp's Last Tape* to illustrate this point, revealing a man who has kept a fastidious record of his memories but now feels only disgust at their recall.

During the 1970s a positive, somewhat naive and sentimental image of reminiscence was projected, which is strongly evident today in the sale of reproduction artefacts and mementoes of the past. The new-found passion for reminiscence was understandable as a reaction to the previous decades' dismissal of the past, well captured in the words attributed to Henry Ford: 'history is bunk'. This is a good example of how fashions can change quickly. Up to and including the 1960s reminiscence was associated with senility, was even seen to cause dementia – of which at the time there was only a rudimentary understanding – and was actively discouraged in residential care work. By the 1980s it was viewed quite differently, as important for the affirmation of personal identity and self-esteem. The changed mood of the time was well captured in the influential (on both sides of the Atlantic) television series *Roots*, which traced an African-American's search for his ancestry back through slavery to family history in Africa.

However, as reminiscence came to be promoted in practice in the 1980s, a major credibility gap emerged, in that, despite plenty of anecdotal accounts of the benefits of reminiscence, controlled studies of its efficacy did not produce significant results (Thornton and Brotchie, 1987). This issue could not begin to be resolved until researchers started making distinctions between different functions of reminiscence.

Because of the continuing importance of this issue we will first review research on the differential functions and effects of reminiscence. We will then focus on the concept of life review, and consider a recent study examining its antecedents and consequences. Finally we will briefly examine research on the evaluation of reminiscence and life review interventions. Reminiscence is one area in the developmental psychology of ageing where there has been much attention to the practical implications of theory and research (Birren *et al.*, 1996; Bornat, 1994). Sometimes, indeed, practice has gone beyond what research has justified. This failing is itself witness to the power of theory and the need for theory to be accompanied by rigorous research.

Types and functions of reminiscence

The study of reminiscence preceded the move towards narrative understanding in social science research (Bruner, 1986; Sarbin, 1986), and it is important that it maintains its distinctiveness as the study of the personal use of the past (Webster, 2001). Developing an accurate and fruitful typology of uses of reminiscence is vital to defining the area. This is a first stage in much psychological research, but in the case of reminiscence important distinctions appear to have been neglected in the rush to demonstrate practical benefits.

This neglect is the more surprising since the basis for a typology of functions was already present in the earliest literature (McMahon and Rhudick, 1967). By the late 1960s there were at least three quite distinct sets of theoretical frameworks proposed for understanding the benefits that reminiscence brought to older people. The first was identity maintenance; this was supported by experiments which showed that older people resorted more to the past in defending their opinions from criticism (Lewis, 1971), but was mainly based on observation of older people's behaviour in threatening situations, particularly in the demeaning circumstances of American nursing homes in the 1960s and 1970s. It was this conception of reminiscence that was seized on by those wanting to enliven elderly care settings. By promoting the natural defence of reminiscence they hoped to combat apathy and depression in institutionalised and otherwise neglected older people.

A quite different notion was that of life review. The idea of the reintegration of the self following the mid-life crisis was strongly present in Jung's writings, but it was Butler's discussion of the topic that was seized upon as a means of justifying and giving dignity to older people's reminiscences. However, whereas the identity maintenance function of reminiscence concerned the role of the past in promoting stability of the self, the life review function pointed to possibilities for change and development. These differences in function were minimised in subsequent studies of the frequency and benefits of reminiscence, and it is likely that the full implications of the concept of life review were not properly considered by most of those who promoted reminiscence in care settings.

A third, more social, aspect of reminiscence was also present in the early literature. It existed in two completely different forms, both in the disengagement theory of ageing and the contrasting theory of social and cultural re-engagement, which developed partly in response to reflection on older people's disengagement in western societies (see previous chapter). In disengagement theory terms, reminiscence was seen as part of the natural withdrawal from social responsibilities with age. It was a way of obtaining solace for the self while ceasing to have an impact on society. At the same time, however, anthropologists were noting the ways in which older people in traditional societies invested themselves with authority in drawing out teaching from their life's experience.

Gutmann's subsequent comparative and longitudinal studies illustrated how older people in traditional societies did disengage from daily practical concerns but only in order to engage more fully at the social and spiritual level, in acting as the spokespersons for the cultural, religious and moral traditions of their society (Gutmann, 1987). Some researchers have provided evidence for hypotheses derived from an evolutionary view of older people's reminiscences – for example, that older people will be more effective communicators about past events, speaking about them in a more digestible mode, and in a voice that will draw the attention of their listeners (Mergler and Goldstein, 1983).

A first attempt to define and operationalise measures for distinct types of reminiscence was made by one of the present authors in a study of naturally occurring reminiscence in older people living in London sheltered housing schemes (Coleman, 1974) (see Table 3.2). This study developed criteria to assess different categories of reminiscence and quantify their presence in transcripts of conversation collected on multiple occasions. Using these methods, the study was able to demonstrate that life review reminiscence had beneficial associations. It was related to higher levels of well-being in those who had more negative views of their past. Culturally informative or transmissive reminiscence was significantly associated with well-being in the men, but not the women, interviewed. In subsequent studies following up the same sample, Coleman (1986) illustrated how, by contrast, other types of reminiscence might be maladaptive. For example, rumination reflected guilt and regret over past events, and memories that were nostalgic to the point of pain were associated with extended grief reactions to bereavement and loss.

Table 3.2 Typologies of reminiscence

Coleman (1974, 1986)	Wong & Watt (1991)	Webster (1993, 2002)
Life Review	Integrative	Identity
		Death preparation
	Obsessive	
		Bitterness revival
Informative	Transmissive	Teach/inform
	Instrumental	Problem-solving
		Intimacy maintenance
Simple	Narrative	Conversation
	Escapist	
		Boredom reduction

This differential approach to reminiscence was expanded by others. In an important study also based on systematic observation of older people's reminiscence at home, Wong and Watt (1991) showed that 'integrative' reminiscence – corresponding to Butler's life review – was related to independently assessed markers of ageing well in a large sample of community- and institution-living elders. They developed a coding manual for classifying each successive 'paragraph' (i.e. self-contained idea) into predefined types of reminiscence (see Table 3.2). Their observations on the negative associations of obsessive reminiscence have proved particularly influential. People can get caught in a vicious cycle of repetition, continually revisiting painful memories but without achieving resolution, and with implications for their adjustment to new health and social problems (Walker and Sofaer, 1998).

As Chris Brewin has noted, there are links between the study of persistent intrusive memories both in post-traumatic stress disorder (PTSD) and in depressed states (Brewin, 1998). PTSD is characterised by uncontrolled recall of memory with many features of sensory immediacy and without any form of reworking. Problems arising in later life as a result of the recall of earlier traumatic events have become a major area for research in the field of older people's mental health (Hunt et al., 1997). This includes specialist areas such as work with holocaust survivors (Hassan, 1997).

Deliberate avoidance of painful memories – a common form of coping with stress but also in itself a sign of PTSD – appears a less successful strategy in the long run. Avoidance has the paradoxical effect of increasing that memory's power to disturb. Nigel Hunt's research on older British war veterans (Hunt, 1997; Hunt and Robbins, 2001a; 2001b) highlights well the different consequences of avoidance as a coping strategy, which tends to break down in late life, as compared with narrative mastery, which brings the memory under control in the form of story. This is not a simple process and seems to develop in stages, as the traumatic memory comes under control, then remains captured in all its detail, before becoming open to processes of development and ageing. Hunt demonstrates how the memories of very old veterans still appear to preserve much of the sensory detail of the original traumatic memory, a quality to which he applies the term 'consummate'.

In recent years there has been a healthy influx of new ideas into this field of research from outside gerontology. These include growing links with the study of autobiographical memory (Bluck and Alea, 2002; Bluck and Habermas, 2000; Bluck and Levine, 1998; Webster and Cappeliez, 1993), life-span developmental psychology (Webster, 1999) and social psychology (Sedikides et al., 2003). If the functions of reminiscence are regarded as particular uses of autobiographical memory, a number of interesting questions arise, such as the development of reminiscence behaviour in early childhood and in adolescence, and the consequences for reminiscence in later life (Habermas and Bluck, 2000). In learning to reminisce what is it precisely that is learned? How do the experiences and skills acquired in early life influence the type of reminiscence that occurs in adulthood and ageing? How do the positive and negative components in nostalgic recall interact and alter over the life-span?

The most notable recent contribution to delineating reminiscence types comes from the attempt to produce more sophisticated and psychometrically sound self-report instruments. Whereas the method of rating conversation transcripts has led to many fresh insights, it is costly in terms of time.

The development of valid questionnaires allows for large-scale studies that can test more sophisticated hypotheses. The best-known example is Jeff Webster's Reminiscence Functions Scale (RFS) (Webster, 1993; 1997). This is a 43-item questionnaire in which subjects indicate on a six-point scale how often they reminisce for different purposes. The items are presented as completions to the stem 'When I reminisce it is ...' (for example, 'to pass the time during idle or restless hours').

As well as functions of 'identity', 'teaching/informing', 'problem-solving', 'intimacy maintenance' and 'conversation', the measure assesses some hitherto little-studied functions of reminiscence: 'boredom reduction', 'bitterness revival' and 'death preparation' (see Table 3.2). 'Bitterness revival' assesses the extent to which memories are used to affectively charge recalled episodes in which the reminiscer perceives him- or herself as having been unjustly treated. Webster (2001) suggests that it may provide a justification to maintain negative thoughts and emotions towards others. It has a clear function, in preparing people to seize the moment of revenge. But it is negatively correlated with measures of personal well-being (Webster, 1998). This observation begins to get at the dark side of generativity, hinted at by theorists such as Levinson and Gould, but relatively little studied (see McAdams et al., 1997) .

Work using the RFS illustrates how a multidimensional instrument brings us closer to more fine-grained hypotheses as more precise definitions accrue and opportunity to build conceptually sophisticated models of reminiscence increases (Merriam, 1993). It is also significant that Webster and colleagues' research is not restricted to older people, and this is a further reason, perhaps, why it points to a number of functions of reminiscence that have not been discussed before. For example, the use of reminiscence for 'boredom reduction' is more often found among the young, and has negative associations.

Consistent gender differences have emerged for the identity function of reminiscence: women score higher than men. Webster (2002) has also considered the issue of racial differences in reminiscence function; he confirmed earlier work by Merriam (1993) that certain ethnic groups – African-Americans, Chinese-Canadians and Native Americans – used reminiscence more. Further research needs to examine to what extent this finding reflects a stronger oral tradition among these groups and/or a greater need to use reminiscence to promote self-understanding, preserve identity and teach younger generations.

Use of the RFS scale has also made it possible to study reminiscence function in relation to other psychological concepts. Attachment theory provides a good example. In a Canadian study, Webster (1998) showed that securely attached individuals scored significantly higher on the teaching/informing factor, and significantly lower on the bitterness revival, identity and problem-solving factors than insecure groups. In a replication using similar methods in England, we have found similar results. Other studies in Canada have shown connections between reminiscence frequency and measures of personal meaning in older adults (Cappeliez and O'Rourke, 2002; Fry, 1991) (see Chapter 5). Negative correlations with variables such as purpose in life, life control and will to find meaning suggest that a struggle to find meaning may underlie much reminiscence in later life. A high level of reminiscence activity may not necessarily be a positive sign. It could indicate a person caught in negative ruminations and needing therapeutic assistance.

Life review, its antecedents and associations

Despite the proliferation of different reminiscence functions, 'life review' remains the foremost developmental concept in the literature. It suggests a distinct task for later life in achieving a rounded evaluation of the life that has been lived. However, life review's universal character as originally proposed by Butler has been questioned by interview studies which suggest that well-being in later life is not dependent on reminiscence (Coleman, 1986; Sherman, 1991), also by evidence that life review demands high levels of inner skills and is therefore not necessarily characteristic of most older people (Lieberman and Tobin, 1983), and even by theoretical considerations of the self's bias towards continuity (Bluck and Levine, 1998; Parker, 1995). Reminiscence, in adulthood, appears to be more often used to reassert previous patterns of self-understanding – for example, in response to threat or challenge – than to create the new understanding arising from life review.

Nevertheless life review in the radical sense enunciated by Butler remains a fascinating concept, perhaps even more so because of its special emergent character. Moody has pointed out that its real origins and appeal are spiritual (Moody and Carroll, 1997). Butler had been influenced by conversations with the Jewish philosopher Martin Buber. His concept of life review thus reflects a Judaeo-Christian concern with repentance and release from guilt. But it also implies a search for meaning through reflection on one's life's experience (Randall and Kenyon, 2001). This cannot be achieved without effort. It may lead to the transformation of goals and to changed values (Freeman, 1997; Freeman and Robinson, 1990). Other recent studies have reaffirmed the developmental aspect of life review, specifically linking it to later life, in reconstruction of the self. Tornstam (1999b) has associated it with his concept of gerotranscendence (see Chapter 2) in arguing for an increased use of reminiscence in later life to unify across time, linking the living with the dead, the past and the future.

Susan Bluck, in arguing for greater interaction between the study of reminiscence and of autobiographical memory (Bluck and Habermas, 2000; Bluck and Levine, 1998), has pointed to the reconstructive role of memory throughout life in addition to its stabilising role. The self is largely constant over time and reminiscence certainly often serves this function, but it is also constantly being revised through the selective accession and modification of memories. It is important to recognise and respect both functions, especially in intervening in people's lives. There are times for reassuring those we seek to help but times also for helping them to move on in their level of self-understanding.

The study of life review, like other emergent features of ageing, should be placed in a life-span perspective. We need to identify, systematically, the developmental precursors and antecedent conditions that foster its expression. Placing it in this context also encourages attention to the different facets of reminiscence. A very interesting example of such a study of the life review has been published by Wink and Schiff (2002). It is based on the Berkeley (California) longitudinal study whose original sample of new-born babies and pre-adolescents was collected in 1928–29 and 1931 respectively. Having been studied intensively in childhood and adolescence they have been interviewed in depth on four occasions in adulthood.

The life-span character of this study gives it special significance. It is difficult to attract scholars to carry out work whose main benefits will not be seen during their working life, and equally difficult to obtain the necessary institutional commitment for prospective studies of the life-span. Systematic longitudinal study of adult life therefore remains rare, and this explains why relatively small-scale approximations such as Levinson's studies remain so widely cited. Within the USA there have been a number of important longitudinal studies of ageing (for example, Palmore, 1970; 1974; Schaie, 1996) but few that have been able to examine ageing in a life-span perspective. The longest-running cohort study in Britain, of those born in March 1946 (Wadsworth, 1991), is still some way off providing data on ageing. For the present we have to make do with approximations to true longitudinal study, namely long-term follow-up studies with or without some element of retrospective reconstruction of lives (Gatz and Karel, 1993; Munnichs *et al.*, 1985).

Wink and Schiff (2002) were able to base their analysis on 172 participants in the Berkeley study while they were in their late sixties and mid-seventies. These constituted 90 per cent of the cohort still available (neither dead nor lost). They derived an assessment of life review activity from the interviews conducted at that time and related it to ratings of personality collected earlier in life. In-depth interviews, lasting on average three and a half hours, were conducted with the participants. In keeping with the previous observations, these covered psychological and social functioning. The interviewer kept to the discipline of a format but also followed up issues that arose, which he or she found psychologically interesting. Two independent judges rated the material for signs of life review using a five-point scale adapted from the work of Sherman (1991). Only 22 per cent of the sample showed clear evidence of striving for a new level of self-understanding (ratings of 4 or 5), 20 per cent were unclear, and the remaining 58 per cent showed no signs at all of striving for new understanding or integration.

Although life review was not associated with self-ratings of life satisfaction, it was positively related to ratings of other characteristics, notably creativity, spirituality and generativity (Wink, 1999). It is to the great credit of this study that it included such characteristics. Considered in terms of its social relevance, creativity, spirituality and generativity are much more important outcomes than well-being. Gerontological research has perhaps been impoverished by an over-focus on individual subjective well-being as the primary outcome variable. The contribution older people make and the example they set to the rest of society are certainly as important.

As one might expect, life review was also related to ratings of 'openness to experience', one of the 'big five' personality traits (Costa and McCrae, 1994), personal growth and to using reminiscence (on the Webster RFS) for identity exploration and problem solving. Most interesting are the links found with psychological characteristics assessed earlier in life, such as observer-based indices of introspection and insight. Life review was also related to a global measure of past negative life events, such as a major bereavement, other personal crisis or illness. Wink and Schiff's thesis, consistent with that of previous commentators (Coleman, 1986; Parker, 1995), is that life review is an adaptive response to ageing in those who have encountered marked difficulties in life, but that for the majority of ageing individuals it is not a necessary adaptation. They take their analysis further by describing in detail and contrasting two individuals from their sample, both with high acceptance of their lives, but the one high and the other low in life review.

Case study analysis is a neglected method of research in psychology but one that can be used not only to illustrate but also to validate theory. Ultimately, psychological propositions have to make sense at the level of the individual person, and need to be employed in understanding individual behaviour. It is a legitimate question to ask whether or not a new theory can be used to illuminate a particular person's behaviour. If it does, this is supporting evidence, which gradually accumulates with additional cases. Important criteria for judging the validity of a case study are the inclusion of corroborating evidence for principal propositions, the coherence of the argument and the theoretical backing provided (Bromley, 1977; 1986; Coleman, 2002).

Such analyses are also likely to raise questions about existing theory and provide suggestions for further hypothesis testing. Exploratory case examination can also be used to point to new areas of enquiry within a given field, and sometimes to chart an unknown area of work. Reciprocal relationships have always existed between idiographic and nomothetic research (Runyan, 1984; 1997). Observations on individuals often provide the stimulus for theory building. Theory in turn provides the focus for data collection and enquiry into the individual case.

Particularly valuable are longitudinal case studies that base their conclusions on data collected over a substantial period of the person's life. Examples exist in adult developmental psychology (Stewart *et al.*, 1988; Coleman *et al.*, 1999) but they are rare. The nature of Wink and Schiff's study means they can draw on data on self-reflection collected throughout the persons' lives. 'Melissa' and 'Frank' are two such cases, with contrasting features.

'Melissa', aged 69 years at the time of the last interview, was a productive artist, with many other interests, including counselling, for which she had recently undergone training. She had been through many difficulties, including divorcing her husband in mid-life. Nevertheless she rated her current life satisfaction as very high, and was hoping that she would be able to find another partner. When interviewed 40 years earlier at 29 years of age, Melissa was estranged from her parents and her marriage was disintegrating. The year before she had begun psychotherapy in response to her distress. She described in detail the difficulties she had growing up with a controlling mother and hostile father, and an abiding sense of betrayal and feeling barely alive. Despite her insecurities about sexuality and about men, she had left home, got pregnant by and married the man who had come close to her in her difficulties. But he turned out also to be as emotionally needy as she was, and became more and more controlling and abusive of her. Only after many years trying to improve the situation and finally realising that he would not change did she separate from him.

Melissa's development as an adult has involved a lot of hard work and painful adjustment in order to become financially and emotionally independent. This had continued right up to the last interview at 69 years, when for the first time she was able to pinpoint her basic sense of betrayal at being sexually abused by her father at the age of three or four, a fact she believes was subsequently covered up by her mother. She never confronted her father with this accusation, but described a cathartic scene shortly before he died when she had shaken him with rage and yelled at him to behave. Back in her car afterwards she had suffered a panic attack. She can now understand better her father's behaviour towards her, also why her mother's reactions were ambivalent, and has also begun to understand her own problems in relationships with men. Most remarkably she has, in Erikson's terms, accepted the 'inevitability' of her life, and created from it a cohesive life story. She also scores high on the measure of spirituality employed in the study (see Chapter 5).

'Frank' by contrast is not interested in introspection or self-reflection. Aged 76 years at the time of the last interview, he had been retired for nearly 20 years from a career in banking. He retired early to concentrate on his passion for writing literary criticism, which he had left behind at college. He has only been moderately successful at this task but still enjoys it immensely. He does reminisce – for example, to relive experiences with his wife or tell stories to his grandchildren. However, he accepts his life story without feeling the need for further analysis. He had wanted to pursue literature and writing, but his parents counselled him to find a stable occupation. He accepted their advice and has not regretted it. His career in banking was hugely successful, thanks to a combination of making right decisions, and having good colleagues and clients. He astonished his friends and colleagues by his decision to retire early. But there was no financial or other need for him to work further, and he and his wife had other outdoor as well as indoor interests they wanted to develop.

His personality – he is an introvert and a loner – and his literary interests might lead one to expect a measure of self-reflection. But Frank has never felt the need to fuse his interests into a cohesive whole. He exemplifies, as Wink and Schiff conclude, a counter-example to the adage that an unexamined life is not worth living. If one compares the two cases, it is apparent that the focus of Frank's reflections has remained firmly on things outside of himself, whereas Melissa's focus has been on her own life experience. Frank's rich and interesting life has been virtually conflict-free. Melissa has experienced abuse, betrayal and rejection in great measure, and has had to learn to cope with a range of conflicting feelings as a consequence. She has experienced pain to the degree that is perhaps necessary for life review to occur.

These are good case studies on a number of criteria, including the clarity of the theme they investigate, the unbiased collection of material on that topic, and the convincing narrative accounts they provide of the persons themselves. They illustrate well the general finding from Wink and Schiff's researches with the Berkeley sample, that life review and other spiritual developments in later life are the product of life's difficulties more than its successes.

Evaluative studies of reminiscence and life review

From its beginning the study of reminiscence has been closely tied to practice. In fact, it is an indication of the applied nature of much of the research that a substantial entry on reminiscence in the widely read Encyclopaedia of Gerontology (Burnside, 1996) focuses on reminiscence as a therapeutic activity. This reinforces the importance of identifying which types of reminiscence should be encouraged and which avoided – for example, the integrative approach focusing on a constructive reappraisal of the older person's past, and the instrumental approach centred on past problem-solving abilities and coping activities. The subject has certainly developed from the position 20 years ago when unsuspecting residents of homes or attenders at day centres might be confronted with disturbing images – for example, from the First World War – as part of a reminiscence-activation programme.

There has been much debate about the strengths and limitations of both group reminiscence and one-to-one interaction. The former, if used sensitively with due regard for individual differences in needs including vulnerabilities, remains the most popular and most effective practice. Its aims are different from dyadic reminiscence, and reflect the support and camaraderie that can develop especially in reminiscence group practice. Burnside (1996) describes some of the techniques, props and triggers that group leaders can use.

Unfortunately most of the early evaluative studies had serious methodological flaws. Aside from the issue of inadequate definition and the absence of differentiation of distinct types of definition, studies suffered from the lack of adequate controls, limited samples, and poor measurement. Indices of reminiscence activity were often subjective ratings of limited validity. The failings were such that even by the late 1980s critical reviews could be published pointing out the lack of convincing evidence for the benefits of stimulating reminiscence activity (Thornton and Brotchie, 1987).

In certain areas of work – for example, with demented elderly people (see Chapters 6 and 7) – there is still a lack of rigorous evaluation to back up the anecdotal reports of the benefits of reminiscence work (Spector *et al.*, 1998). This is frustrating for practitioners, who feel as a consequence that their efforts are not sufficiently appreciated. Nevertheless, overall, there have been noticeable improvements in the methods employed, particularly in the development of standardised instruments and the provision of comparative control samples undertaking alternative activities to reminiscence (see McKee *et al.*, 2003). More attention has also been given to consolidating findings by providing systematic reviews.

Barbara Haight has been a pioneer researcher-practitioner in this field in the USA, including rigorous evaluations of the time-limited life review interventions she has developed for use by nurse practitioners both in the community and in nursing homes (Haight, 1988; 1992; Haight *et al.*, 2000). She has also provided regular reviews of the reminiscence literature (Haight, 1991; Haight and Hendrix, 1995; Hendrix and Haight, 2002) and helped launch the International Institute for Reminiscence and Life Review as a centre for communicating ideas, practice and research findings.

A good early example of the more rigorous style of research on reminiscence interventions is Fielden's (1990) report of a project conducted in a sheltered housing complex in England. This was a small but well-controlled study, conducted by a clinical psychologist, in two sheltered housing complexes four miles apart. A 'reminiscence package' of pictures and slides was used over nine weekly sessions in the communal lounge of one scheme, whereas in the other a 'here and now' group looked at pictures and slides of present activities and holidays. In both cases residents were encouraged to bring in their own pictures and memorabilia.

In contrast to the group that did the present-centred activities, the reminiscence group showed marked improvement in well-being over the course of the programme. Significant changes also occurred in patterns of socialisation and intimacy. It is not possible to assess whether these social changes accounted for the change in well-being or vice versa, or whether both were independent effects, but it is a plausible explanation that the reminiscence-based activity was more successful in creating relationships. It gave something more significant to talk about. Of course, it is important to replicate studies such as this. There may have been special circumstances in one or both of the sheltered housing schemes that accounted for the significant effect.

The field of reminiscence interventions is now so large that it has become necessary to examine more critically the nature of the various interventions employed, and to assess their benefits for different client groups. There are already a number of different procedures in use. The method of life review advocated by Haight (Haight *et al.*, 1995), for example, is a one-to-one approach, but also a time-limited series of six sessions covering the whole life course, including a final integrative session. Both positive and negative themes are addressed. The design of this programme explicitly takes into account the time constraints operating on health and social welfare workers as well as the needs of their clients.

By contrast, the 'guided autobiography' groups, pioneered by Birren and colleagues (Birren and Deutchman, 1991; Randall and Kenyon, 2001) are much more extensive in terms of the time and social skills (such as written composition and creative listening) required. Participants are typically made up of people who are from the outset well motivated to explore the major themes of their lives in company with others (Ruth *et al.*, 1996). The therapeutic benefit of writing is now a well-established theme in health and clinical psychology (Niederhoffer and Pennebaker, 2002).

Thanks to recent advances in research we can now see more clearly how the specific outcomes of reminiscence will depend on the types of memory recalled (Bluck and Levine, 1998). Accessing some memories will encourage self-acceptance, accessing others will actually stimulate self-change. Much, then, depends on the aims of the intervention and the techniques used. Life review in the sense in which Butler originally described it is more concerned with the possibility of self-change than with maintaining present self-conception. It would be possible to change one's sense of self by drawing on a different, often forgotten, set of memories to the ones on which the present self is based; but this is a difficult and anxiety-provoking task as Butler realised and emphasised by means of the literary illustrations with which he accompanied his original description (Butler, 1963). It is more possible when someone is already dissatisfied with life or is already seeking self-growth, but for most people it is hard to give up a theory of the self in which they have long invested. Life-review techniques to encourage this process have, understandably, been little tried with older people.

In this as well as the previous chapter we have considered ideal models of ageing, and developments that are beneficial not only to the individual but also to the society around and to future generations (i.e. which are generative). It is appropriate to close with a focus on the witness to past truths and future values that older people provide in their reminiscing. Objective truth is an important element in establishing the story of one's life (Coleman, 1999), and the incorporation of techniques that do loosen the hold of the 'totalitarian ego' (Greenwald, 1980) would be important additions to methods of reminiscence work. Persons are potentially much more than the current stories they tell of themselves.

What, for example, makes a good life story? It is important to devise criteria for judging the quality of reminiscence on its own terms, and not only through the consequences for the individual's subjective sense of well-being. Coleman (1999) as well as Habermas and Bluck (2000) have emphasised the importance of coherence as an essential characteristic of an integrated and satisfying life story. Habermas and Bluck proposed four types of global coherence: temporal, cultural, causal and thematic.

Temporal coherence describes the manner in which remembered experiences are temporally related to one another and to external historical events. Cultural coherence refers to the normative cultural facts and events that define conventional life phases (e.g. births, marriages and deaths). Causal and thematic coherence, on the other hand, refers to the evaluative and meaning-making components of the life story. For example, when causal links are not established, life appears to have been determined by chance and will be experienced as meaningless. Ruth and Öberg (1992) and Coleman (1999) describe lives that are perceived as disconnected, consisting of a series of events rather than a story, not seeming to flow, and being outside the person's control.

However, it is possible to work with people on 'restorying' their lives (Kenyon and Randall, 1997) so that negative experiences become opportunities for development and the acquisition of wisdom (Randall and Kenyon, 2001). Even emotionally disturbing events can become an occasion for transformation. Tedeschi and Calhoun (1995) have gone so far as to coin the term 'post-traumatic growth'. This is consistent with what we know of human potential from biographical studies, and appears, as we have seen, to lie at the basis of the attitude-changing reminiscence that has come to be called life review.

Recent studies on lives disrupted by the historical events of the Second World War and the recent collapse of the Soviet empire, itself a product of that war (Andrews, 1997; Coleman, Hautamäki and Podolskij, 2002; Keller, 2002; Kruse *et al.*, 2003), illustrate both how such historical events interfere with normal identity processes, but also the potential resulting from such experience for appreciating and communicating new insights and values. The three developmental themes we have emphasised in this chapter – wisdom, generativity and reminiscence – are closely interrelated. The continuing resonance of these themes suggests that the pursuit of a developmental psychology of ageing remains valid also in contemporary society.

2
Ageing and adaptation

Forming a coalition between the human mind and society to outwit the limits of biological constraints in old age seems an obtainable and challenging goal for cultural evolution ...

(Baltes and Baltes, 1990)

4 Theories of ageing and adaptation

Problems, deficits, losses and declines in later life have been well documented in the gerontological literature. Biologically, ageing is defined as a deteriorative process. Socially, relationships disappear as older adults lose parents, spouses and other close friends. Previous work and family roles that the individual enjoyed may no longer be salient after retirement and when children leave home. Multiple losses, challenges and problems can place a significant strain on the individual, particularly if these occur in quick succession. It is not surprising that adjustment, adaptation and various expressions used to refer to the individual's experience of well-being, morale, life satisfaction and depression are some of the most commonly used terms in social and psychological studies of ageing.

But as research findings have accumulated, it has become clear that adults in later life are not as anxious, depressed or fearful as might have been expected (Dietz, 1990; Kunzman et al., 2000; Thompson et al., 1990). For example, we carried out a longitudinal study in Southampton from 1977–78 and found remarkable stability in participants' self-esteem and well-being. Rather than becoming more anxious or depressed, these older people generally retained high levels of self-esteem and autonomy (Coleman, Ivani-Chalian and Robinson, 1993). Similar results are evident from cross-sectional studies comparing different age groups. Asking 300 older (mean age 74 years) and 300 younger (mean age 24 years) people to carry out sentence-completion tasks in Germany, Freya Dittmann-Kohli (1990) discovered that older participants were more positive towards themselves than younger participants. Younger people were typically more derogating and harsh towards themselves by comparison with older people, even in regard to physical appearance, where one might expect younger people to think they had a distinct advantage. A recent large-scale survey of the American population found a marked decline in self-esteem in adolescence, followed by gradual consolidation, with those in their sixties showing peak levels of self-esteem (Robins et al., 2002).

Early researchers in the study of stress assumed that negative effects would be related to the amount of stressful experience. However, as the result of the work of Lazarus and colleagues, a more sophisticated understanding of stress and coping has developed (Lazarus, 1966; Lazarus and DeLongis, 1983; Lazarus and Folkman, 1984). Lazarus argued that the experience of stress could be represented by three processes:

1. primary appraisals of the potential threat to the self
2. secondary appraisal of possible responses to the perceived threat
3. coping as the process of responding to the perceived threat.

Consistent with the theories and studies reported in Chapters 2 and 3, the limited comparative research carried out on stress and coping in different age groups suggests that the use of intrapsychic methods, involving the control of emotions, becomes more common with age, and problem-focused approaches decline. However, it has to be borne in mind that sources of stress change with age. Folkman *et al.* (1987) reported that younger adults experienced significantly more hassles in the domains of finances, work, home maintenance, personal life, and family and friends than older adults. Older men and women reported proportionately more stress related to environmental and social issues, home maintenance and health. Nevertheless, this study did show that age differences in styles of coping remained even within individual areas, which tends to support a developmental interpretation of changes in coping methods with age.

However, consistent age differences in psychological functioning tend not to be large. Even in the limited field of cognitive functioning there is a considerable amount of variation among individuals, and much more so in the field of personality studies. Most striking is the consistency over time within individuals (Staudinger, 2005). As a result, recent investigators have become less interested in looking for normative age differences than in accounting for the processes of self regulation that underlie continued stability as well as the determinants of eventual change.

Differential ageing

The perspectives on ageing of Jung, Erikson and those who followed them in elaborating normative stage theories of adult development were in part a reaction against the negative stereotypes of ageing predominant in the late nineteenth and early twentieth century. Their response was to propose positive models of ageing. Both views assumed a large degree of generalised age changes. The dominant school of life-span developmental psychology that has developed over the last 30 years in North America and Europe has come instead to emphasise differential ageing, as well as the influences of societal and historical factors on age-related expectations (Baltes, 1987; Baltes *et al.*, 1980; Dannefer, 1988; Maddox, 1987) (for general accounts of life-span developmental psychology see Heckausen, 2005; Sugarman, 2001). Thus it has become possible to understand better why it is that some older adults do show characteristics similar to the negative stereotypes of age, whereas others age much more positively. This has led to the coining of terms such as 'normal', 'pathological', and 'optimal' or 'successful' ageing.

Figure 4.1 Quantitative relation of gains and losses across the adult life span: percentages and absolute numbers (insert) (Heckhausen *et al.*, 1989)

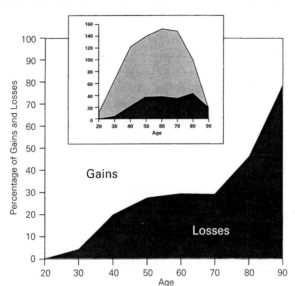

The last term – 'successful ageing' – refers to optimal physical, psychological and social possibilities for living, to an experience of ageing where health, activity and role fulfilment are better than found within the population generally (Rowe and Kahn, 1998). Within this framework, researchers are interested in finding ways in which adults can not only offset problems or challenges, but also function to maximum potential in their later years (Baltes, 1987; Baltes and Baltes, 1990). Death is seen to occur at the end of a full and active life, in ways comparable to a clock that simply stops ticking (Baltes, 1991). The opposite model of pathological old age assumes a much more pessimistic outlook for the self in which increasingly poor health and lower levels of psychological and social functioning can be expected. This would include ageing with dementia.

The 1990 article by Paul and Margret Baltes from the Max Planck Institute of Human Development in Berlin sets out clearly both their theoretical and research agenda. They stress two concepts as having influenced their thinking about successful ageing: 'interindividual variability' and 'intraindividual plasticity'. 'Systematic age-related shifts in the extent of variability and plasticity are cornerstones for a developmental theory of human adaptation' (Baltes and Baltes, 1990: 1). Significant, too, is the emphasis they give to beliefs and attitudes about ageing. 'Optimism about old age influences research and personal action by directing it toward the search for positive aspects of aging' (1990: 2). As we shall argue in the following chapter this is a key topic for future research. Figure 4.1 shows the shifting balance in gains and losses that adults attribute to the later periods of the life-span, with an increasingly larger number of losses. But even in very old age, some positive changes are expected – for example, in terms of wisdom and dignity (Heckhausen *et al.*, 1989). Such attitudes are influential on actual outcomes, but also themselves malleable.

Baltes and Baltes cite the essay 'De Senectute' ('On Old Age') of the Roman philosopher and statesman Cicero as a prototype of productive thinking about ageing. In this, Cicero challenges the negative stereotypes of ageing in his own time relating, for example, to illness and forgetfulness as overgeneralisations, and points to the importance of motivation, values, good habits and social encouragement for optimising human potentialities in the later years. Baltes and Baltes conclude:

> although his [Cicero's] stoicist optimism about the power of the human mind is certainly an oversimplification of the mind–body interface, forming a coalition between the human mind and society to outwit the limits of biological constraints in old age seems an obtainable and challenging goal for cultural evolution.
>
> (Baltes and Baltes, 1990: 27)

It is clear that many factors, both biological and social, influence the experience of ageing (Rowe and Kahn, 1998). European sociologists following Townsend (1981) have come to refer to the structured dependency of older adults (Phillipson and Walker, 1986; Walker, 1999). For instance, retirement from paid work is very often forced upon older adults in such a way that it weakens both their financial and social status. The current emphasis of policy within the European Union has switched in recent years to 'productive ageing', by which is meant keeping people in the labour market longer. Whether this is intended primarily to benefit older people rather than to combat ever increasing pension costs is doubtful. Older people have often been the passive victims of abrupt changes in public policy. The collapse of pension values in the former Soviet Union is a recent extreme example of political change gravely affecting older people's quality of life.

There are probably limits to the optimising of age. Certainly in the near future it is hard to imagine that ageing will not continue to be marked by physical, psychological and social losses. However, gains and losses accompany each other throughout the life-span (Baltes, 1987; Dannefer and Perlmutter, 1990), and it is in studying the interaction between them that most insight can be gained into the nature of development. As far as later life is concerned, this means understanding better strategies of adaptation and coping. Successful adaptation and coping with the stresses and changes of life are principal markers of mental and emotional health in people of all ages. The psychology of ageing has been defined by Birren and Schroots (1996) in terms of the ability of the individual to adapt to changing circumstances during adulthood. Many adults have concerns about their own future old age and death. That such potential worries are managed – even to the limited extent of avoiding thinking about such topics – is important if individuals are to maintain a sense of well-being. Health professionals, too, if they are to help their clients, need to be aware of the strategies that can be used to create a sense of control, predictability and safety. Learning about the different possibilities for adaptation is likely to be useful in helping older adults who are adapting less well.

The ways in which people regulate and manage threats connected with their own old age are likely to develop over many decades. The following quote from Pearlin and McKean Skaff illustrates this view:

> Because stress processes and the changes they encompass may unfold over considerable spans of time along the life course, they become inherently intertwined with and indistinguishable from what we ordinarily think of as development and ageing. Therefore, when we examine changes prompted by stress, we may at the same time be observing changes that can also be described as life-course developments.
>
> (Pearlin and McKean Skaff, 1996: 239)

By understanding better the ways in which adults respond to age-related threats we may also gain further insights into the mechanisms leading to many of the positive attributes that can occur in the latter part of the life cycle, such as wisdom and mature forms of integrity. This is because some of these positive attributes may only arise when potential threats to do with own old age and death are successfully regulated. For instance, the attribute of wisdom may only arise when the individual has overcome fears around the finite nature of life, and successfully integrated such fears with an appreciation and urgent awareness of the positive things life has to offer. By understanding better the positive attributes and experiences that can come with age we may be in a better position to encourage the development of these experiences in more people.

The most substantial early study into older people's styles of coping was the Bonn longitudinal study of ageing (Rott and Thomae, 1991; Thomae, 1976; 1987). This investigated stresses in the areas of health, family, housing and income, among a sample of 222 people of 55 years and over, followed up over periods of 20 years and employing in-depth interviews. The investigators developed the concept of 'hierarchies of coping responses' with which to describe their observations over time. Considerable consistencies were demonstrated, but also changes. 'Hope for change' and 'active resistance' diminished, whereas 'revision of expectancies' and 'asking for help' increased. However, differences between areas of stress in the coping methods employed remained significant. For example, 'asking for help' did not increase in regard to problems of income, perhaps because older people, of this generation at least, found it too demeaning a solution to their problems. The investigators also found a significant decline both in 'depressive reactions' and in the number of 'resistance' responses to health stresses in their female group (who had initially scored higher than the male group on both indices) in the course of ageing. They postulated a process of learning on the part of these women to cope more effectively with health problems (Rott and Thomae, 1991).

Subsequent studies in Germany have developed further this approach to the study of coping – for example, Kruse's studies of persons coping with chronic disease, caregiving and war trauma (Kruse, 1989; 1991; Kruse and Schmitt, 2000; Kruse *et al.*, 2003). These studies, like the earlier Bonn studies, are characterised by careful delineation of typologies of coping. People respond in diverse ways to what appear objectively similar situations. Their coping styles also become increasingly specialised and different from others' over time.

In developing theory about ageing and adaptation, such researchers seek to understand the basis of these differences. The sections to follow examine some of the major theories devised for explaining the way people manage the latter part of the life course. These include selective optimisation with compensation, the shifting balance between accommodation and assimilation, and socio-emotional selectivity theory. Patricia Crittenden's dynamic maturational model of attachment is also outlined as an example of a theory from child developmental psychology that we believe could be applied with profit to issues surrounding ageing. As we emphasised earlier, there is always need for fresh theoretical insights in psychology, and these can often be provided by other, especially adjacent, areas of psychology.

Selective optimisation with compensation

Strong claims have been made by various theorists (Baltes and Baltes, 1990; Birren and Schroots, 1996) for adaptivity, the potential and preparedness for dealing with a variety of demands, as a criterion of successful ageing. In the contemporary western world such a measure appears more acceptable as an objective criterion of successful ageing because it does not imply a single outcome but rather the ability of the system to meet demands. It includes a range of characteristics, involving cognitive as well as social abilities.

The importance of adaptivity was emphasised much earlier in the history of gerontology, in the pioneering writings of Anderson, for example, who approached the study of ageing after a career working on child development (Anderson, 1956). Anderson stressed that in the course of our development we purchase efficiency at the cost of versatility, and that the regressive processes to be found in extreme old age simply represent the cumulative effect of all the restrictive choices made in the past, which cause an increased reliance on habit. Kastenbaum has also referred to ageing as 'habituation', a decreasing attention to repetitive stimuli in one's life: 'what we recognize as "aging" or "oldness" is the emerging tendency to overadapt to one's own routines and expectations rather than to adapt flexibly and resourcefully to the world at large' (Kastenbaum, 1984: 105).

In contrast to these pessimistic pictures of the life-span, other theorists consider how adaptivity may be preserved in the course of ageing, and how it may be enhanced with the strengths that come from the increased expertise, specialisation and individuality of age (Baltes, 1987; Shock, 1977). The best-articulated and investigated model of this type is the model of selection, optimisation and compensation (SOC) developed by Paul and Margret Baltes (Baltes and Baltes, 1990; Freund and Baltes, 1998; Marsiske *et al.*, 1995). This theory provides a prototype strategy of successful ageing, of adapting to the constraints and losses of later life by optimising favourable outcomes for the self.

The strategy, as its name suggests, involves three components. 'Selection' refers to the adaptive task not only of the person but also of the society – in this way, Baltes follows Erikson in emphasising the reciprocal character of development – to concentrate on those domains that are of high priority to the individual, and also that suit their skills and situation. With growing restrictions on their powers, individuals should select only the most rewarding interests and commitments, ones that can be performed without great effort. However, the choices made should not be determined only by subjective preference but also as a result of objective judgement. A particular individual may make the wrong choice, and focus on activities that do not optimise their sense of identity, meaning or even pleasure.

Within the theory, selection is further defined in terms of elective and loss-based selection. Elective selection is defined in terms of 'regulative processes that are involved in selection from a pool of alternative developmental pathways' (Freund and Baltes, 1998: 531). Loss-based selection occurs in response to a decline in resources and is defined in terms of a downward shift to less important goals.

The process of selection implies a continual narrowing in the range of alternative options open to the individual. Although this narrowing of options may occur throughout the life course, including childhood, it is likely to be more salient in old age given the pressure of increasing constraints on the self as a consequence of decreases in ability and energy, and the declining effectiveness of the culture in supporting older adults (Baltes, 1997). By reducing activities to high-efficacy domains, the activities can be as enjoyable as before they were reduced in number (Baltes and Carstensen, 1996). The process of selection is initiated by the anticipation of change and restriction in functioning brought by age.

Losses or decline in several areas call for a concentration of the limited resources into areas of behaviour of great importance for the individual. The selection presupposes a re-evaluation of goals, and can be reactive as well as proactive. That is, it may pertain to adjustment to limits or to actively overriding them by saving the resources for the most important tasks. A performer such as a singer or a musician may find it fruitful to select a more limited repertoire, performing only those pieces that were always performed well. Pianist Arthur Rubinstein has described how he actively selected the piano repertoire he performed in the latter part of his career, and how he at that time abstained from performing very tricky pieces (Baltes and Baltes, 1990).

Optimisation is linked to behavioural plasticity and the ability of the individual to modify the environment, both to create more favourable or desired outcomes for the self and to meet the continual challenges and changes being experienced. Examples of optimising outcomes can be understood at an age-graded level (e.g. maturation and the accumulation of experience), or at a history-graded level (e.g. improvements in health care and education) (Marsiske et al., 1995). Optimisation strategies can also be understood at physical, psychological and social levels. An example within the physical sector would be a person who is overweight, and whose health therefore is in danger. Optimisation in this case would be to keep to a strict diet or to exercise more or to avoid situations that elicit eating behaviour.

An example from the psychological sector would be persons who feel that their memory functions are disturbed. Optimisation would mean reducing stress if overstimulated or possibly getting help with a masked depression that might cause these problems. An example of optimisation from the social field would be an older person who has considerable difficulties in maintaining functional autonomy in everyday living activities. Optimisation and functional autonomy would mean asking for more help from a spouse, getting home-help care from a providing agent, or, if living in a residential or care home, forming an alliance with the caretaking personnel and delegating the performance of household activities to them (see Baltes and Carstensen, 1999).

When some capacities are reduced and lost in old age, the third principle of compensation will be used to aid adaptation. The principle of compensation involves the use of alternate means of reaching a goal, making increased use of the 'tricks of the trade' to keep performance at desired levels. The strategy of compensation reflects the recognition of constraints or challenges in the environment and the need for adults to respond to these constraints or losses by taking counter-steps so that any potential impairment is lessened. Examples of compensatory mechanisms include the use of hearing aids, glasses or walking sticks. Similarly, a pianist like the aforementioned Rubinstein, who still wants to perform at the top level but has problems with the slowness brought on by age, has to find alternate ways of performing fast passages particularly at high levels. A compensatory mechanism for the ageing pianist would be to slow down his performance prior to such a passage, to give the impression that it was being played faster than was actually the case.

Another example of compensatory strategies is where a ballet dancer, who 'ages' very early in his or her profession, might turn to substitute activities within the same field. Even if a career as a performing artist is over as the ballet dancer approaches mid-life, this can be compensated for by taking up a new career as a ballet teacher. Despite serious disability in physical performance the ageing teacher can show the right movements by using the barre for support, or by showing the more demanding movements on videotape. Verbal instruction and correcting the students' inaccurate movements by pointing out their mistakes will be the main modes of instruction in many ballet situations.

There has been little empirical research examining selective optimisation with compensation. Nevertheless, within the last five years, this situation has changed in consequence of two new SOC measures, a 12- and a 48-item measure of the SOC strategies. Both scales have a similar format: participants choose one of two responses that most resembles their strategy of adaptation. Internal reliability scores for the SOC-12 tend to be low. In a study with young professionals under 36 years, Wiese, Freund and Baltes (2000) found internal reliability scores for this measure to be only around .5. Internal reliability scores for the SOC-48 tend to be higher at .67 and above (see Freund and Baltes, 2000). Test-retest reliability scores for these measures have also been found to be at an acceptable range (Freund and Baltes, 2002; Wiese et al., 2002).

The uses of SOC strategies are being examined in a growing range of contexts and with different age groups including young adults. SOC strategies have been found to be significantly related to health and to successful ageing. For instance, in a study by Freund and Baltes (1998; 1999) with older adults (mean age 83 years, SD 6.8) as part of the Berlin Ageing Study, the relationship between engagement in SOC strategies and outcome measures was examined. The SOC strategies were significantly correlated with measures of subjective well-being, positive emotions and absence of loneliness, even when a range of other rival variables were controlled, e.g. extraversion, neuroticism, control beliefs and intelligence. Freund and Baltes (2002) conducted two further studies with German participants from younger, middle-aged and older groups. Self-reported use of SOC strategies was found to be associated with display of positive emotions, environmental mastery, purpose in life and self-acceptance.

The model of selective optimisation with compensation focuses on the personal meaning the individual ascribes to different arenas of action in late life. 'Successful ageing' is thus defined by personal goal attainment and the development of individualised strategies to accomplish favoured tasks and behaviour. Whether an individual ages successfully or not cannot be predicted in a generalised fashion, but is dependent on the striving of the individual and the domains of functioning he or she considers it important to keep intact in late life. Agreeing with Jung and Erikson, Baltes and Carstensen (1996) suggest that finding meaning is the major developmental task of old age. Meaning is a multifaceted concept, however, and may refer to reaching a cognitive congruence between values, goals and actions in the retrospective recollections and interpretations of life. An element of self-discovery may enhance personal meaning in late life.

The possibility of defining successful ageing in terms of the flexible and multicriteria approach that this model proposes seems to be one of its most fruitful aspects. According to the model, success can be defined by different agents (individual–society), different criteria (subjective–objective) and different norms (ideal–functional). Internal or external strategies may be developed to support the individual when a wide range of activity or a high level of performance is needed to reach a preferred goal.

This model is also informative about the strategies adults use to achieve more favourable outcomes for the self into later life even under increasing constraints. By restricting the range of options and selecting only those experiences or activities that are most important or enjoyable for the self, adults can gain a lot of enjoyment and pleasure into advanced old age. This is also likely to result in better health and an associated higher quality of life. In contrast, through the notion of compensatory mechanisms, the above model is also sufficiently complex to recognise the losses and limitations that can also occur into later life and the strategies that need to be taken to overcome them. There is evidence that the use of the above strategies can be functional in maintaining or promoting successful ageing, i.e. in maximising positive or desired outcomes for the self (e.g. self-esteem, life satisfaction) and minimising or avoiding negative outcomes (e.g. loneliness).

A potential problem with this model is its lack of detail about either the nature of the processes involved, or the contexts within which these are likely to take place. Although goals may need to be reduced with age, the mechanisms involved or conditions needed to achieve this reduction are not yet sufficiently well understood. For instance, it is not yet clear why some people might be more successful than others in using these strategies. Perhaps adults most likely to engage in the above strategies are those who are currently experiencing the least amount of stress and threat in their lives. An alternative explanation is that adults who do not engage in the above strategies have lower levels of knowledge about the nature of old age and the opportunities this time of life can offer for continued development and functioning. One reason for this uncertainty may be the lack of empirical research examining this model. As noted by Marsiske *et al.*, 'the status of this model (selection, optimisation and compensation) in the literature, to date, has largely been conceptual' (1999: 35). Given its potential importance for older people's health and psychosocial functioning, more research exploring these issues is urgently needed. Such work is now proceeding in various countries both in Europe and North America.

Future research in this area could include studies exploring adaptation and possible use of strategies of selection, optimisation and compensation in adults who have experienced particular problems – for example, adaptation following falls or a hip replacement. The development of questionnaire measures of selection, optimisation and compensation has made possible their inclusion in a variety of studies dealing with issues from coping with cognitive decline to financial preparation for later life.

Shifting between assimilation and accommodation

In related but independent work to that just described, Jochen Brandtstädter and colleagues at the University of Trier in Germany (Brandtstädter and Greve, 1994; Brandtstädter and Renner, 1990; Brandtstädter and Rothermund, 1994; Brandtstädter et al., 1998) have attempted to explain the ways in which developmental losses or self-discrepancies with age can be reduced by two interrelated processes: assimilation and accommodation. Their work is based on the assumption that later life has many biological, social and psychological challenges and losses that place 'considerable strain on the individual's construction of self and personal continuity' (Brandtstädter and Greve, 1994: 52). Their theory also draws on the work of Markus and Wurf (1987) on representation of possible selves in the future and on protective strategies to enhance and maintain the self.

Assimilative coping refers to strategies where the individual actively attempts to change the environment in ways congruent with his/her own goals and expectations. Strategies of assimilation can include behavioural changes. Brandtstädter views the processes of selection, optimisation and compensation as well as socio-emotional selectivity theory (see next section) as sub-patterns of assimilation, because these strategies enable the individual to engage in their preferred activities at a high level of functioning. In addition, they help the individual to 'realize, maintain, and stabilize established self-definitions' (Brandtstädter et al., 1997: 108).

However, when threats or losses with age become too demanding and too difficult to maintain, Brandtstädter argues that it may be necessary for the individual to move towards processes of accommodation. Accommodative coping refers to strategies of readjusting goals or aspirations downwards in the light of constraints and limitations within the environment or the self – for example, as a result of physical ill-health or reductions in mobility. Examples of accommodative strategies include reappraisal of experiences or the attribution of positive meaning to new goals and experiences, and the making of self-enhancing comparisons (Brandtstädter and Greve, 1994).

Underpinning strategies both of assimilation and accommodation are immunising processes; these refer to mechanisms that can influence the process of receiving information relevant to the self, such as beliefs about the self, the availability of alternative interpretations or the rejection, or euphemistic interpretation, of self-threatening evidence. Further distinctions within immunisation processes can be made between processes of encoding and interpreting evidence in ways that reduce or deny its relevance for the self (i.e. data-oriented immunisation) and the reshaping or reorganisation of items of evidence so that these are excluded from its range of application (i.e. concept-oriented immunisation). The latter form of immunisation tends to occur when data-oriented immunisation strategies are not available.

Brandtstädter and colleagues have developed two scales to test the processes of assimilation and accommodation: the tenacious goal pursuit (TGP) and flexible goal adjustment (FGA) scales. In cross-sectional pooled research with nearly 4000 participants, Brandtstädter and Greve (1994) report a linear relationship with age for both the TGP ($r = .19$, p .001) and FGA ($r = -.22$, p .001). They found that older adults are increasingly likely to engage in accommodative processes, whereas younger adults are more likely to engage in strategies of assimilation. In addition, both scales were positively correlated with measures of optimisation, life satisfaction and absence of depression.

Empirical research exploring these strategies is still scarce. However, in a study with 120 chronic pain patients (aged 18–68), Schmitz, Saile and Nilges (1996) sought to examine the relationship between assimilation and accommodation, and the experience of chronic pain. Assimilation and accommodative coping strategies were measured by tenacious goal pursuit and flexible goal adjustment respectively. Additional measures of depression, pain intensity and pain-related disability were included. Results indicated that accommodative coping (i.e. adjusting personal goals) attenuated the negative impact of the pain experience on well-being, and helped maintain a positive life perspective in these patients.

Brandtstädter's theory makes an important contribution to our understanding of the nature of later life, particularly in his analysis of the processes of accommodation as the self comes to experience more serious threats, constraints and limitations to continuity of functioning. We shall come back to this theory in Chapter 6 when we focus on adaptation in advanced old age. Like the theory of selective optimisation with compensation, it assumes that individuals play an active role in their own development and experiences until late in life, and that they are not just the passive recipients of circumstances.

Despite its strengths, the above model also has some limitations, not least in explaining the mechanisms involved in the above strategies. Brandtstädter and colleagues, for instance, argue that one of the key factors in the development of strategies of assimilation and accommodation is flexibility in adjusting goals and expectations in the light of the context in which the individual finds him/herself. However, researchers need to be more precise about the mechanisms involved, and why some people might be more successful in using these strategies than others. Specifically, it is not enough to propose that these strategies develop over time and generally occur outside conscious awareness. There are times when persons do not make optimal responses – when, for example, resistance rather than accommodation may be the most appropriate response for the type of constraints or limitations being experienced within the environment. More research is needed to understand better how these strategies come to be selected, their relationship to experienced change in the environment, and consequences for their functioning.

Research also needs to be undertaken to examine these strategies within a range of contexts – for example, with older adults of lower and higher socio-economic status, in various psychological conditions, and especially of different degrees of frailty. Exploring differences in strategies of adaptation among adults in urban and rural areas would also be interesting. People in rural areas may have qualitatively different lifestyles and different means of accessing services. Researchers must take more account of the actual life experiences of older adults and the ways these experiences are represented psychologically. More interdisciplinary research undertaken together with sociologists, anthropologists and geographers would be valuable.

Future studies also need to find ways of interlinking different theoretical approaches. We have already mentioned the possible interrelationship between the concepts of assimilation and accommodation and the theory of selective optimisation with compensation. Another even more closely related framework is the theory of control and its model of developmental optimisation in primary and secondary control (Heckhausen, 1999; Heckhausen and Schulz, 1995; Schulz and Heckhausen, 1996; 1999). This theory is based on the assumption of the existence of a fundamental motivation for primary control, i.e. producing effects in the environment contingent on one's own behaviour. The concept of secondary control refers to the person's internal world and maintaining resources needed to be able to exert primary control. Individuals vary in their ability to regulate their control strategies and this impacts on their mental health and affective well-being (Heckhausen et al., 2001). Assimilation is similar to primary control in that it refers to active efforts on the part of the person to influence the situation. However, the primary function of the former is consistency of goals, and hence sense of identity, over time, rather than control over the environment. We shall return to the concepts of primary and secondary control in Chapter 5, and to the related concept of autonomy when discussing care of dependent elderly people in Chapter 6.

Socio-emotional selectivity theory

Developed by Laura Carstensen, socio-emotional selectivity theory (Carstensen, 1991; Carstensen et al., 1999) claims that reductions in social contact across adulthood are volitional and result from changes in the salience of specific social goals, i.e. a preference for present emotion-based relationships rather than relationships based on knowledge acquisition.

Information acquisition and the regulation of emotion are two principle classes of goals that are achieved through social contact. The essential premise of this theory is that the relative importance of these goals changes as a function of perceived time. When time is perceived as largely open-ended, future-orientated goals such as information acquisition are of paramount importance. When time is perceived as limited, adults adapt by prioritising present-orientated emotion-based relationships. Age is associated with preferences for emotionally satisfying contact, which is preferred over other types such as information-rich contact.

To illustrate their theory, Carstensen *et al.* (1999) compare relationships across the life-span. The first-year student invests much time and energy in establishing new friendships. Maximising experience allows more satisfying choices to be made. A newlywed couple, if they are sensible, will devote a lot of time to their relationship and to solving problems as they arise within it. Although this may take considerable effort, this is balanced in the longer term by the lessening of future conflicts. An elderly couple, by contrast, 'often decides to accept their relationship as it is, to appreciate what is good, and ignore what is troubling, rather than seek new solutions to problems' (Carstensen *et al.*, 1999: 167). The difference can be understood in terms of a greater present rather than future orientation, and maximising emotional satisfaction.

This theory suggests that age-related differences in anticipated future time influence developmental trends in knowledge-related social goals. In childhood and youth, much new information is gained through contact with more experienced and knowledgeable individuals. A teenager is especially dependent on the views and ideas of his or her peer group. As the years go by, social interaction will be needed less and will also be less effective in obtaining information. The individual is better educated in many ways, and access to new information shifts to more specialised sources such as books, journals and data banks. Thus, the function of social contacts as gateways to information is reduced, and relied on only in some special situations, such as asking a physician friend for advice on some medical symptoms or an accountant friend for advice on some tax matters. Some information gained from friends may be potentially useful, but on the whole, argues Carstensen (1991) that this kind of 'banking information for the future' is of less use in old age. Lang and Carstensen (1994) have produced evidence to support their view that older people proactively manage the decline in the size of their social network as they age. When time is limited, familiar social partners are preferred because they are best able to influence emotional states in the short term.

We partly disagree with Carstensen concerning this information-acquisition aspect of her theory. Some evidence has emerged that confirms the continuous need for information acquisition in decision making in old age. Older adults, particularly those who are well educated, can be very skilful decision makers; this skill can be developed through reliance on a large social network of well-educated friends, who can give expert advice in difficult situations. Birren, for example, has shown that age per se does not have the impact on decision making in consumer affairs that education has. The autobiography groups that he has also pioneered demonstrate the value of forming new reciprocal relationships for self-development in later life (Birren and Deutchman, 1991; Randall and Kenyon, 2001).

Our identities and self-images are also constructed according to how we perceive that others perceive us. Throughout life, we get the building blocks for our self-images in the mirrors that significant others provide for us. Expressed in another way, our identities are negotiated with important others in our immediate life-space. As we get older, however, there are fewer and fewer persons that can confirm our long-held views of ourselves. Many social partners cannot provide us with confirmatory feedback because of differences in experiences, values or preferences, or because they hold stereotypic views of how older persons are. Carstensen gives the example of an older woman who has always been interested in the latest fashions and who likes to wear heavy make-up, but who might be viewed as holding up a mask against ageing if we did not know her personal history (see also Featherstone and Hepworth, 1991).

A central function of our socially acquired self-knowledge is regulating and controlling our emotional states (Markus and Herzog, 1991). When we encounter negative information, we achieve a sense of continuity and stability by defending our favoured views of ourselves. In old age, our self-schemes tend to be well elaborated and delineated. A sign of this is the fact that we have a better memory for personal biography, especially in the case of emotionally charged life events, than for other types of material (Cohen, 1991; Ruth and Vilkko, 1996). We also have a more developed understanding of emotional context and meaning in old age (Labouvie-Vief, 2005).

There are reductions in contacts with co-workers after retirement, and contact with grandchildren can also be somewhat reduced. But stability can be established in the amount of contact with one's own children. Siblings represent another important group of attachment figures, and they help out in many practical matters. Low-income groups in particular rely on the help of siblings because of fewer alternative resources. Generally, in both Europe and America families do not abandon their elderly members. Most of the friends that old people stay in contact with seem to be old friends. There are substantial differences in the preferences for social activities and social contacts, however, and some of these differences can be explained by gender, ethnicity and, above all, health status (Carstensen, 1991).

Studies have shown that the social networks of the elderly are similar in structure to those of younger age groups, but that the number of contacts within the networks are fewer for older people. They tend to prefer contact with their own children or friends, or other familiar persons, whom they contact often. In these relationships there are quite intense emotions invested, and there are few data to support the idea of 'emotional flattening' in old age. However, there does appear to be a reduced interest in interacting with acquaintances or a new partner. The patterns of avoiding initiating new contacts with non-familial persons is clearly visible in nursing homes and other institutions. There might be quite a risk involved in contact seeking in old age: conversations become more difficult, for instance, if the other person has difficulty hearing as a consequence of sensory loss. According to Carstensen, withdrawal represents an adaptive response in an overcrowded or unpredictable social environment. That is presumably why interventions to activate contact seeking have often only a temporary effect in institutions. The older person does not perceive the need for increased activities; this need is felt only by relatives and care staff.

A central principle of Carstensen's selectivity theory is the reliance on old social contacts to maximise the possibilities of positive emotion in encounters with significant others. Far from being emotionally flattened, older people appear to be emotionally conscious, making judicious decisions about activities and giving thoughtful consideration to their functions as affect regulators (Carstensen, 1991: 210). Aversive social feedback has an even greater impact on the well-being of the aged than a passive response. Actively choosing our social partners reflects our adaptive efforts to optimise the positive outcome of our social interaction in old age.

Even if people are social by nature, there are changes in social activity with age; this need not be perceived as loss, but simply as adaptive. Carstensen argues that the lesser amount of social activity in old age is deliberate, it is actively chosen, because it benefits older people and therefore can be considered 'successful'. Of course, many of the newly retired elderly and even some of the oldest of the old are providers of care, services and money to the middle-aged generation, although this reciprocity is insufficiently referred to in gerontological research.

Health seems to be the main variable explaining the changes in social activity in old age. Carstensen states that 'in many cases healthy older people do not show the supposed patterns of social aging. Indeed, a number of otherwise compelling psychological theories have been reduced to corollaries of health' (1991: 201). As an example, she mentions retirement, which was earlier considered as having a deleterious impact on well-being. Now we know that this is not the case, but when sick people retire (early), their illness will negatively affect their well-being.

Carstensen has collaborated with Margret Baltes in arguing for the complementarity of the theory of socio-emotional selectivity with that of selective optimisation with compensation (Baltes and Carstensen, 1996). The latter describes processes that are necessary for the realisation of goals, but does not refer to the criteria involved in the initial selection. Socio-emotional selectivity theory is involved in explaining this selection in the domains of emotions and social relations.

Future research in this area should examine in more detail the mechanisms through which differences in relationships occur. For instance, it is well known that women have more social contacts, and especially more intimate friends or confidantes, than men. Those who take the role of confidante tend to be women, both for other women and for most men. The difference in life expectancy between the sexes in many western countries is around five years (in some countries the difference is bigger, such as Finland, where it is eight years). This means that older women often live alone, while most older men are married. It also means that women are primary caregivers to a greater extent than men, even if many men nowadays also act as caregivers. It is not clear what role gender plays in socio-emotional selectivity theory, or indeed other variables such as chronological age, geographical location or socio-economic status. Nor has much connection been made between selectivity in social relationships with age and consequences for health and well-being. These and other questions should be addressed in future studies.

The dynamic maturational model of attachment

As a final example of theory in the field of ageing and adaptation we look at the potential contribution of a major theory designed to explain behaviour earlier in the life-span. Attachment theory, as developed by the British psychiatrist John Bowlby (1969; 1977; 1979; 1988), draws attention to the development and operation of the primary human motivation for safety and protection. Drawing on a range of evidence as diverse as psychoanalysis, ethology and cognitive psychology, Bowlby hypothesised that a biologically rooted, universal need was present in all human beings to attain or retain proximity to other preferred individuals. Bowlby argued that this propensity to form strong emotional bonds with particular individuals was desirable, and had protective value throughout the life course, from 'the cradle to the grave' (Bowlby, 1979: 129). Particularly under conditions of threat or danger, this need for closeness with others is hypothesised to manifest itself in certain behaviours used functionally to increase the probability of attaining or retaining proximity to the preferred individual. Bowlby also developed the construct of internal representational models to explain the continued importance of early attachment experiences in later health, development and behaviour. Specifically, Bowlby argued that individuals had a number of representational models linked to specific relationships and different memory systems. These representational models, Bowlby argued, would guide behaviour and development under different conditions.

A major contribution of Mary Ainsworth to attachment theory has been to recognise individual differences in patterns of attachment (Ainsworth, 1989). To assess individual patterns of attachment Ainsworth developed the

'Strange Situation' (Ainsworth *et al.*, 1978). This assessment involves a videotaped laboratory situation when the child is left either alone, or in the company of an adult unknown to them. Usually, on about two occasions, the mother or other attachment figure will depart when a stimulus such as a knock has been signalled by the researchers. For a very young child being left in a strange environment, alone or with a stranger, is an anxiety-provoking experience. The Strange Situation procedure above has shown that there is a range of individual differences in patterns of attachment. Children with the so-called Type B relationships welcome their mothers' return and are happy to begin playing again after a brief reunion with them. Children with the Type A pattern of attachment tend to ignore the departure and return of their mothers, while children with a Type C pattern of attachment are those who are highly anxious and fearful when their mothers depart, and are ambivalent on their return.

Although researchers in attachment can view Type A and C patterns of attachment in terms of pathology (e.g. the inability of the child to regulate his/her emotions), Patricia Crittenden views these responses differently. In her dynamic maturational model of attachment the Types A and C patterns of attachment are not necessarily viewed in terms of pathology, but as appropriate and successful strategies to manage particular difficulties and problems being experienced. Specifically, critical to survival is the ability to identify the probability, extent and nature of danger soon enough to take protective action while having appropriate strategies in place either to protect the self and others, or reduce the risk and extent of the danger.

Crittenden draws on diverse areas of evidence from cognitive psychology to evolutionary biology and child development, to examine and document these strategies. Within the Crittenden model, childhood patterns of attachment can persist into adulthood, where they remain (so long, that is, as they continue to enable the individual to feel a sense of control, predictability and safety in their environments). Within the Strange Situation, therefore, each pattern of attachment is seen to reflect sophisticated and adaptive responses to particular kinds of danger and threat. Crittenden has also developed and extended the value and use of attachment to encompass any issue or experience where the self is under threat (Crittenden, 1995; 1997; 1999; 2000).

Crittenden (1997) argues that early experiences of danger can retain their impact on later development and functioning, given the immaturity of the central nervous system, along with a tendency to overestimate the probability of danger. However, for Crittenden, early childhood experiences do not always predict experiences in relationships as adults. To the contrary, through a process of maturation, mental capacities develop greatly through adolescence and adulthood. Young children have a limited capacity to identify impending danger and do not have wide repertoires of available protective responses. By adolescence, individuals can process information in increasingly complex ways.

The most common method for assessing patterns of attachment in adulthood is the Adult Attachment Interview (AAI). This interview was first developed by Mary Main and colleagues – Kaplan and Cassidy (Main *et al.*, 1985) – but then further developed and extended by Crittenden (1999), who added a range of new categories and classifications. The AAI is a structured interview that sets out to examine semantic, episodic and working (integrative) memory systems. These memory systems are addressed systematically through the interview, so that comparisons can be made between them. Each memory system can be evaluated independently, but discrepancies between memory systems provide the clearest guide to the speaker's mental functioning and the way information is being used to protect the self. Semantic memory is probed by requesting five adjectives to describe the relationships with each parent. Episodic memory is probed (i) by asking for early memories to support each adjective, and (ii) through probing of specific sorts of incident, e.g. being hurt, rejected or separated from parents. Integration is assessed in a range of ways, for example by asking speakers to think about changes over time (e.g. how early experiences influenced current development and functioning) or the validity of different perspectives on a given situation.

In addition, although the AAI is often referred to as one instrument, it has several components, including a particular set of questions and a specific way of analysing data. It is possible therefore to substitute one component of this interview for another, e.g. using the questions as originally developed but changing the data-analysis strategy, or substituting the questions on attachment for those in a different field, but retaining the method of discourse analysis based on comparisons between different memory systems.

Within Crittenden's system adults can be classified into A, B or C patterns of attachment; they can also be categorised in more refined and detailed ways. For instance, individuals classified as dismissing can be coded as idealising (A1), derogating (A2), compulsively caregiving (A3) or compulsively compliant (A4). Adults can also use some of these strategies in particular instances, e.g. be idealising with reference to one parent, and compulsively compliant with the other. Further categories of the Type A classification are available for clinical populations (see Crittenden, 2002). Similar levels of detail are available for the Type B and C patterns of attachment (see Crittenden, 1995; 2000; 2002).

Adults classified as Type A dismissing have transcripts in which negative affect such as anxiety and fear is omitted. The mechanism through which this is done will vary by sub-component (e.g. idealising or derogating). Within Crittenden's framework, the Type A individual will try to distract him/herself from negative affective states by not thinking about the stressor or by blocking the stressor from vision. In the context of ageing, a Type A response might be one in which individuals react in a falsely positive and

Figure 4.2 Crittenden's dynamic maturational model of attachment

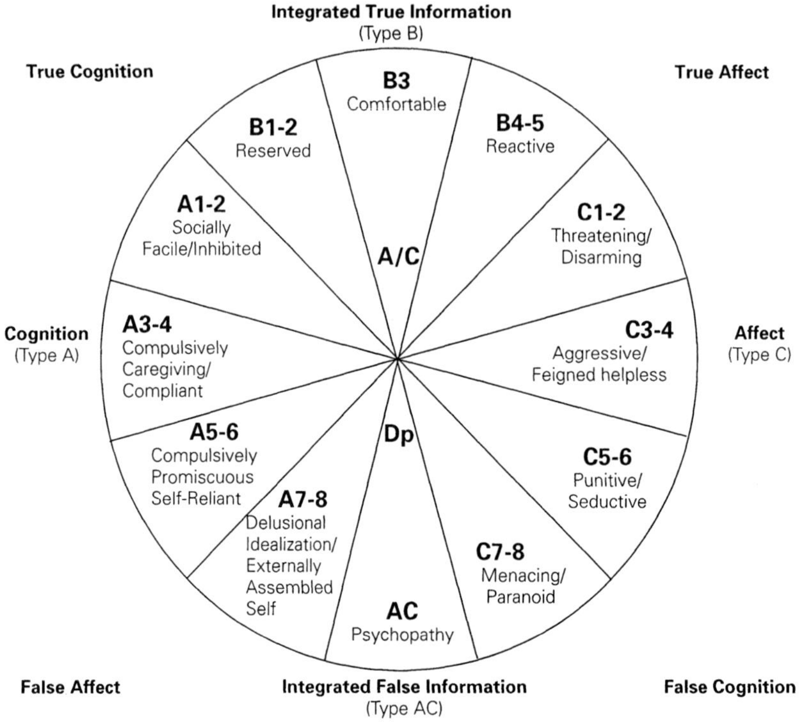

optimistic way, without necessarily having the evidence and means to support such positive views. Such adults may also learn from an early age to
inhibit their own negative feeling states (to avoid anger) and to organise
themselves around 'if/then' contingencies (e.g. 'If I exercise and maintain a
good diet then my old age will be fine'). Nevertheless, although such strategies can be functional, the individual can still feel anxiety and worry, which
can be exacerbated because he/she feels unable to communicate this negative affect to others.

For the adult classified as Type C within the Crittenden system, a different strategy of adaptation is seen. Inconsistent responses from caregivers or
attachment figures as a child, along with continued inconsistency and
unpredictability from close others as an adult, mean that the person with a
Type C attachment cannot trust temporal (if/then) information and,
instead, adaptation occurs around intense affective displays (i.e. anger, fear
and the desire for comfort). Adults using the Type C strategy know that the
probability of help or attention from others in the environment increases
with heightened displays of negative affect. The purposeful heightening of
affective display occurs because this produces results where a milder display
of affect will fail. The problem is that when habituation occurs (others get
so used to a certain level of provocative behaviour that they then ignore it),

the individual needs to escalate into ever increasing self-endangering behaviours to secure the needed attention or support. The specific strategy of negative affect entails the alternation of affective displays around anger, fear, and the desire for comfort (C1–4), such that one feeling state is exaggerated above others and/or then alternated. Further C patterns are available for clinical groups (C5–8; see Figure 4.2).

The above two main strategies of adaptation arise because of problems and challenges being experienced in the environment. Where such challenges are not so evident, adults do not need to develop strategies of adaptation, and in such cases, can cope with challenges using a balanced integration of both cognition and affect, i.e. a Type B pattern of relationships.

Although there is little empirical work on Crittenden's model to date with adults, it has promising implications. Crittenden's contribution to attachment has been to develop and extend the use of attachment to encompass any issue or experience where the self is under threat. Specifically, rather than solely or primarily being about separation and loss, attachment theory is relevant for understanding any experience where the self is threatened, including threats around own prospective old age. Crittenden also developed earlier classificatory systems to reflect the increased number of strategies adults are using in response to a wider array of potential threats. The potential contribution Crittenden makes to the gerontological field lies in the application of this model to understanding the ways adults experience and respond to challenges they associate with their own old age.

The benefits and strengths of this model lie in its complexity and detail. In contrast to earlier views of the representational self as being unitary and integrated, Crittenden joins other researchers who assume a much more complex model of the self. For instance, Markus and Wurf describe how researchers have moved away from a static and fixed model of the self and towards an understanding of the self-structure as an 'active ... multidimensional, multifaceted dynamic structure that is systematically impacted in all aspects of social information processing' (1987: 301). Crittenden also makes reference to the self as an 'organisational process ... never completely finished, stable or even "true" ... [adapting to] life's ever changing challenges'. Also, the method of assessment lies in a series of comparisons between memory systems, which are outside the conscious awareness or control of most individuals.

Consequently, this model addresses criticisms put forward by Biggs (1999), among others, warning against the use of self-report assessments. It does, however, necessitate detailed and complex training. The complexity of the training is not necessarily a problematic issue. Researchers always need to be increasingly detailed and refined in their observations of behaviour and experiences, and it should not be surprising that the achievement of such sophisticated insights does necessitate detailed training. We shall describe further the value of this conceptual framework in describing research on attitudes to ageing in the next chapter.

Analysis of the AAI is also time-consuming, although this will become less problematic with the use of voice-recognition software. Areas for future research include finding a new self-report measure. This would save time and increase the use of this model in a wider array of settings.

In this chapter we set out to review a select number of strategies relevant to understanding adaptation and management of the self into later life. There are a large number of other theories that have been found useful in understanding adaptation and management of the self into later life, including self-regulation (Carver and Scheier, 1998) and social production function theory (Lindenberg, 1996). (For a brief review of theories on self-regulation of development in adulthood and ageing see Heckhausen, 2005.) It is understandable why adaptation has become such a popular topic for researchers. Understanding the skills and strategies many older adults use to successfully regulate threats posed by their own prospective old age is information that can be used to help adults who are adapting less well to an experience that is expected to become almost universal in the course of this century. Furthermore, given that many positive attributes associated with ageing may only arise as a consequence of facing anxieties about one's future, research exploring the regulation of threats is clearly central to many other areas in the developmental psychology of ageing that were discussed in Chapter 2. In Chapter 5 we shall consider in more detail three current research themes that help us understand better the experience of ageing.

5 Current research themes on ageing and adaptation

In the previous chapter we saw how contemporary theory on adaptation to ageing in later life has rejected the view that old age is intrinsically a difficult time of life. Older people by and large adjust well to the changes that occur, find ways of maintaining their principal goals and meeting their needs for competence, control and relationship. In later chapters we shall focus on the problems and challenges of advanced old age, but even in circumstances of frailty, most older people impress by their ability to cope. Why is this so? In some ways the resilience of the old in the face of decline and death is paradoxical. They appear happier than they should be, happier than younger people would be if faced with the same physical and social losses (Diener *et al.*, 1999). In this chapter we discuss empirical research relating to three burgeoning themes in the study of ageing and adaptation, which will help us to understand this paradox.

The first theme concerns adults' attitudes towards ageing and old age, and the role that such evaluations can play in influencing well-being. Researchers have found that participants with more negative attitudes towards their own old age have reported greater anxiety and worry about ageing, lowered subjective well-being when followed up longitudinally, and even reductions in the will to live. This is not a minor issue. A substantial number of adults in western societies do have serious concerns about their own future old age and about what this time of life will mean for them. Research exploring the nature and origins of positive attitudes could be applied in helping adults with less positive attitudes.

The second theme is the role of personal relationships in adjustment to ageing. Relationships are one of the most significant sources of meaning and enjoyment in later life. They have the potential to impact on a wide range of human experiences and behaviours, including emotional well-being, recovery following physical illness and mortality rates. We consider three areas of research within the relationship literature:

1. spousal relationships, and particularly the factors that might influence adjustment following bereavement
2. the nature of wider social networks into the latter half of the life cycle and the factors sustaining such relationships

3. older people's perception of their own position within their society and culture, illustrated in particular by studies on the social factors affecting adaptation in the aftermath of major historical events such as war and war-related trauma.

The third theme is the study of personal meaning and spirituality. As the study of stress and adaptation has developed to take more account of the subjective interpretation of life events, so there has been a greater need to assess the whole intrapersonal context. This was well recognised by the pioneer stress researcher Richard Lazarus:

> Throughout life people struggle to make sense of what happens to them and to provide themselves with a sense of order and continuity. This struggle is centered in divergent personal beliefs and commitments, shapes cognitive appraisals of stressful transactions and coping, and therefore has profound consequences for morale, social and work functioning, and somatic health.
>
> (Lazarus and DeLongis, 1983: 246)

Of the various sources of existential meaning (i.e. the meaning that justifies a person's existence in his or her own mind), the most widespread are those provided by religious and spiritual beliefs. Yet religion has been a neglected area of ageing research since the early studies of Moberg (1968). That situation has now changed as gerontologists, particularly in the United States, have recognised the power of religion in sustaining older people's lives.

Attitudes to ageing and older adults

With people living longer than ever before, there is an increased urgency to identify the factors likely to influence health, autonomy and well-being in later years. These factors can include adults' attitudes towards their own ageing and future old age. Attitudes can be understood as multidimensional constructs, reflecting 'a psychological tendency that is expressed by evaluating a particular entity, object or experience with some degree of favour or disfavor' (Eagly and Chaiken, 1993: 1). Attitudes can be divided further into beliefs, feelings and behaviours; this additional sub-division means that researchers can be increasingly refined about the nature of adults' attitudes, and the ways specific attitudinal components relate to other variables and outcomes.

Research on attitudes to ageing is important given their impact on later development, health and mortality. People who evaluate their own ageing negatively are likely to feel a lack of control, predictability and safety about their futures; yet these attributes are central to the occurrence of health and the absence of pathology. They are also less likely to recognise or appreciate the many positive attributes and experiences that can occur in later life, such as increased experience and wisdom (see Chapters 2 and 3 of this book). The inability to appreciate the experience and insights that adults gain over many decades of life can have serious consequences for relationships and family functioning, particularly given the vital role that older adults can play in the lives of their children and grandchildren (Gutmann, 1987; 1997). Adults with more negative attitudes may also be less motivated to prepare financially for later life, or to engage in more healthy lifestyle choices in terms of exercise and diet behaviours. The latter is especially serious given the role that health behaviours can play in later morbidity and mortality. In a US-based longitudinal study, Levy *et al.* (2002) found that perceptions of ageing were strongly predictive of mortality up to 23 years later.

Early attitudinal researchers tended to focus on attitudes towards older adults, and particularly the attitudes of younger adults towards older people (Rosencranz and McNevin, 1969; Tuckman and Lorge, 1953). Attitudes were often found to be negative. Golde and Kogan (1959), for instance, asked open-ended questions of undergraduates and found that students tended to characterise older people as being lonely and dependent on others. However, other studies found few differences in attitudes between younger and older adults, and so researchers began to examine the contexts and situational influences on attitudes and stereotypes of older adults. Weinberger and Millham (1974) found that attitudes were more negative when the target person was a 'representative' older person rather than a specific individual. Similarly, attitudes can be more negative when measures focus on the physical characteristics of older adults or their economic welfare rather than on personality traits.

A difficulty with this early research, however, was that it was not guided by any strong theoretical framework. Theory is important for integrating knowledge, explaining the relationships between phenomena and making predictions about what is not yet known or observed. Furthermore, as noted in Chapter 1, theory can also be valuable in providing new perspectives on experiences and behaviours. Without theory, we get inconsistencies in research findings and few insights into what is known about a given topic.

Beliefs about the self over time

Ryff (1991) was one of the first researchers to examine perceptions and beliefs about adults' own ageing rather than beliefs about ageing generally. She also offered one of the first systematic attempts to draw on theory, in an examination of age differences in adults' perceptions of their own functioning over time. Ryff sought to compare actual and ideal self-ratings over the adult years. She based her research within the social-psychological framework of possible selves, defined as evaluations about what people can become, what they would like to become and what they are fearful of becoming (Markus and Nurius, 1986). She also drew upon the self-narrative work of Gergen and Gergen (1988), which aims to understand individual development over time.

Perceived functioning for the self can remain stable, show improvements or show decrements. As well as providing a base for current evaluations of the self, these perceptions can motivate future behaviour and choices. Ryff also examines the possibility that discrepancies between the actual and ideal self diminish with age; the actual self refers to attributes individuals believe they actually possess, while the ideal self refers to attributes that they would ideally like to have. Diminishing discrepancies between these two selves with age is an interesting issue that may have significant implications for understanding and facilitating better health for older adults.

In her study, Ryff (1991) recruited adults from both genders and across the age range: younger adults (mean age 19 years, n = 123) were recruited through an educational institution, while mid-life and older adults (mean ages 46 and 73 respectively) were recruited through community and civic organisations. Perceptions of improvement or decline in functioning over time were assessed by self-report scales measuring six dimensions of psychological health: life satisfaction, autonomy, personal growth, self-acceptance, environmental mastery and positive relations with others. Participants completed the scales under four conditions, in terms of: (i) the present, (ii) the person they would most like to be (i.e. their ideal selves), (iii) what they were like in the past, and (iv) what they felt they would be like in the future. Ratings of the past and the future referred to the generational group closest to the present, i.e. the past for younger generations was adolescence, while for mid-life and older adults the past was defined as young adulthood and mid-life respectively. Similarly, for young and mid-life adults, the future focused on ages 40–50 and 75–80 respectively; while the future was defined for the older age group at 10–15 years later. Psychometric properties for these measures were good.

Ryff's results indicated that each generation has different views of themselves at various time points. The young and mid-life age groups rated present functioning higher than the past. These perceived improvements from the past to the present occurred in most domains: autonomy, positive relations with others, life satisfaction, environmental mastery and personal growth. The young and mid-life age groups also foresaw continued progress and gains on these domains of functioning from the present to the future. For older adults, past ratings were similar to present evaluations, indicating stability in functioning, however older adults had significantly higher past ratings than did the two younger age groups on self-acceptance, autonomy and positive relations with others. Future assessments indicated that older adults generally saw stability in some aspects of functioning such as self-acceptance, but declines in others such as purpose in life, environmental mastery, positive relations with others and personal growth.

These findings suggest that adults' perceptions and beliefs about their progression through the life course are generally realistic; however, by linking theory in social and developmental psychology, Ryff gives us more sophisticated insights into the nature of these beliefs and perceptions. In young and middle adulthood health typically remains good and opportunities are often more plentiful; as such, continued development and high levels of functioning are valid perspectives to hold. Although later life can offer many opportunities for continued development and enjoyment of life, this time of life can also bring with it constraints and losses. Older adults seem typically to accept changes and challenges that occur, and adjust their expectations accordingly.

The integration of the perspectives from social and developmental psychology alerts us to the complexity of adults' attitudes and perceptions about ageing. In addition to the range of views adults can have for themselves in different contexts, multiple selves theory also suggests that adults' perceptions and attitudes consist of a range of evaluations including their hopes, fears and goals. These perceptions can guide and shape later behaviour and decisions, so it is important that they are understood in their complexity and detail. Theory also needs to be able to make predictions about future beliefs and behaviour, and a challenge for researchers will be to identify the ways specific attitudinal components influence and predict later behaviour and health.

Ryff also found that older adults have the lowest discrepancies between their actual and ideal selves. Ratings for the ideal self were higher than ratings for the self in the present; however, the difference between these ratings showed progressive decrements with age group so that the ideal selves of the oldest age groups were closest to their assessments of themselves in the present. This trend remained the same for all six of the psychological well-being sub-scales. These results are consistent with the view that development continues into the latter part of the life course towards greater acceptance of the self, even with greater awareness of flaws and limitations. Such a view has echoes in the work of other researchers. Labouvie-Vief *et al.* (1995), for instance, argue that changes can occur in self-representation from self-representations that are relatively poorly differentiated to representations that are more complex, including attention to process, context and individuality.

A strength and a limitation of Ryff's work is her focus on positive health for the self in different contexts. Other studies have often defined and measured health solely or primarily in terms of illness, i.e. varying degrees of deviations and malfunctioning in individuals (e.g. Groves and Pennell, 1995; Hopton and Hunt, 1996; Prosser and McArdle, 1996). Ryff's emphasis on positive functioning is not unproblematic however, particularly for researchers who want to understand the relationship between health and the process of ageing. For instance, by exploring perceptions of the future in terms of positive relations with others, it becomes difficult to examine the role or influence of relationships on the ways adults evaluate and view their own future old age. Similarly, if one wishes to examine the role of self-esteem or self-efficacy in influencing positive attitudes into later life, there is an overlap in constructs that is problematic.

Future research needs to explore and examine the ways age-associated changes are interpreted and evaluated. For instance, when attitudes to age-ing are very negative, it is not yet clear whether these evaluations are based on erroneous information about later life, a pragmatic realism, or other vari-ables such as current mood state or neuroticism. Similarly, the nature of positive attitudes also remains unclear. Positive attitudes may reflect a naiveté about potential problems; as awareness of problems but the use of certain strategies to manage these; or genuine growth and acceptance, earned through any number of mechanisms still to be understood. Research examining the ways adults interpret and evaluate unwanted age-associated challenges and changes is discussed next.

Attitudes towards own prospective old age (anxiety, worry, threat)

Although people can associate the latter part of their lives with unwanted problems and losses, it should not be assumed that these associations are always pathological or in need of change. Not only are some negative expec-tations for later life realistic, but there is growing evidence that older people are typically highly skilled in successfully managing problems and challenges (see Chapter 4). In addition, there is evidence from history and anthropology that gives testament to the creativity and resilience of human beings, not only in overcoming adversity and danger but also in creating more favourable out-comes for the self and others (Garliski, 1975; De Vries, 1995). Future studies may find that under certain conditions, negative attitudes are important pre-cursors to continued development and health in later years. This is because positive attributes such as wisdom and integrity may only occur when fears and worries associated with ageing have been addressed and resolved.

Nevertheless, people can view the latter part of their lives in negative and fearful ways. In a study with a group of nurses for instance, Bernard (1998) found that many respondents were highly anxious about their own ageing and future old age and viewed their later years with 'trepidation' (p. 637). Gething, Fethney, McKee, Goff, Churchward and Matthews (2002) exam-ined nurses' attitudes towards their own ageing and stereotypes of older adults; they found that participants' views were 'in the main … negative' (p. 74). Rabbitt (1999) provides further evidence that later life can be evaluated in very negative ways; 'early recognition that ageing is not at all a benevolent process compelled me to realise that a determination to stress any possible (positive) aspect of this condition … is a betrayal of science and of responsibility. All of us who are lucky must put up with ageing as best we can, but to do anything useful about it we must recognise and understand all of the extraordinary unpleasant things that it does to us and the ways in which these contract the scope of our lives. ... [Ageing is] an unpleasant condition that, if we are lucky, we will all experience at first hand' (pp. 180–181).

Given the ways negative attitudes can impact adversely on heath (see opening paragraphs of this section), there is a surprising paucity of research in this area. For instance according to Treharne (1990) 'little research is published in this country about the social and psychological issues faced by the elderly' (p. 780). Similarly, sociologist Thompson (1992) concluded that his book on the experience of ageing stands 'strangely alone' (p. 26). One reason for this paucity of research may be because researchers and gerontologists themselves view old age in negative and aversive ways. For instance, according to Bernard (1998) 'if we indeed are so afraid to ask it of ourselves [old age], then perhaps this helps explain why we have so little research on this issue' (p. 635). Another reason for the paucity of research in this area is because there are so few measures available to researchers. For instance, some researchers in this field have used the Facts on Aging Quiz (Palmore, 1977) to measure attitudes, but there have been concerns about the psychometric properties of this scale (O'Hanlon, Camp & Osofsky, 1993). Another scale often used is the Opinions About People Scale from the Ontario Welfare Council (1971). Despite acknowledging the limitations of this scale (including low internal reliability scores), Wullschleger *et al.* (1996) have defended its use in their research by stating that this scale is more recent than two others developed in 1953 and 1961 respectively.

O'Hanlon sought to contribute to this field by carrying out a series of studies exploring, measuring and explaining adults' attitudes to their own ageing and future old age. Although there is little research exploring and examining positive attitudes to ageing, O'Hanlon was especially interested in negative attitudes given the possibility that these have more immediate and adverse consequences on functioning and well-being.

In exploring adults' attitudes to ageing, O'Hanlon (2002) used a series of open-ended questions administered via the internet (n = 942). A second group of participants completed the same questionnaire but via the more traditional pen and paper format; no significant differences were found on the quantitative measures between the two groups, which suggests that the web is a useful and quick method of data collection. In both formats, participants were asked to describe the likely process of their own ageing to advanced old age; participants were also asked what aspects of ageing and old age they found, or expected to find, positive, and what aspects they found or expected to find worrying or of concern. Participants were also asked how they felt about the general experience of their own ageing and future old age. In responding to the last question, many participants responded positively, but many others were highly anxious and worried: 'I am terrified of getting older, not only for health reasons or for financial reasons, but because of so much loss – of loved ones and just about everything else' (Martha, age 57); 'How do I feel about getting older? Anxious. Worried. Afraid. … I dread old age with a phobia that nearly consumes me at times' (Sally, age 40) and 'I will take increasing physical risks as I age and hopefully end my life in an extreme manner so I don't have to face old age' (Mike, age 36).

O'Hanlon used the rich data set above to develop a number of scales measuring attitudes to ageing in different ways. Measures developed by O'Hanlon (2002; O'Hanlon & Coleman, 2004) included: the General Attitudes to Ageing Scale (GAAS); the Physical Social and Psychological Ageing Scale (which measures attitudes to physical, social and psychological experiences of ageing); the Constraints, Losses and Positive Ageing Attitudes Scale (which measures attitudes to possible constraints, losses and positive experiences in later life); the Fears about Own Ageing Measure (FOAM) and the Ageing Controllability Scale (which measures perceived control over potential positive and negative experiences in later life). A list of possible items for these scales were generated from the initial exploratory study; these items were then critically reviewed on several criteria including their clarity and meaning, and their content coverage in terms of reflecting the constructs of interest. In discussions with others, items were then revised, rephrased or removed before being piloted on participants recruited from a range of settings and contexts; these settings included the high street, church groups and community-based social and health activities. Across studies, these measures were repeatedly found to have good psychometric properties, e.g. the scales had good internal reliability, and were significantly related to other measures in the expected directions. With just five to six items each, these scales are also short and easy for participants to rate and researchers to score.

Using the above measures, O'Hanlon sought to understand and explain adults' general attitudes to their own ageing and future old age. For instance, it was queried whether general attitudes to ageing could best be explained by physical, social or psychological concerns and threats about ageing. Physical threats were examined in terms of physical health challenges and fears about death; social threats included problematic experiences in relationships while psychological threats included experiences such as a more urgent awareness of the finite nature of time. If negative attitudes to ageing are best explained solely by physical concerns people have, then it may be more correct to speak of attitudes to physical health or attitudes to physical changes with age, rather than attitudes to ageing itself. To examine the relationship between physical, social and psychological aspects of attitudes, a convenience sample was recruited in the US and the UK. Results indicated that all three types of experience – physical, social and psychological – predicted attitudes to ageing, even when controlling for the others. For example, concerns around psychological experiences including identity and regrets predicted general attitudes to ageing, even when controlling for physical and social concerns and worries. These results are especially interesting given that few cross loadings were found, i.e. all measures were relatively independent of each other meaning that these results cannot be explained by similarities or overlap between scale items. Furthermore, in terms of culture, attitudes towards the physical aspects of ageing (but not psychological or social aspects of ageing) were more negative for participants in the US by comparison with their British counterparts.

O'Hanlon also sought to examine whether general attitudes could best be explained by the constraints and losses associated with later life, or by adults' attitudes towards possible positive experiences. Constraints were defined in terms of confines/restraints/limitations on the self (e.g. of time, opportunities, health or social expectations), while losses were defined in terms of the irretrievable and demise/passing of something critical to the physical, social or representational self, e.g. independence, life. While the focus for constraints and losses was on negative experiences, positive experiences were defined in terms of enjoyable, constructive and/or affirmative experiences typically associated with later years. In this study a convenience sample of participants was recruited from the high street; participants were approached individually and invited to take part in a questionnaire study on adult development and ageing. Where participants declined involvement they were asked if they would be willing to answer several brief questions on the spot, hence in terms of generalisability, it is possible to say that participants who declined involvement in the study were not significantly different from participants who took part on a range of demographic and health variables. Results indicated that the constraints, losses and positive experiences subscales had few cross loadings with each other and with the GAAS; furthermore, each of the constraints, losses and positives contributed significantly to the variance in general attitudes to ageing scores, even when each was entered last into the regression model. However, although this study will need to be replicated, results indicated that general attitudes were predicted most strongly by constraints and losses associated with later life rather than positive experiences.

O'Hanlon carried out a final study, in order to attempt to explain adults' attitudes to their own ageing; possible explanations of interest included demographic factors (gender, chronological age, education), attachment-related variables (representations of self and others, and coping strategies), and rival variables (knowledge and information about ageing and old age, neuroticism and expected financial status). Participants were community-based adults of all ages who completed questionnaires in their own homes (n = 350). Using structural equation modelling, a model was proposed through which experiences in early childhood predicted current representations of self and others (Bartholomew, 1990) and coping strategies

Figure 5.1 Model mapping the influence of attachment-related variables and rival variables on age-associated attitudes (O'Hanlon, 2002)

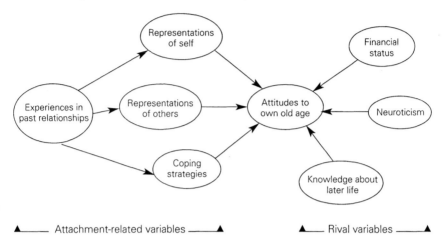

▲——— Attachment-related variables ———▲   ▲—— Rival variables ——▲

(Crittenden, 1999), which in turn predicted adults' attitudes towards their own ageing and future old age (see Figure 5.1). Demographic variables were found to explain only a small proportion of the variance in scores, and rival explanations such as expected financial status or neuroticism did not increase the fit of the model. Attachment-related variables were found to be important predictors of general attitudes.

To encourage participants in the above studies to report accurately their concerns and worries, O'Hanlon did not ask them for any identifying information. Participants were also told that questionnaire items were based on statements made by other people, thus normalising participants' fears and worries. However, to reduce the probability that participants would respond very negatively, questionnaires were balanced to ask about both positive and negative experiences in later life. Gifts, raffle prizes and/or cash were offered to participants to encourage those adults to take part in this research who might not otherwise be inclined to do so.

Few researchers have examined the ways adults evaluate and interpret age-associated challenges and changes in the context of threat. One exception is Brandtstädter and colleagues, who sought to examine age-associated threats in terms of their consequences and implications for identity (Brandtstädter and Rothermund, 1994; Brandtstädter et al., 1993; 1998). In contrast, Lasher and Faulkender (1993) found that anxiety about one's own ageing was significantly related to knowledge about ageing. Montepare and Lachman (1989) found that fears about ageing were significantly related to discrepancies between the subjective and actual ages of individuals in the attitudinal literature.

Future research can examine why ageing is more threatening for some people than others and why attitudes can have the impact they do on later development and functioning. By drawing on theoretical frameworks as diverse as evolutionary biology and life-span developmental psychology, this research would have a real possibility of facilitating our understanding about the nature of adults' age-associated attitudes, their antecedents and the consequences for behaviours and health.

Future research in this field is urgent given the ways in which attitudes can influence later development and health. For instance, if adults view their own future old age as intrinsically a time of decline and loss, there may be little motivation to invest in exercise routines or a more healthy diet. The welfare of other generations, as well as older adults, can also be influenced by age-associated attitudes. Older adults have a vital role in teaching, guiding and supporting younger generations, but negative attitudes about ageing may mean that older adults do not recognise their strengths, and do not have the confidence to offer their skills and experience to younger generations. Research should examine in more detail the nature of people's attitudes towards their own future old age, the origins of these attitudes in earlier life experiences, and the consequences of different attitudinal components for health and well-being, including financial and social preparedness for own old age.

Primary and secondary control strategies of adaptation

The ways adults perceive and evaluate their own ageing can be related to the range of coping strategies available (Lazarus, 1999). One coping strategy that may have much value in facilitating health in later life is primary and secondary control (Heckhausen and Schultz, 1995; Rothbaum et al., 1982; Schultz and Heckhausen, 1996). Primary control involves the use of proactive strategies directed towards overcoming obstacles and attaining the individual's chosen goals. Examples of primary control can include getting help and support, investing more time and effort to achieve preferred goals and targets, and prioritising goals to do only those activities that are most satisfying and enjoyable. Secondary control refers to strategies directed towards managing and influencing emotions and perceptions. Secondary control strategies can include positive reappraisals (e.g. seeing the positive side of a bad situation), lowering goals and expectations, and accepting declines and losses. Heckhausen and Schultz (1995) note that the factor that most distinguishes primary and secondary control is that the former involves strategies directed towards the external world of the individual, while the latter involves strategies directed towards changes directly within the individual.

Wrosch, Heckhausen and Lachman (2000) sought to examine the occurrence of primary and secondary control strategies, and whether these strategies were related to well-being at different ages and in different contexts (i.e. where individuals experienced either health or financial stress). Data was collected on a national probability sample of non-institutionalised

English-speaking adults from households in the United States (n = 3490, age range 25–76 years). Data collection took place by telephone interview and by mailing questionnaires to participants. Primary control was examined in terms of persistence in goal striving, while secondary control was examined in terms of positive reappraisals and the lowering of aspirations. In the appendix of their paper, Wrosch and colleagues give the items for three sub-scales measuring these primary and secondary control strategies. These sub-scales can be useful tools for researchers, as they have acceptable internal reliability scores and each sub-scale is easy to use, having just four or five items. To measure health stress participants were asked to indicate whether they had experienced any of 28 health problems. Financial stress was measured by asking participants if they had enough money to meet their needs and whether they had difficulties in paying monthly bills. The subjective well-being scale was the composite score of five items including a rating about present life satisfaction, satisfaction with self, worry about life and disappointment about their achievements in life.

The researchers found that there was a significant effect of control strategies for each of three age groups: younger adults (aged 25–39 years), mid-life adults (aged 40–59) and older adults (aged 60–76). Older adults were found to be more likely than the younger or mid-life group to report lowering aspirations, and more likely than the younger age group (but not the mid-life group) to report using strategies of positive reappraisal. The greater use of secondary control strategies by older adults is assumed to reflect the functional value of this strategy in later years when there is a greater probability of unwanted and unavoidable challenges occurring. In contrast, primary control strategies are directed towards the attainment of goals and so were expected to be most salient and functional for younger adults who typically have a wide range of opportunities and developmental pathways available. Contrary to expectations, however, younger adults did not report greater use of persistence in comparison to their older counterparts. Instead, the highest mean scores for the primary control strategy of persistence was achieved by the oldest age group.

Other researchers have also examined the relationship between age and use of control-related strategies. The results, however, have been inconsistent. In this literature, chronological age has been found to be significantly related to an increase (Freund and Baltes, 2002), stability (Heckhausen, 1997) and a decrease (Brandtstädter et al., 1993; Freund and Baltes, 1998; Gignac et al., 2000) in primary control-related strategies. These studies used small convenience samples, which can have an important place in gerontological research (for example, in providing useful and informative insights), but which lead to limitations of generalisability. Wrosch and colleagues rightly believed that the discrepancies in this research evidence could be addressed in their study through the recruitment of a large and representative sample of US-based adults.

Evidence that there was an effect for age on the use of different control strategies is informative. Such results challenge negative stereotypes of older adults as being passive or helpless in their own experiences, behaviour and development. Instead, older adults continue to be actively engaged in managing their experiences and adapting to the age-associated challenges that arise. The findings of Wrosch and colleagues also offer further insights into the nature of control strategies. These are not static constructs that people tend to have in greater or lesser quantities. Instead, control strategies are seen as being dynamic constructs that change with different experiences as people progress through the life course. But does this fluidity extend to having a differential impact on health for adults in different age groups? This was another question Wrosch and colleagues sought to address.

As later life can bring many unwanted changes and challenges, Wrosch and colleagues examined whether secondary control strategies would be most strongly related to health for adults at different ages and in different stress contexts. In young adulthood, when opportunities are typically high and constraints low, it was expected that there would be a strong relationship between persistence and well-being for younger adults rather than for older adults. In contrast, when these circumstances are reversed, such as in later life, it was expected that secondary control strategies would be most salient for well-being for the older age groups. Consistent with expectations, findings indicated that primary control strategies (persistence) had no effect on well-being for older adults, but a significant effect was found for mid-life and younger adults. In contrast, secondary control (reappraisals) was found to be associated with well-being for mid-life and older adults; this effect, however, was much less strong for young adults. Lowering aspirations, though, were found to be negatively related to well-being, independently of age. These results remained even when controlling for gender, educational level and race.

Evidence that control strategies have a differential impact on well-being adds to our knowledge about this construct and about the importance of context. Other researchers have found primary and secondary control strategies to be related to health (Freund and Baltes, 1998) but, typically, these researchers have not examined whether these relationships vary by age (for an exception, see Lang and Heckhausen, 2001). Central to the control theory of Heckhausen and colleagues is the notion that control strategies are related to age-graded constraints and opportunities for development (Heckhausen and Schultz, 1995). Consequently, control is being examined in a dynamic and interactive way, with consideration for experiences of the individual, whether these are chronological age or other specific experiences such as health or financial stress. These results then go beyond those of other researchers, who have examined control strategies without necessarily considering the broader developmental or health context within which control strategies can operate.

Adults in later life scored highest on all measures of primary and secondary control; increases in the endorsement of control strategies with age may help explain why adults are able to maintain levels of health and wellbeing, even in the face of significant difficulties, constraints and losses. Such findings again highlight the ways in which adults are actively engaged with their own experiences, development and health. Given this complexity, researchers need to develop increasingly sophisticated designs and studies to begin to examine the relationship between multiple variables while controlling/holding steady the impact of other variables such as health or financial stress.

Some practical and theoretical limitations in the study by Wrosch and colleagues can be addressed by future research. For instance, in their study, old age is defined in terms of adults in the age group 60–76 years, but this grouping is problematic. As people are living longer and more healthy lives, traditional views of old age beginning at around age 65 have been extended. As such, for many researchers the age group of 60–76 years would be seen as reflecting adults in late mid-life rather than old age, while the older adults segment would only be seen to begin at around the age period of 70–75 years and upwards. Researchers have made further distinctions between the 'middle old' and the 'very old' (i.e. adults in the age period of 75 to 85 years, and adults aged 85 years and over). Given these issues, additional research examining the use and impact of primary and secondary control strategies with adults in these older age groups could be very interesting and informative. Not only would such studies facilitate further theoretical insights into the nature of these control strategies, such research could also have value in helping us understand and facilitate better health and autonomy for current generations of adults in early and late old age.

There are new research questions that urgently need to be addressed if health professionals and researchers are to work together to facilitate optimal development and health for adults in later years. To date, the mechanisms involved in the use of primary and secondary control strategies remain unknown. It is not yet clear why some people are better able to use these strategies than others; also, factors that might influence this relationship have yet to be identified. We do not know whether primary and secondary control strategies have a differential impact on later well-being for particular domains of functioning. Lachman and Weaver (1998) found that adults perceived themselves as having increasing levels of control for some experiences, such as finances and marriage, but declines in control for other domains, such as relationships with children. Future studies that examine the relationship between control strategies and well-being within different domains of functioning would have much theoretical and applied value.

The protective role of personal relationships

Warm relationships with others are an important part of most people's lives and crucial to successful ageing. In addition to the meaning and joy they can give to people, relationships are important because they serve a protective function. The direct protective role of close family relationships is evident across a range of psychological and physical experiences in later life; these include occasions when actual physical risks occur, such as recovery following a fall, or when potential risks to the representational self are higher, such as transitions around retirement or moving into a care home. Relationships also serve a protective function socially, in terms of shared friendships and sources of meaning, particularly in long-term relationships that can last several decades. This protective value of relationships also occurs at a cultural level in terms of the opportunities made available for help and support.

Just as older adults need support from younger generations, younger adults also benefit from the skills and experience that older people can develop over several decades of life. This point is made strongly by Gutmann (1987), who draws on ethnographic, cross-cultural and anthropological data to argue that as a consequence of maturation and experience, older adults have their own unique strengths and talents that should be used, particularly in helping, supporting and teaching the next generation. Gutmann takes this perspective, particularly in light of the 'parental emergency' (1987: 7) – that is, the difficulties and problems involved in raising emotionally healthy children without the support of extended family and friends. In this way, Erikson's notion of generativity is being echoed – that is, the need many adults have to care for, guide and support the next generation (Erikson *et al.*, 1986). Yet although many older people are providers of care, services and financial support to young and mid-life adults, these actions have so far benefited from surprisingly little research. (Further discussion on the expertise adults develop over time and the ways older adults can care for and guide younger generations can be found in Chapters 2 and 3, in the sections on wisdom and Eriksonian generativity.)

In later life, however, relationships are lost, constrained or impaired. Personal work roles and relationships that the individual had and enjoyed may no longer be salient or relevant, such as when children are grown up and leave home. Similarly, adult children may divorce and separate so that older people can lose links with younger family members (Drew and Smith, 1999). Furthermore, given compulsory retirement, one's work friends and acquaintances may have to be surrendered, and adults in later life are more likely to experience the loss of parents, spouses and/or other close relationships through bereavement.

Early researchers typically associated changes in relationships with unfavourable and aversive conditions including poor health. For instance, in outlining their disengagement theory Cumming and Henry (1961) believed that reductions and withdrawals in the frequency and nature of relationships with others were a consequence of the ageing process, including increases in health problems, decreases in mobility and energy, and ultimately the death of the self. Declines in relationships were similarly believed to occur as a consequence of the loss of contemporaries and reduced opportunities for social contact, and declines in cognitive functioning (Craik and Byrd, 1982).

Yet although relationships can change and become lost in later life, negative social images and stereotypes have been revised by many current researchers in this field. Assumptions of crises in mid- and later life (e.g. 'empty nest syndrome') have little empirical evidence to support them (Antonucci *et al.*, 2001). Indeed, a contrasting view is that problems and challenges occur throughout the life course and not just in later life. In addition, even when challenges and losses in relationships occur in later years, negative stereotypes need to be revised to take into account both the ways expectations and interests change over time, and also the resilience and creativity of older people in managing their own experiences. Furthermore, many rewarding relationships can be sustained or be formed in later years, including new romantic and sexual relationships. However, little is still known about new romantic relationships in later years, and the characteristics in these relationships which are more typical of older couples, e.g. the attitudes and (un)willingness of older women towards remarriage. The research discussed next offers insights into the nature of different types of relationship changes and challenges: spousal relationships and adaptation following spousal bereavement; relationship changes in close social and friendship networks; and the functional role of relationships in particular cultural contexts.

Factors influencing well-being following spousal loss

Spousal relationships can play a significant role in adult health and psychosocial functioning offering older couples decades of close friendships, sexual intimacy, and shared memories and lifestyles (Carstensen, Gottman and Levenson, 1995). The loss of such experiences when a spouse dies can be very painful and traumatic. Widowed persons are more likely to experience disability and to have health problems, including limitations in activities of daily living, hypertension and stroke. Widowhood is also associated with unhealthy behaviour changes such as increases in smoking and drinking behaviours (Bowling, 1987). Furthermore, Goldman and colleagues (1995) note that widowed persons have higher odds of dying in comparison with their married counterparts. Although the experience of death and bereavement can occur at any time through the life course, the death of a spouse is a stressful experience more likely to occur in later life, and to be an experience most salient for older women given gender differences in longevity.

There are some discrepancies in the literature about whether men or women are most at risk of health problems following bereavement. Some researchers believe that women do less well than men following the death of a spouse (Umberson *et al.*, 1991); this may be a consequence of perceived greater proneness to psychological distress and depressive symptomatology among women, alongside greater financial difficulties. Other researchers, however, have found that men become more distressed following the loss of their spouses. Lee *et al.* (2001) drew on data from the 1987–88 National Survey of Families and Households to select a sub-sample of respondents aged 65 and older who were married or widowed (n = 1686). These researchers found that gender was significant in explaining the variance in depression, with older men adapting significantly less well than their female counterparts.

There are a range of experiences that can influence well-being following spousal loss. These can include the quality of the relationship with the spouse (Carr *et al.*, 2000), the level of stress associated with the bereavement, and contextual or situational factors including the suddenness of the death (Gamino *et al.*, 2000) and the level of social support available (Litwin, 1999). The passage of time can reduce the distress and sense of loss that can occur with bereavement. Although under-researched, existential issues may also influence well-being following spousal loss. Existential issues can include experiences such as optimism, purpose in life, religious involvement and spirituality.

In a longitudinal study on adjustment and coping patterns among older adults, Fry (2001) sought to examine the contribution of existential factors to the prediction of well-being following spousal bereavement. It was expected that existential factors would be stronger predictors of well-being following bereavement than would demographic variables and rival factors; the latter included social support and physical health. It was also expected that existential variables would be more strongly related to well-being for widows rather than widowers, given earlier findings to indicate that women can have wider social networks than men and have more psychosocial resources available to them.

To examine these issues, Fry interviewed 101 widows and 87 widowers aged 65–87, who were all between 6 and 24 months post-bereavement. Existential assessments included self-report measures of meaning in life (having a purpose), optimism, religious involvement and spirituality. Psychosocial well-being was determined by the use of a composite measure that included questions about depressed mood, anxiety, happiness, autonomy and self-esteem. Other possible rival predictors of well-being included self-report measures of physical health problems, social support and the frequency of negative or upsetting events.

Fry found that existential factors were significant predictors of well-being for both widows and widowers. In a regression analysis, demographic variables were entered in the first block, followed by rival explanations and then existential explanations; existential explanations were entered last because they had not been examined before and because it was of interest to see how much additional and unique variance could be explained once demographic and rival explanations were entered and controlled. The interaction of existential variables and physical health was entered in the last block. Once demographic and rival explanations had been entered, existential factors were found to explain an additional 28 per cent and 27 per cent of the variance in well-being for widows and widowers respectively. Spiritual beliefs and practices, comfort from religion, personal meaning, optimism and the importance of religion, were all found to be related to well-being for widows, but only the latter three variables were related to well-being for widowers. Access to religious support was not related to well-being for either group, nor was a sense of inner peace. Neither was there any additional variance explained in an interaction between the existential and health variables.

Fry's study contributes to the field by highlighting the important role that existential variables can play in influencing well-being following spousal bereavement. Her results do not negate the important role that other variables such as physical health and social support play in the occurrence of well-being following bereavement. Nevertheless, Fry showed that existential factors are important predictors of well-being following spousal loss, even when several of these rival variables and explanations have been examined and controlled. Fry's work builds on that of other researchers who found that post-bereaved adults experienced existential confusion and incoherence following the bereavement (Dershimer, 1990) as well as having reductions in the will to live (Raphael *et al.*, 1993). The mechanisms through which existential variables impact on well-being are not yet clear, but possible explanations could be via their roles in alleviating symptoms of depression or anxiety.

Fry's (2001) study also highlights significant gender differences in the experience of spousal loss. Although the psychological well-being of widowers was lower than the health of widows, Fry asked about the factors that are related to well-being for both groups. She found that widowers were less likely to participate in religious activities, and had fewer social contacts by comparison with widows. However, widowers also reported having fewer physical health problems and experienced fewer negative life events.

Men can, traditionally, be more reluctant to take part in research, or to talk about their experiences of bereavement. Fry addressed this problem in an enterprising if controversial way by offering her participants two group sessions in bereavement counselling. This incentive may raise questions about the potential for biases in recruitment towards adults more distressed and maladjusted. Nevertheless, this incentive may be particularly appropriate and useful in encouraging participants into the study who otherwise might not have taken part.

Fry also offers suggestions for clinicians seeking to help adults who have experienced bereavement through spousal loss. She advises clinicians and health professionals working in this area to find ways to stimulate and encourage purpose in life and the will to live. This may be achieved by encouraging attendance at religious organisations or venues, or through other organisations or relationships that encourage personal growth and questioning of existential-related issues. This work may facilitate positive gains in terms of continued development and growth. As an example, in a study with 85 mourners (mean age 59 years), Gamino and colleagues (2000) explored the factors that were associated with personal growth following the experience of bereavement; these included the ability to find positive aspects resulting from the death, and positive memories of the deceased.

There are many methodological challenges that researchers need to consider. These include biases in retrospective recall, as participants may believe they should respond with the distress and anxiety congruent with social expectations following the loss of a spouse or other close relationship. Ideally, one could address this by designing large prospective studies whereby participants are assessed before as well as after the bereavement. An alternative and more modest way to address possible biases in recall is to have independent coders comment on participants' attitudes, or else to have a control sample. Having independent raters comment on participants' attitudes or relationship prior to the bereavement could be easy to do. Having a control group is more difficult, but such a group could have many benefits. It would mean that the researcher could compare the well-being of bereaved spouses with that of others, perhaps of similar age and background, who have experienced a different stressor. In this way, a control group might shed light on the experiences, health and coping strategies unique to participants experiencing spousal loss by comparison with other stressors and challenges.

Future studies should examine other factors influencing well-being. For instance, Fry did not include assessments specific to the nature of the attachment relationships with the lost spouse, neither did she include measures of situational or contextual factors such as the suddenness of the death or the amount of financial/social/practical resources available to manage the loss. Further research is needed to explore the above issues with other sample populations, including less typical groups such as those involved in same-sex relationships or among single adults mourning other lost relationships. The latter may be particularly important given the growing numbers of adults remaining single. In examining the relationship between bereavement and subsequent well-being, researchers also need to control for the specific type of relationship being examined; this is because variables found to be important in influencing well-being following the death of a spouse, may not be so important following the death of a close friend or colleague.

Changes in relationships over time

The essential premise within Carstensen's socio-emotional selective theory is that age-related reductions in social contact occur as a consequence of motivational processes or goals that influence adults' social preferences and behaviours (Carstensen, 1991). These motivational factors are the acquisition of information and the regulation of emotion; the salience and importance of these two factors in relationships are seen to change through the life course as a consequence of perceived time. The theory proposes that as people approach endings, including the end of life, they are motivated to prioritise present goals through relationships that are emotionally supportive and satisfying. In contrast, when time is perceived as being largely open-ended, people are motivated to prioritise future-orientated social contact such as information-rich contact. But is Carstensen's theory correct?

In four studies, with over 1000 participants recruited in the United States and Hong Kong, Fung, Carstensen and Lutz (1999) sought to examine selectivity theory, by exploring whether declines in social networks into later life could be explained in part by participants' preference for emotionally close significant others rather than for information-rich social relationships. In Study 1, participants in the USA aged 8–93 years were recruited from the telephone directory. They were presented with hypothetical scenarios when time was unspecified and open-ended (e.g. imagine you have half an hour with no pressing commitments ...), and when time was expanded (new medical treatment means living 20 additional years in reasonably good health). Participants were asked to choose from social partners who they would like to spend time with; these partners included a family member, or new people, including the author of a book just read.

To examine cultural differences, Study 2 participants were recruited from Hong Kong and asked about an unspecified time condition as in the first study, and a time-limited condition (e.g. emigrating in the next few weeks). In Study 3, participants were recruited and interviewed by telephone as for Studies 1 and 2. The questions were similar, but without the time-limited option; also, the timing was just prior to the handing over of Hong Kong back to China. Study 4 was similar to Study 3, but took place one year after the handing over of the colony to China.

Results from these studies provide compelling evidence that older adults have stronger preferences for close relationships with others, which is not shared by younger adults, except when there are constraints on time. In Study 1, younger and older adults differed in their choice of partners in the open-ended conditions, with 52 per cent and 66 per cent respectively showing a preference for familiar rather than novel social partners. When time was expanded, social partner choices changed only for the older group, with just 50 per cent of older participants choosing the familiar social partner. Study 2 results indicated that in the unspecified time condition 47 per cent of younger participants chose familiar social partners, whereas this rose to 59 per cent for older adults; however, when time was constrained by imagined impending emigration, the preferences for both cohorts were the same, with 89 per cent and 90 per cent of participants in both age groups preferring the familiar social partner. Study 3 results indicated that when time was unspecified, both the younger and older participants (interviewed two months before the handover of the British colony) expressed a preference for familiar social partners. The percentages for both age groups were 62 per cent and 70 per cent respectively, a non-significant difference 12 months prior to the handover. Study 4 showed that one year later this difference was significant again, with 48 per cent of younger adults preferring familiar social partners compared with 76 per cent of older adults.

The above results show that constraints on time motivate a preference for emotional goals. Consistent with socio-emotional selectivity theory, they support the view that older adults can actively prefer meaningful relationships such as those available with family members and close friends, rather than other types of relationship, such as those relating to the pursuit of information. However, this significant age difference is lost in unconstrained conditions – that is, all age groups expressed a preference for emotionally close relationships with constraints or time limits (such as the imminent political handover in Hong Kong).

These results offer new insights into older theories such as that of Cumming and Henry (1961), which assumed that social networks declined in later life as a consequence of inevitable age-associated losses and constraints. Instead, underpinning socio-emotional theory is the assumption that social networks are influenced by changing social preferences; adults in later life can have a preference for emotionally close relationships. Also underpinning this work is the recognition of the complexity of relationships and their interaction with changing preferences and goals as individuals progress through the life course. The factor that influences these changing preferences is not the process of ageing per se, but rather time. It is also interesting to note that these results were similar with participants recruited in both American and Asian cultures; the replication of these results suggests that these findings may have a wider generalisability to other groups and populations, although further testing of this is needed.

Nevertheless, many of the participants in the above research did not respond in ways congruent with socio-emotional selectivity theory. For instance, even when time was constrained, 10 per cent of the participants in Study 2 still expressed a preference for novel rather than familiar social partners. Similar trends were found for participants in the other studies who chose novel rather than familiar social partners, even when time was constrained. More research is needed to understand the choices people make with regard to relationships and social partners.

Methodologically, one of the strengths of the empirical research by Fung *et al.* (1999) is their strategy of testing and retesting essential aspects of socio-emotional selectivity theory across different samples and different countries. Researchers do need to be critical of their own work and to be rigorous in testing the context and conditions under which certain relationships might occur. To improve theory it is important that quantitative researchers attempt to falsify their own hypotheses. Yet when results are replicated across sample groups, and across cultures and countries, it is then possible for the reader to be more confident in accepting the findings as being accurate. Another interesting implication of this empirical finding is the positive interpretation and implications placed on potential problems and constraints. For instance, from losses and potential problems, further growth and development can occur. This issue is discussed later in this chapter, when positives and gains following spousal bereavement are discussed.

Future research should refine and clarify the nature of relationships across adulthood, and the impact that social motives and other factors might have on influencing and shaping the quality and nature of relationships with others. Research using both qualitative and qualitative methods is important to explain individual differences in the nature of personal relationships and why some people do not respond in ways congruent with socio-emotional selectivity theory. It will be necessary to replicate the above findings in other countries and population groups; and to explore other factors that might influence the ways adults experience and view relationships, such as the role of reciprocity in relationships, caregiving and support, shared interests and the experience of potential problems such as hearing loss.

Relationships within a cultural context

Culture can be a significant variable in understanding relationships. It can influence not only the kinds of questions being addressed, but also the ways in which a given experience or behaviour is viewed and interpreted. As an example, let's look at the impact of relationships on post-traumatic stress following the experience of war.

A significant cultural and personal event in the lives of many older adults was the Second World War (1939–45). Huge numbers of people died and many others suffered serious and traumatic injuries, both of a physical and psychological nature. Intrusive and traumatic memories from this time can still be prevalent for many older people, and even become more recurrent and distressing in later life without the distracters of family and work life (Coleman and Mills, 1997). It is important to understand these experiences given their adverse impact on the health and lives of current generations of older people. In addition, traumatic war memories can impact adversely on the lives of younger generations because the consequences of traumas such as war can continue through later generations (Hass, 1990; Bar-On, 1995). However, rates of post-traumatic stress disorder (PTSD) from the Second World War are more salient for some cultural groups than others. Finland, for instance, has a relatively low rate of PTSD from the Second World War in comparison with other European countries such as Britain. There has been little research examining these discrepancies.

Hautamäki and Coleman (2001) explored the role of cultural ties and relationships in resolving trauma in a group of Finnish war veterans. A total of 30 volunteers, ranging in age from 71 to 94, were recruited from a hospital and a rehabilitation centre. On two occasions, participants were interviewed using questionnaires including the Impact of Events Scale (Horowitz *et al.*, 1979), the General Health Questionnaire (Goldberg, 1978) and a Medical Problems Questionnaire (Jerram and Coleman, 1999). Interviews began with open-ended questions about the participants' military careers and allowed them to elaborate on war experiences and the meanings attributed to them both then and retrospectively. Interview data were recorded and transcribed verbatim, and analysed using discourse markers developed from the Adult Attachment Interview (AAI) (Crittenden, 2002; Main *et al.*, 1985). Within Crittenden's framework, discourse is seen to reflect the individual's internal mental state and particularly the strategies he/she is using to predict danger and protect the self (see also Chapter 4). The researcher examines the discourse for evidence for markers such as distancing speech (e.g. omission of the self from sentences), the clarity of if/then phrases (e.g. 'if you were noisy, then father would get angry'), preferences for cognitive or affective information and discrepancies between different memory systems.

The trained coder draws on multiple instances and examples to identify patterns of discourse that reflect balanced, dismissing or preoccupied strategies of adaptation and coping. These strategies can often be outside the conscious awareness of even the speaker. Transcripts from autonomous (securely attached) individuals are seen as balanced in the ways information is being processed. In contrast, transcripts classified as from either dismissing or preoccupied speakers are characterised by an imbalance, although in different ways (see earlier pp. 99–103).

Results from the above study indicated that only a small number of veterans had traumatic war memories and health problems. On the Impacts of Events Scale, two participants out of 30 scored above the PTSD cut-off point of 30, while just three scored above the cut-off point for health problems on the GHQ. Looking at PTSD scores in relation to the AAI strategies that were coded, Hautamäki and Coleman found that avoidance items ('I tried not to think about the war') and preoccupied items were the best predictors of PTSD scores. This echoed views by other researchers that PTSD can be understood in terms of the alternation of dismissing and preoccupied strategies to manage the trauma.

For example, one veteran with a PTSD score of 26 described anxiety and disturbing dreams from the war:

> ... one had always a kind of feeling of being constantly on the alert. ... I do have a dream about the war ... only a week ago I [dreamt] I was fighting in Kriev in a trench ... and then suddenly had two Russians ... and I shot them with sustained fire – like this [waving arms] – ... and I woke up screaming.

The episode given by this speaker to support continued disturbing dreams about the war is believable. This visual image given of fighting in the trenches is still emotionally arousing; involving animated gestures (waving arms) and strong negative affect (screaming); images with a frightening quality are more typical of higher subscript preoccupied speakers. Nevertheless, in this short part of the transcript there are discourse markers more typical of dismissing speakers, such as coherent discourse, with temporally ordered information including a sound conclusion (waking up). If such a pattern is repeated elsewhere through the interview, it may show that this person is using both dismissing and preoccupied strategies to adapt and manage trauma following the war.

Future research could examine in more detail the nature of those alternating strategies, including the nature of the strategy, the specific subcomponent strategies being used (such as A3/C2) and the focus or people around which this strategy occurs (such as A3/C2 $_{John}$ to indicate this particular strategy only when speaking about his friend John).

Other participants, however, spoke freely about the war, with coherence and balance between cognition and affect so that their views have credibility to a trained listener. Consistency was also found between scores on the quantitative measures (indicating low trauma) and their interview transcripts. For instance, one participant (PTSD score of 0) spoke about the war as follows:

> I can say that surely the war left some kind of mark on me, because more than ten years after the war, if I had drank more than moderately ... or let's say a lot of alcoholic beverages ... those war memories popped into my mind ... they just returned. I found myself always in

Hatjalajti, fighting against the Russians. Or so my wife told me. [War operations came to mind] some twelve years after the war. Since then they didn't come back.

Unlike dismissing and preoccupied transcripts, which each have a preference for cognitive and affective information respectively, this short transcript shows a balanced integration of both cognition and affect. Although slightly run-on, there are no dysfluency markers such as stutters or speech delays (where defended-against information almost slips into the dialogue, which can indicate difficulties of integration); the story has a temporal logic to it (distinctions are made between the past and the present, with no blurring of time), and there is an acknowledgement of true negative affect in the time immediately after the war ('a mark being left'). If similar patterns are found at other times through this transcript, it is possible to accept with greater levels of confidence that such veterans do not suffer from PTSD.

An explanation for the low levels of PTSD could be the social and cultural relationships between the veterans in terms of a shared meaning about the war and the general support offered to the veterans. Despite physical and medical problems, veterans generally scored high on positive health. Many participants made reference to the 'Finnish fighting spirit' and the responsibility they had as fighters to leave a positive legacy for future generations of Finns; this sentiment can be summed up in the following quote: '[Fighting] was the task of our generation – to save Finland as an independent nation. And now our children and grandchildren have a good country to live in' (former lawyer, with a PTSD score of 6). Social support for these veterans came from many sources; one participant stated: 'they [hospital staff] take such good care of me. ... Everybody is saying "Hey Peter, hallo, Peter! Do you feel fine and how are you?" All the doctors sit here from time to time. I am treated so well here.'

The above research has many interesting features. In using both questionnaires and interviews, it is a nice example of the effective use of mixed-method research. Questionnaires can be used to examine the relationships between different variables, while interviews can be used to explore and examine a given issue or theme in more detail. In examining the role that cultural support and relationships can have on the lives of those affected by trauma, the authors also discuss the potential for further development; even though many veterans have been through very traumatic experiences, it can be possible with support from others to integrate these experiences and move forward with new insights and a greater appreciation of the basics in life.

A strength of the Hautamäki and Coleman (2001) study is that they did not accept directly what participants said. Instead, they drew upon recent thinking in one branch of discourse analysis, to make distinctions between appearances that might be offered and the reality based on an assessment of the available evidence in the interview transcript. Adults can use personae or masks in portraying themselves, as they may not always wish to communicate their true thoughts or feelings. The AAI coding allows the researcher to distinguish appearance from reality and to see beyond any masquerade or personae individuals might use. Potential difficulties include the demands it places on the researcher, particularly on memory given the multiplicity of comparisons that need to be made between the responses of the same participants at different points through the interview, as well as comparisons between participants' responses to the same question.

More research is needed that examines the influence of culture on experiences and attitudes, and the mechanisms by which these influences carry their effects. Culture can be difficult to define and measure; it does not have to be studied in wide geographical areas, however, but can be studied between different groups of individuals in the same town. Culture can have its effect in terms of relationships, support, shared meanings, socioeconomic resources, geography or history. Researchers need not assume differences will occur between different cultural groups, but instead should include a measure of the cultural variable that interests them. Relationships could be examined in terms of what experiences and support older people have in their own personal lives or the ways in which people elicit support at a social or national level. With advances in technology such as the use of the World Wide Web, research examining the role of culture should become more feasible in future years.

Personal meaning and spirituality

Since gerontological studies got under way after the Second World War, there has been a search to identify the key factors that underlie ageing well. The early years were marked by debates about the relative benefits of high activity levels versus disengagement as a mode of adjustment. But from the 1960s attention came to be focused on self-perception, in particular maintenance of self-esteem and subjective control. Both characteristics have proved to be remarkably resilient with age (Bengtson et al., 1985). In recent years more consideration has begun to be given to perception of meaning (Reker and Chamberlain, 2000; Wong and Fry, 1998). This is an area where perhaps more individual difference is to be found. It is also an area where decline with age is more evident (Ryff, 1995). Societal change contributes to this. Jerrome's comments from her study on the protective role of older people's organisations in a southern English city are pertinent:

The sentiments of envy, disapproval, and bitterness toward post-war generations displayed by cohorts born early this century are intrinsic in the modern ageing process and are to be found in all cohorts as they increasingly inhabit a world they have not made.

(Jerrome, 1988: 77)

The same challenges are evident in the new world too. As Busse commented at the end of the Duke Longitudinal Study of Ageing, 'the legacy of a long life appears to be a confrontation and struggle with the value of living. The issue for older people may well be not just survival but meaningful and purposeful existence' (Busse, 1985: 220).

One of the pioneers in the psychological study of existential meaning has been Viktor Frankl, who witnessed the holocaust of European Jews at close quarters (Frankl, 1964). On the basis of his studies he argued that any trauma could be survived so long as some meaning could be found in the situation. His comments have obvious relevance to ageing as well, and the experience of loss and impending death that is intrinsic to it. Religion is one of the traditional sources of meaning to ageing. Psychologists on the whole have tended to give unsympathetic consideration to the value of religion (Pargament, 2002b). However, some major early figures as James, Jung and Erikson acknowledged its importance, for example: 'No matter what the world thinks about religious experiences, the one who has it possesses the great treasure ... that provides him with some of life's meaning and beauty' (Jung, 1938: 113). But religion is not the only source of existential meaning, and especially in the contemporary western world the search for alternative sources, often spiritual in character but outside the boundaries of orthodox religious faith, has become more evident.

The study of perceived meaning is a diffuse area. It includes the issues of perception of purpose, value and commitment, applied to one's own life and to the society around. The time perspectives may be limited (i.e. the goals of my present actions) or very broad (i.e. the meaning of life in this universe). Humans appear naturally inclined to ask questions about purposes and ends, and to apply them to the world around them. Considerations of personal meaning used to be subsumed under the study of the self-concept, but are increasingly separated (Freden, 1982). They seem to point to a different dimension of experience that, perhaps as people age and find the need to answer questions about meaning more insistent, becomes more salient and distinct from self-perception.

The increased concern with issues of personal meaning is one area in which gerontological studies could benefit other fields of psychology. Western society is obsessed with happiness, and as a result is demeaning of experiences and actions that do not bring ever higher levels of happiness. But one should be wary of thinking that it is the only or most important element in quality of life. There are other valid emotions, as Frankl illustrates in his book *Man's Search for Meaning* (Frankl, 1964). People can make great personal sacrifices for the well-being of others. Their pursuit of particular goals may involve considerable hardships. It is the process of living with purpose that is important. The pursuit of happiness is only one possible goal or value in life, and one that much traditional wisdom suggests is best approached indirectly. Research on quality of life should take more account of such considerations. The study by Wink and Schiff (2002) on life review (discussed in Chapter 3) is a good example of what we have in mind.

In this section we first examine attempts by researchers to conceptualise and define personal meaning and related concepts. Conceptual clarification is an important research task that is often neglected in the rush to operationalise and assess. Although not specific to gerontology, the perspective of ageing gives added salience to the study of meaning. A concept to which we devote particular attention is spirituality. The significance of the spiritual dimension in human adjustment is being given increasing attention in ageing studies (e.g. MacKinlay, 2001; Marcoen, 2005; Moberg, 2001), but the concept of spirituality is not straightforward. In the succeeding sections we will examine studies investigating age as well as gender and racial differences in meaning and spirituality, and the role of religious and spiritual beliefs and practices in coping with later life stresses.

Conceptualising spirituality, religion and meaning in ageing research

The study of personal meaning has developed through the careful drawing of distinctions. For most of the time the meaningfulness of our lives is not something we actively consider. Our goals and their value are implied in our actions. Such harmony of action and intention is captured in Csikszentmihalyi's (1990) discussion of 'flow' as the key to peak experience, where there is total congruence between the activity and ability of the person, and the impact on the environment around. Meaning is central to this experience. The person is achieving his or her purpose, what he or she feels called to be.

When life becomes problematic, the meaning of our activities ceases to be implicit, and the values and commitments that characterise our actions become the object of examination and evaluation. Marcoen (1993) makes a useful distinction between the surface or provisional meanings that reflect immediate goals, and the ultimate meanings, the wider values, hopes and concerns that give meaning to our present goals. Often, loss of meaning relates to a perception of dissociation between the implied meanings of our present actions and our underlying aspirations. As we develop a personal meaning system through adult life there are likely to be clashes with the values we have previously adopted from the society around. Later life provides fresh incentives, as a result of greater experience, freedom from outside pressures, and disillusion with previously accepted values, to develop our sense of meaning further.

The importance of the study of the personal meaning system for research on ageing was first signalled strongly by Reker and Wong's review article in the 1988 volume *Emergent Theories of Aging* (Reker and Wong, 1988). In their chapter they recognised the heterogeneity of personal values and commitments, also the creativity and hardiness of individuals who find meaning within contexts of changes and adversity, and the possibility of changes in later life as a result of greater introspection on sources of ultimate meaning. They defined meaning in terms of its cognitive, affective and motivational components. They also reviewed different approaches to assessing personal meaning, including their own scales, which have made a major contribution to the advancement of the subject. These are based on operationalisation of Frankl's concepts, including life purpose, existential vacuum, life control, death acceptance, will to meaning, goal seeking and future meaning (Reker, 1999).

A noteworthy element of these measurement scales is their freedom from religious language. It is therefore possible for someone who is not religious, but who has developed a strong philosophy or ideology of life, to score highly. Nor do all people who practise a religion necessarily possess a highly developed meaning system. In practice, particularly in North American society, most people who do score highly on these scales are religious. But it is most important to have established a way of assessing personal meaning that does not assume religious belief. This is particularly the case now that religion and spirituality have become major topics in the psychology of ageing in their own right. Until relatively recently they were comparatively neglected topics, but this has changed with a growing recognition of the significance of belief systems to well-being in later life (McFadden, 1996a).

Religion is one of the great providers of meanings in life – an ultimate perspective on life's final goals and purposes, against which present failures and disappointments can be set. It provides a justification for the value of individual action, whatever the obstacles in the way, hope for eventual resolution of difficulties, and peace of mind. Despite indifference and hostility on the part of successive generations of psychologists, there are now increasing signs that religion is coming to be regarded as an important subject for scientific enquiry (Hinde, 1999; Miller and Thoresen, 2003). This is not to deny that religious belief can also be associated with negative psychological characteristics, such as inducement to excessive guilt and low self-esteem (Pargament, 2002a), but as a contribution to a sense of existential meaning its benefit is clear.

With ageing in particular, religion and spirituality allow older people to experience their lives as meaningful despite challenges to quality of life. Life's tribulations can be reinterpreted in a positive light, and new meanings can be created to replace meanings that have succumbed to events. Particularly when the capacity to exercise other forms of control diminishes, religion provides elderly people with continued control over meaning

(McFadden, 1996b).

However, it is not so easy a matter to obtain satisfactory definitions of religion and spirituality. Previously they were closely intertwined concepts, but with increased autonomy in belief systems as well as more open critique of the functioning of religious institutions, spirituality has acquired a greater independence of usage (Heelas, 1998; Zinnbauer et al., 1999). Some have gone so far as to equate spirituality more with personal meaning than with religion. Thus it has been conceptualised, for example by Frankl, as the human drive for meaning and purpose or, more recently, 'the motivational and emotional foundation of the lifelong quest for meaning' (McFadden, 1996b: 164).

Gerontologists and others working in closely related fields – for example, in health care (Miller and Thoresen, 2003; Sloan et al., 1999) – appear to be turning to the language of spirituality because it raises important questions about well-being, especially in later life. These are issues that tend not to be raised within purely psychological, sociological, economic or political frames of reference (Howse, 1999). The language of spirituality is more holistic, and stresses issues of value, meaning and relationships.

Bruce (1998) describes the following as distinct qualities of spiritual well-being: moments of transcendence (that is, feeling one's perspective to belong outside the natural world); having a sense of connection with something beyond the individual; experiencing feelings that are deep and mysterious; experiencing moments of awe and wonder; being concerned with deeper values; finding some meaning in life; feeling that the universe will endure; having a point of reference from the individual to the universal. Although such experiences can be described in a religious framework, they need not be.

It is doubtful, though, that a common definition of spirituality can be constructed on this basis. The concept will necessarily be used differently by those who ground their experiences in a non-material reality, whether defined as transcendent or immanent (i.e. sensing God's presence within creation), and by those who wish to accept them simply as psychological experiences to which humans are inclined.

Zinnbauer, Pargament and Scott (1999) criticise the tendency to separate religion from spirituality, and especially to evaluate the latter as superior to the former. Religion is by definition concerned with spiritual matters, and treating it merely in terms of formal group membership, as some researchers are inclined to do, loses sight of its dynamic operation in the lives of individuals. Similarly, treating spirituality solely as a personal matter loses the social context in which it arises and is nurtured. Religion most typically constitutes that social context, providing 'convoys of love and caring that accompany [people] over the lifespan' (Zinnbauer et al., 1999: 905). Religious communities, of course, need to ask themselves to what extent they constitute this ideal. In support of the close interconnection between religion and spirituality, studies both in America and Britain show that most people, and particularly older people, identify themselves as both spiritual and religious.

A concept important to both religion and spirituality is that of the 'sacred', which typically refers to an experience of deep value whose source lies outside the world as we ordinarily experience it. Pargament prefers a definition of both religion and spirituality that brings out this interrelationship in these terms, spirituality being a 'search for the sacred', whereas religion involves a 'search for significance in ways related to the sacred'. An important point to stress about these definitions is that they are both active, not passive, concepts. Spirituality is the more straightforward concept. Pargament's definition is reflected in the work of other researchers. For example, Wink and Dillon (2002), in assessing signs of spirituality on the basis of interview material, draw on Atchley's (1997) definition of spirituality as 'engagement in a personal quest toward an understanding of the ultimate ground of all being that involves an integration of both inner and outer life experiences through systematic practice'.

Pargament's definition of religion is, by contrast, more complex. This deserves reflection, because often the opposite is assumed (i.e. that religion is simply the practice of a particular faith or belief). In reality, religion is much more than that. It is a resource that can be used in different ways to provide not only meaning to life but also other benefits. It offers various strategies for responding to the exigencies of life, including the challenges and trials of later life. At the same time it points to the ultimate ends of this search by means of rituals, narratives, symbols and belief structures. But from the point of view of research, it is most important to realise that religion is used for secular as well as spiritual purposes. Benefits often flow from use of religion, but not always. Religion can be misunderstood, it can also be misused, and it can harm people.

For this reason Pargament dislikes the long-standing distinction made in the psychology of religion between intrinsic and extrinsic religiosity, originating with Allport's work (1966). According to these definitions, substantive religion is engaged in for its own sake, whereas functional religion is engaged in as a means to an end, such as psychological support, social belonging or political control. But in fact, Pargament argues, religion is always used for some purpose, spiritual or non-spiritual, and most of the time its purposes are mixed.

Pargament's is one interesting approach to the question of definition in this area of research. But it would be misleading to imply that a clear consensus has now been achieved. The most common approach to studying religion and spirituality is to employ a multidimensional model in which a variety of religious and spiritual characteristics are assessed, incorporating belief, ritual, experience and knowledge (Koenig, 1993; McFadden, 1996b). These are typically grouped as indicators under the term 'religiosity'. What it is important to realise, however, is that the way a phenomenon is described in itself determines the research questions that are likely to be investigated. As we shall see later, Pargament's approach to religion raises questions about its positive and negative uses in later life, questions that do not arise if it is treated, for example, merely as a demographic or attitudinal variable.

For research purposes we consider that it is probably necessary to accept this close relationship of religion and spirituality, and their distinctness from perceived meaning in life. Spirituality is concerned with higher levels of meaning, value and purpose in life, but it is usually associated with belief in a power or force beyond the material world. Perceiving meaning in life, on the other hand, does not depend on belief in a transcendent power. Thus one can justifiably distinguish philosophical beliefs, which exclude any such reliance, from religious and spiritual beliefs. The term 'existential meaning' is perhaps the most useful generic term to refer to the perceived purpose of one's own life, whether provided by religious and/or spiritual beliefs and/or philosophical, community, family or other principles, values and goals.

Age, gender and racial differences in uses of religion and spirituality

The historical and scientific literature would suggest that issues of meaning and spirituality become more salient as people age. Older people tend to score higher on meaning scales (Reker, 1999). However, older people also indicate more problems with perception of purpose (Ryff, 1995). It would appear more important to older people to have answers, or at least strategies, for dealing with questions about life's meaning. National surveys, in the USA, Britain and other countries of western Europe, indicate that age is associated with both religious practice and religious belief (Davie and Vincent, 1998; McFadden, 1996a). Many of these differences could be cohort effects reflecting social changes in attitudes to religion particularly over the past century. Most likely, cohort and ageing effects are both present.

Longitudinal evidence remains limited in scope but suggests that non-organisational religious activities such as prayer and religious reading increase in later life, as if in compensation for decreased public religious activity. McFadden (1996b) stresses the need for better types of data collection, employing qualitative as well as quantitative methods of analysis. More specifically, standardised instruments may not be as effective as in-depth interviews in elucidating religious trajectories. Also more use should be made of secondary analysis of data sets for references to religious and spiritual issues. Of particular interest in this context is a recent report from the Berkeley longitudinal study of adult life, which found that spirituality defined in terms both of interest in spiritual questions and engagement in spiritual practices did increase over the life-span (Wink and Dillon, 2002). This analysis also found an association between experience of negative life events and subsequent spiritual development.

Particularly pertinent to the theme of adaptation is the evidence on uses of religion and spirituality in coping with life's problems. In some US studies (e.g. Koenig *et al.*, 1988) turning to religion was mentioned most often, ranking higher than other strategies such as seeking support from family and friends, seeking professional help, and accepting the event. But evidence on age differences in religious coping is less certain. Few studies have investigated the subject, and of those that have only some have produced results indicating that older people use religious resources more often.

The most intriguing evidence comes from Pargament's research programme on religion and coping (Pargament, 1997; Pargament *et al.*, 1995), which we will refer to in greater detail in the next section. This found that age was associated with the type of religious strategy used. Older people were more likely to use spiritually based ways of coping (e.g. looking to religion for different ways to handle a problem), do good deeds, seek support from clergy or church members, and try to avoid their problems through religion (e.g. pray or read the Bible to take their minds off the problem). Older people were less likely to voice their discontent with God or the church and plead with God as ways of coping with their negative events. Of course, these too could be cohort rather than age effects.

General conclusions about the relationship between age, religion and spirituality should not be used to mask diversity. Hazan's ethnographic studies (1984) illustrate how older people can abandon as well as embrace the path of religion. A recent longitudinal study of a British cohort also indicated a marked distancing from religion in this group of people (Coleman *et al.*, 2004). Partly this may reflect disillusionment with religious organisations, particularly in their response to older people (Coleman and McCulloch, 1990). The majority of British older people, although brought up to follow the teachings of a church, agreed with the statement that the state of the modern world made it difficult to believe. Religious doubts can surface at any age, and should be taken as normative not exceptional; it is important to devote more research resources to understanding how people respond to them, and the factors affecting their religious and spiritual trajectories throughout life (McFadden, 1996b).

Much stronger than the association with age is that between gender and religion, at least in western societies (Davie and Vincent, 1998). In both old and new forms of religion, women practitioners outnumber men. They also rate their own religious activities as more meaningful to them, and they are more likely to turn to religion as a way of coping with life's difficulties. Explanations for this phenomenon include women's greater socialisation to expression of emotion, and their greater caregiving role and consequent need for support within this role (McFadden, 1996a).

Women's greater religiosity remains one of the most central and important facts about the psychology and sociology of religion. It has attracted surprisingly few analysts. Yet it may well offer the key to the nature of spiritual and religious identity. Certainly it has major implications for ageing. Religious organisations can expect to minister to growing numbers of older women in the population. They should also reflect on what more could be done to minister to the spiritual needs of men. Theory with evidence to support it suggests some gender cross-over effect with age, with men becoming more receptive to belief in advanced age, and women more sceptical (Coleman *et al.*, 2004; Gutmann, 1987; Henry, 1988).

Age and gender are not the only important demographic variables in this area. As McFadden (1996a) stresses, researchers need to be cautious in drawing conclusions about religion, spirituality and ageing from limited sample groups. There is a large variation in religiosity between the USA and western Europe, with church attendances in the former greatly exceeding those in the latter, and also between different parts of the USA and within the nations that make up the UK (Davie, 2002; McFadden, 1996a).

It is also necessary to consider different ethnic and occupational groups within a society. Religion is a potent source of identity, particularly in migrant populations. To older migrants it offers cultural support and continuity. In Britain, for example, two-thirds of older African-Caribbeans attend church regularly, a far higher proportion than found in the host community, and the importance of the local faith community is emphasised in studies of other ethnic groups (Davie and Vincent, 1998). In the United States there are higher levels of both organisational and non-organisational religious activity among elderly blacks, even when key socio-demographic variables are controlled for (Chatters and Taylor, 1994; Taylor *et al.*, 1996). For Hispanic elders, their Catholic faith constitutes a major source of both social and psychological support (Maldonado, 1995). Relevant to understanding the benefits of religion are the differential associations of religious activity between ethnic groups – for example, with stronger relationships between religiosity and self-esteem, and a greater reduction of depression among older blacks with cancer (Chatters and Taylor, 1994; Musick *et al.*, 1998).

Religion, well-being and coping in later life

The significance of religion for mental health is another area in which gerontologists have been at the forefront of research. Studies on older people provide both the largest and most coherent body of evidence about the effects of religion on health (McFadden and Levin, 1996). However, there are also theoretical reasons for examining the relationship of religion to adjustment in older people. As Pargament, Van Haitsma and Ensing (1995: 47) state,

> many of the greatest religious dramas are played out by those in the

later years of life. These are pivotal times, when people of greatest maturity meet situations of greatest challenge. It is in these moments that people move from the abstractions of a religion in theory to the concreteness of a religion in action.

People do not come to ageing, or to any crisis point in life, empty-handed. A person's religion, their spiritual belief system, their philosophy of life are important resources. They shape the way they interpret and deal with situations. Much, of course, depends on the way the belief system has been nurtured throughout life.

One reason for the particularly large lead that US research has in this field is the high level of religiosity of American people, and especially American older people. Despite the health-related declines in organisational participation among the oldest cohorts, findings from national surveys show high and increasing rates of religious attendance among the older groups. The 1990 US General Social Survey revealed that at least weekly religious attendance increases with successive older age cohorts, and among those aged 65 years and older it is over 46 per cent, which is a rise of nearly 10 per cent over 1978 data (Levin, 1995). Among respondents aged 75 years and older, nearly three-quarters pray at least daily.

Reviews of US research on spirituality and health show consistent links between religious practices and reduced onset of physical and mental illness, reduced mortality, and likelihood of recovery from or adjustment to physical and mental illness (George *et al.*, 2000; Levin, 1994a; 1994b). Interpreting findings on older people is particularly problematic, however, because religious practice, and especially attendance at religious services, also reflects better functional health. The literature on religion and ageing also suffers from an absence of studies on those hostile or indifferent to religion, and assessments of the beneficial or other effects of non-religious and non-spiritual perspectives on life's meaning (McFadden, 1996b). It is likely that people continue or adopt religious practices in part at least because of the benefit they perceive they obtain from them. Therefore the only fair comparison is with people who claim benefits from other forms of belief, not from those who find little benefit in religious practice.

It is also important not to rely solely on US studies – on a society in which spiritual belief and church membership is the norm. There is evidence from less religious societies such as Britain that spiritual belief is not necessarily associated with favourable health outcomes (King *et al.*, 1999). This may reflect differences in degree of belief. Uncertain levels of belief, for example, are known to be associated with death anxiety (Kalish and Reynolds, 1976). Our recent study on older people's adjustment to spousal loss showed higher levels of depression in those with low to moderate levels of strength of spiritual belief than in those with very strong or no beliefs (Coleman, Hautamäki and Podolski, 2002). Subsequent case study analysis suggested that problems with belief had preceded rather than followed the bereavement. Krause's large-scale survey on religiosity and self-esteem also suggests a curvilinear relationship between self-esteem and religious coping. Feelings of self-worth tended to be lowest for those with a little religious involvement (Krause, 1995b).

George *et al.* (2000) have reviewed the evidence for the mechanisms underlying relationships between religion/spirituality and health. Besides the meaning-giving qualities of a spiritual belief system, they also identify religious influences on healthy behaviours – for example, respect for the body, avoidance of harmful substances and risky sexual and violent behaviour, and the provision of social support from incorporation in a social network of other believers. However, in those studies that have looked at all factors together, the sense of coherence provided by religion/spirituality and the positive mental attitudes it engenders appear as the most significant.

Kirkpatrick (1992) has suggested an interesting theoretical integration of the literature on religion and well-being in terms of attachment theory. Religion can be conceptualised as an attachment process, in which religious practice provides a sense of security, confirming that there is a caring presence in the person's life. As McFadden and Levin (1996) point out, theistic religions are essentially relational. The child is typically introduced to God by parents, and God functions as an extension of the parental figures, usually for the better (more powerful, more forgiving, more understanding), but sometimes for the worse (more demanding, more judgemental, more punishing). Even those who appear the least religious seek safety and help in situations of extreme stress, such as warfare, in appeal and prayer to God.

Approaching religion via the concept of attachment appears particularly promising, accounting for many of the striking and beneficial features of religious belonging. The tangible social support provided within well-functioning religious communities is an extension and confirmation of divine care. Participation in community acts of worship is of a particularly high level among older people before they reach the age of frailty, and often continues afterwards despite the difficulties of accessing places of worship. The considerable investment of time and energy older people give to attending religious services is rewarded by the improvement to emotional balance that acts of public worship provide. The religious building functions as a safe haven, providing a place of 'sanctuary'. Even passing the building or anticipating entry may be sufficient to induce positive feelings. Also, many aspects of private religious observance can be understood as an extension of belonging to a worshipping community.

However, it is no longer sufficient to examine the links between religiosity, well-being and positive health outcomes. The evidence is now sufficiently strong to justify more detailed studies of religion in action. Coping with stress is a prime example. Religious coping is commonly reported in

US studies, and people experiencing high levels of stress report more favourable well-being if at the same time they indicate high levels of spiritual support. Pargament's project on religion and coping has examined how several hundred members of mainstream Protestant and Roman Catholic churches coped with the most serious negative life event they had experienced in the past year (Pargament, 1997).

Pargament *et al.* (1995) have also reviewed the evidence on the benefits of religion to older people in different fields, in coping with one's own as well as the spouse's illness, in bereavement, and with one's own anticipated death. They have proposed ways in which religion may achieve these results: by maintaining integrity of the self, exchanging personal mastery for surrendering to God's will, overcoming fear of dying in His presence, and through a sense of growing intimacy with Him. This may imply the need to change religious coping styles with age from active to more passive forms of coping.

Evidence is now being collected on areas where religiosity appears to be less helpful or even detrimental. Strawbridge *et al.* (1998a) reported findings from a large longitudinal study in Alameda County, California, strongly indicating that whereas indices of religion buffer associations with depression for health-related stressors and also financial problems, they appear to exacerbate the stress caused by family crises, such as marital and child problems. This is consistent with Ellison's (1994) perspective on religion and stress; this proposes that those stressors that raise conflicts with the values emphasised by religious organisations may be especially problematic for members to confront. Faced with unruly children, difficult marriages or even caring for an older parent, religious persons may feel more at fault.

A significant feature of Pargament's current research programme is his acknowledgement and active investigation of maladaptive religious coping (Pargament, 2002a; Pargament *et al.*, 1998; 2000). To this end he has constructed scales of 'positive' and 'negative' patterns of religious coping. The former were based, for example, on a sense of secure relationship with God, a belief that there is a meaning to be found in life, and a sense of spiritual connectedness with others. The latter, by contrast, reflected a view of a punishing, abandoning and absent God, and expressions of anger and discontent with Him and others. Pargament has also tested these scales with older hospitalised patients coping with moderately severe medical illness. Better adjustment was related to a number of religious coping methods, such as benevolent religious reappraisals, religious forgiveness/purification and seeking religious support. Poorer adjustment was associated with reappraisals of God's powers, spiritual discontent and 'punishing God' reappraisals. Both positive and negative religious coping were associated with poorer health status, perhaps reflecting the fact that religious responses were elicited more frequently by serious conditions.

Clearly there is much more work to be done in order to satisfy theologians that such measures do justice to the complexity of religious experience, in which negative and positive thought and feeling are often interrelated. But there is no doubt that uses of religion are not all positive, and further refinement of these types of scale as well as closer examination of people in stressful situations should lead to better understanding of 'beneficial' and 'damaging' religious responses to stress.

Other authors besides Pargament have called for more distinction between health-promoting and health-damaging religious/spiritual beliefs and practices (Koenig, 2001). Crowther *et al.* (2002) have sought to delineate a concept of 'positive spirituality', distinct from religion and spirituality, which they argue should be included in conceptual models of successful ageing. They criticise previous theorists in this area (e.g. Rowe and Kahn, 1998) for neglecting the spiritual dimension. The publication of special issues on the subject of religion, spirituality and health within major psychological journals, such as *American Psychologist* and *Psychological Inquiry*, indicates that the study of religion has finally entered mainstream health psychology.

Future research in this field should also give more attention to comparing different religious groups and cultures, rather than proceeding on the assumption that all types of religion function in the same way. Even within Christianity there are important distinctions to be made. In his lectures on William James' *The Varieties of Religious Experience*, Charles Taylor has pointed to the differences between James' Protestant focus on religion as an individual experience on the one hand and, on the other, a Catholic understanding of 'collective religious life, which is not just the result of [individual] religious connections, but which in some ways constitutes or *is* that connection' (Taylor, 2002: 24). Little or no work has been done on non-Christian religious traditions. Any comparative work, inevitably controversial, has to be preceded by careful description of the coping characteristics of religious cultures. An illuminating example of such work in the field of ageing studies is Rory Williams' *A Protestant Legacy* (1990), a detailed study on attitudes to death and illness among older Aberdonians. This illustrates how these elderly Scots drew on themes from their religious background in facing the predicaments of later life.

The three research themes we have addressed in this chapter all provide insight into the paradox of well-being and ageing that we mentioned at the beginning of this chapter. The process of adaptation to ageing is fostered by a growing acceptance of its products, including a wider and less egocentric perspective on life, and a realisation that at every stage (except perhaps the very last) the experience of ageing exceeds expectations. As contemporary society hopefully develops a more positive attitude to the potential of age, we can reasonably expect these aspects of the experience of ageing to be enhanced.

Social relationships remain crucial until the end of life. These are threatened by successive bereavements. Although contemporary society offers older people more possibilities for new types of friendship, there is no evidence that their traditional reliance on the family has diminished.

Religion and culture are important sources of existential meaning that may grow in importance in later life. There is a strange contrast in this regard between North America and western Europe. In the latter, religion has a diminishing importance. Yet it is a pertinent question whether alternative sources of existential meaning for older people can be found that match the power of religious belonging.

3

Towards a developmental psychology of advanced old age

So here it is at last, the distinguished thing ...

(Henry James, in Edel, 1985)

6 Key concepts in the study of late life

We now move deeper into the experience of ageing, to what is increasingly referred to as the 'fourth age', when issues of disability and frailty come to predominate the lives of older people. This is 'old age' proper, the time of life when people finally do ascribe the adjective 'old' to themselves. It is what many have been waiting for all along, expecting it with varying degrees of apprehension (see Chapter 5). As he incurred his first stroke, the Anglo-American novelist Henry James said that in the very act of falling 'he heard in the room a voice which was distinctly, it seemed, not his own, saying, "So here it is at last, the distinguished thing"' (Edel, 1985: 706). Thus opened for him the last stage of life, one of which to be fearful but also in some sense to be respected.

The fourth age can begin dramatically, with an event such as a major stroke, but it can also show a more gentle gradient of approach, as one becomes aware year by year, month by month that one's energies and capabilities are diminishing. Probably most people would prefer the latter, if only because it allows more time for adaptation. Many might also prefer a quick death, without awareness, 'to cease upon the midnight with no pain' (Keats), although that too has its sorrowful aspect, in the lack of opportunity for farewells. We know relatively little about people's preferences in this regard. They remain for the most part unspoken. That is why Henry James' remark has such resonance. We know immediately what he is talking about, even though it has not been mentioned before, and maybe will not be mentioned again.

In fact, Henry James, in the almost three months he remained alive after his stroke, went through many struggles. A second stroke produced some brain damage, and he was concerned not only that he had become mad but that people would notice the change. He seemed to one friend who knew him well to have lost 'his own unmistakeable identity'. He was unsure of his surroundings, thinking of himself at times in various places he had visited during his life in Europe and America. The diaries of friends and relatives record 'a kind of heroic struggle to retain his grasp on reality in the midst of death-in-life' (Edel, 1985: 709). This reflected that 'terror of consciousness' he had been attempting to describe in his unfinished novel *The Sense of the Past*, which in fact he been working on in the evening before his first stroke. But there were also periods of peace as, looking out from the window of his apartment in Chelsea on the barges passing along the River Thames, he imagined that he himself was on a boat, voyaging and visiting foreign cities.

Advanced old age has been an extremely neglected field of study. Even within gerontology relatively few researchers, and especially few developmental or health psychologists, study these later stages. The opportunities of the third age, of continued employment, occupation and interest, arouse more interest than managing more appropriately the decline to death. But as death itself has become a much more ready topic for discussion in recent years, so perhaps more attention will be given to the period preceding it.

Because until recently the very old were a numerically insignificant part of the population, the issue of declining health status was less important. Signs of ageing and disability were more prevalent throughout the second half of life. In the Middle Ages many working people would have appeared old and worn out physically by the age of 50, if not earlier; they probably did not live very long in that condition, however. Advanced age was for most people a relatively short, terminal phase of life.

There is continuing controversy over whether or not this stage of life is lengthening in duration. In the 1970s concern was expressed that as the population aged and more people lived into their eighties and nineties, the period in which they would suffer from disability and chronic disease before death would lengthen as well. Studies were cited which suggested that this indeed was happening, that there was a relationship between age of death and the preceding period of disabled living. The older one died, the longer one was disabled beforehand. However, evidence from studies conducted in the 1980s and 1990s has lessened many of these worries. Disability and functional limitation prevalence rates among older Americans have been in decline, despite what appear to be continued increases in reports of chronic disease (Freedman and Martin, 2000). This is reassuring as it suggests that increased longevity does not necessarily mean increased disability. However, as Schoeni, Freedman and Wallace (2001) have pointed out, data are not consistent over time. Periods of decline in disability prevalence rates have alternated with periods of stability and thus rising numbers of disabled older people in the population.

Clearly the question of the association between age and disability is crucial for the future of ageing. The health of the world's older population needs to be monitored regularly to check trends in illness and disability, and also to discover factors – for example, in people's nutrition, and social and behavioural circumstances – that are conducive to good and poor health in late life. At this point in time all that can be said with certainty is that people are currently living longer in most of the world's societies. Very few are reaching the upper limits of the human life-span, which is regarded as being around 120 years, but many more are reaching their eighties, nineties and one-hundreds. Figure 6.1 shows the rising numbers within the older popu-

Figure 6.1 Older population by age group in the United States 1990–2050 (Poon *et al.*, 2005)

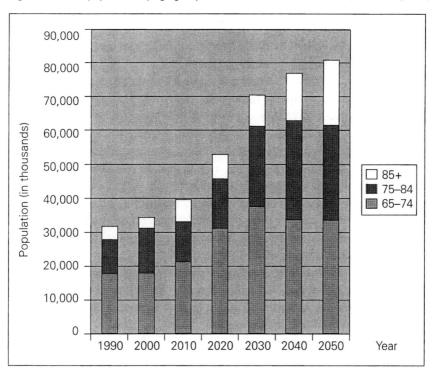

lation of the United States, split across three age groups (65–74, 75–84, and 85 years and over), and projected until the middle of the twenty-first century. The most extreme example is Japan, whose population's average life-span doubled in only 50 years from an average of 42 years at the time of the Second World War to over 80 in the new millennium. By 2050 it is expected that one in every three older Japanese adults will be 85 years and older (Poon *et al.*, 2005).

In Britain the proportion of those over 85, typically now taken as the dividing line for the 'oldest old', has risen from 0.1 per cent to 1.8 per cent of the population in the course of the twentieth century (Coleman, Bond and Peace, 1993). This number may still seem relatively small, but if it has been accompanied by an equivalent tenfold increase in disability, or even a significant fraction of this, its significance becomes clearer. In the USA it is estimated that approximately one-third of the over-85s are healthy enough to live independently in the community, one-third are functionally impaired, and one-third are extremely frail and disabled (Kramarow *et al.*, 1999). Other features of this sector of the population that strongly distinguish them from the rest are the greater proportion of women – 4.2 males for every 10 females in the USA compared with 8.5 males in the age group 60 to 69 years – and living alone – 57 per cent of women and 29 per cent of men among the oldest old live alone (Poon *et al.*, 2005). The oldest old are disadvantaged in various ways, with much higher proportions living on limited finance and in institutions. Correspondingly greater levels of resilience are needed.

Because of the relative lack of attention to the last stage of life this chapter will be somewhat different from Chapters 2 and 4. We will be referring less often to fully formed theories of ageing and development, and rather more to useful ideas and key concepts. Academic disciplines have, along with other cultural institutions, moved slowly to adapt to the new social challenges. For Paul Baltes, one of the most prominent contemporary theoreticians in the field of psychogerontology, whose contributions we have already referred to (in Chapter 4), this is part of a cultural lag. Human development is insufficiently supported in its last stages. Baltes' metaphor is that of an ill-designed building whose vulnerabilities become more manifest after a certain time. 'Neither biological nor cultural evolution has had sufficient opportunity to evolve a full and optimizing scaffolding [architecture] for the later phases of life' (Baltes, 1997: 367). The result is that – paradoxically – 'historically speaking, old age is young'. A major investment of resources – social, material and technical – as well as improved psychological and spiritual understanding, is required to support human development and adaptability in its last stages.

Perhaps such support will never be sufficient, because the processes of human development and ageing are fundamentally incomplete – as people through history have lamented, the advantages of age do not fully compensate for the losses of youthful vigour. The discrepancies between human wishes and human potentials widen, so that, eventually, death is a blessing, a release from decay. This is a theme of stories in many cultures. A good example in Anglo-Irish culture is Jonathan Swift's account in *Gulliver's Travels* of the Struldbruggs, a race condemned to live forever with all the defects of old age, including susceptibility to disease and loss of memory (see Moody, 1995: 164). But the fact that we shall eventually encounter failure in our attempts to maintain quality of life in old age does not mean that we should not seek to promote human development in extremis.

Mental frailty (dementia) is a major concern and fear at this stage of life, but it is important not to let this concern exclude consideration of physical frailty since the experience of ageing is only in a minority of cases an experience of severe mental frailty. Sometimes, of course, physical and mental frailty coincide, as in late-onset Parkinson's disease.

Lack of attention to advanced old age has led to an imbalance in ageing theories. Our discussion in Chapter 4 indicated that a major focus of recent developmental literature on ageing has been on the concept of 'successful ageing' (Rowe and Kahn, 1998). But one consequence of this has been to stigmatise further the very old. The nature of the criteria employed in this discourse – including avoidance of disease and disability, preservation of higher mental function, and active engagement with life – means that, sooner or later, many people fail the test. Positive meanings also need to be found for this last stage of life, not only for the sake of the old themselves but also because failure to do so casts a shadow over the preceding stages of life.

Already, 20 years ago, the cultural historian Tom Cole referred to the stigma of late life, despite improving attitudes towards ageing:

> Today's 'enlightened' view of aging, which encourages older people to remain healthy, active, independent etc. ... harbours potentially pernicious effects. ... Unless the attack on agism is amplified to address the existential challenges and tasks of physical decline and the end of life, we will perpetuate a profound failure of meaning.
>
> (Cole, 1984: 335)

This is the issue of cultural failure that Baltes (1997) and others refer to. Sheldon Tobin asks the key question 'What comes after successful ageing?' (Tobin, 1999: 31). The development of the concept of the 'third age' (Laslett, 1989) has required a further concept of the 'fourth age'. This sense of something missing from current developmental theories of ageing is widely felt. As we have noted before, Erik Erikson himself towards the end of his life questioned whether the eight psychosocial stages he had delineated were sufficient for the realities of ageing; in particular, whether there was a stage 'beyond integrity' (see also Rosel, 1988).

All this is not to say that there have been no previous contributions to understanding the psychology of late life. The first major theoretical developments came with studies of institutional care in the USA in the 1960s and 1970s, in particular those carried out by Sheldon Tobin and Morton Lieberman. Both were part of the Chicago group of gerontologists, together with Neugarten, Havighurst and others, and they brought a fresh and respectful attitude to the phenomenon of psychological survival that they studied. Although demonstrating considerable insight into the condition of the older people they investigated living within American institutions, the inherent biases in the picture they present have taken a long time to be corrected by more representative studies of community-living elderly people (e.g. Johnson and Barer, 1997). For many years the study of the developmental psychology of advanced old age was the study of institutionalised elderly people.

Robert Atchley's review chapter on 'The influence of aging or frailty on perceptions and expressions of the self' (Atchley, 1991) was an important indicator that the psychological differences between the various stages of ageing were being taken seriously by gerontologists. He distinguished, perhaps for the first time unambiguously, between the experiences of ageing and of frailty. The different challenges of the latter raise issues that are much harder to deal with. Atchley reviewed the literature on the self and ageing, and articulated a theoretical position in which the experiences of normal ageing influenced the self in many ways, mostly for good, until the onset of frailty. Older people can be expected to have a more tested, stable set of processes for managing the self, as well as more robust self-concepts. It is frailty that poses more serious challenges to self-esteem. As Atchley pointed out, older people do not become by virtue of their age expert at dealing with problems of disability.

The problems posed particularly by sudden frailty and/or disability are immense: interrupted continuity in way of life, greater need for more extreme coping methods, reduced capacity to use defences such as selective interaction, difficulty in identifying new possible selves, depersonalisation of the social environment, changes in reference groups, and rusty skills in using feedback from others to fashion new self-conceptions. The very stability and long continuity of the self that have been achieved and preserved through adulthood make adjustment more difficult now that real change is required. Self characteristics that are particularly highly valued in western societies, such as competence and self-reliance, are less easy to maintain than interpersonal skills such as warmth and humour.

Studies that we are now conducting into elderly people who refuse care that is offered to them show how devastating can be the experience of suddenly requiring help. They demonstrate the considerable psychological disturbance and confusion of elderly people finding themselves in age-segregated services. Thus one woman admitted to an elderly care ward after a stroke commented when offered home-help services, 'I don't want them. I don't want to turn it into an old people's home.' She said that she 'couldn't bear the thought' of considering what she would like to happen if she became unable to manage on her own. 'It was a terrible blow to go into hospital and realise I was geriatric!'

One reason for the neglect is that this is a stage of life that it is difficult to study using standard quantitative methods. Longitudinal studies of ageing have typically given an overoptimistic view of the later stages of life because of selective drop-out. Those willing to respond to long schedules in their late eighties and nineties tend to be the fit old, those with high self-esteem and low depression ratings, who perceive much continuity with their earlier lifestyles and activities. It is only now that we are getting a more representative picture of this age group from studies that typically rely more on qualitative interview and observation (Johnson and Barer, 1997; Kaufman, 1987).

This chapter will deal with these initial attempts to establish psychological theories about adaptation to states of dependency in late life, especially in institutional care settings. These emphasise the often extreme methods older people employ to preserve and enhance the self in conditions of physical frailty. Coping and development are evident even in the trials of extreme old age. We close the chapter with a consideration of dementia and the preservation of the self despite mental infirmity. It is important to realise that development can be observed even in the trials of late life. First, though, we must be more precise about when the fourth age begins.

When does advanced old age begin?

Formal differentiation between the later stages of life is a relatively recent matter. Shakespeare's Jacques distinguished the fifth age of 'the justice … full of wise saws and moral instances' from the sixth age of the 'lean and slippered pantaloon' and the seventh age of 'second childishness and mere oblivion, sans teeth, sans eyes, sans taste, sans everything'. But even if such systematic change in people as they aged was common knowledge, it was not seen to have practical implications. Up to the late 1970s policy-makers at the Department of Health in London based projections on health and service needs solely on figures of those above the male retirement age of 65 years. This demarcation line is ultimately attributable to Bismarck's innovation of a pension system in Germany in the late nineteenth century. There was no need for any further distinction within the ageing population beyond that required by the institution of retirement and the payment of pensions. The implications of increasing life expectancy beyond 65 years seem to have caught both welfare service and pension planners by surprise.

It was in fact Bernice Neugarten, one of the pioneering developmental psychologists of ageing we have already mentioned (in Chapter 2), who used national data on disabilities to make first the distinction between those she referred to as 'young-old' (65–75 years) and 'old-old' (75 years and over). But already, by the 1980s, data showed acceleration of disabilities to begin at 85 years rather than 75 or even 80, although perceptions of health do not necessarily decline with age (Halpert and Zimmerman, 1986). Clearly, experience of ageing is relative to the particular societies and historical periods one lives in. There is no fixed chronological age when people move from one state of being to another. Perceptions of age in western culture in particular depend critically on the state of the physical body (Dittmann-Kohli, 2001). In the past, people could be seen to be old at 50 years, after a life of heavy labour and limited protection from the elements. For the future it is possible to imagine, especially with improvements in skin and hair care, societies containing young-looking octogenarians and nonogenarians. Further progress ultimately depends on unlocking the secrets of biological ageing.

In the UK, the lack of differentiation between 'young-old' and 'old-old' meant that no plans were put in place to deal with the increase in the older categories of the population, which caught the country by surprise in the 1980s (Murphy, 1995). The consequences were felt dramatically in the failure of residential and community care provision to cater for the increasing numbers of elderly people requiring help. The UK government's decision to allow social security payments to be made to older people entering private care homes was a measure of desperation but with wide-reaching implications in the rapid growth of the initially unmonitored sector of private care.

It is important to realise that level of disability is not the sole determining feature of advanced old age; younger people become disabled too. Moreover disability is not necessarily a progressive characteristic of people's lives. Many of those who suffer severe injury when young and become disabled as a consequence can hope to live full lives within the limits set by their disability. Much more indicative as a concept applicable to late life is 'frailty', a term that has appeared with increasing frequency in the gerontological literature in recent years (Campbell and Buchner, 1997; Hamerman, 1999; Strawbridge *et al.*, 1998b). Disability is a much more limited concept, and does not necessarily indicate the person's need for care or supervision. He or she might have difficulty walking yet be functioning well on all other accounts. The greater usefulness of the concept of frailty to gerontology is that it encompasses 'a combination of deficits or conditions that arise with increasing age and contribute to making the elderly person more vulnerable to changes in the surroundings and to stress' (Nourhashemi *et al.*, 2001: M448).

There is as yet no consensus on how frailty can be most usefully operationalised. Strawbridge, for example, has used a concept of frailty that corresponds to functional loss in at least two of the following domains: physical and nutritional status, cognitive function, and sensory function. Although this is an arbitrary dividing line, it does demonstrate a sharp increase in later life. Whereas only 20 per cent in the 65–74 age group and 32 per cent in the 75–84 age group were classified as frail on this definition, 49 per cent of the over-85s were. This corresponds with clinical perceptions that half of the very old are in need of practical help that, if not forthcoming from family and/or friends and neighbours, needs to be provided by organised welfare services. The key point about frailty, unlike disability, is that it constitutes an unstable state with a risk of functional loss. As it threatens quality of life, regular monitoring is essential.

The rise in disability and frailty thereafter makes 85 years a convenient age to define late life at the present time in most western societies. However, it is important to bear in mind that there are large numbers of disabled and/or frail people below this age, and those who are not disabled or frail above it. In studying this age group it is important to bear in mind their special characteristics. First, they are survivors. Those aged over 85 represent only 25 per cent of their original birth cohort (those aged over 95 represent 3 per cent) (Smith and Baltes, 1997). The survivor effect might be thought to decrease variability among them, but as the findings from the recent Berlin Aging Study show, this does not appear to be the case (Baltes and Mayer, 1999).

Another significant recent observation, from a Finnish study, is that by 85 years most participants feel that they have crossed the line into old age

(Heikkinnen, 2000). This is an important finding because we have surprisingly few studies on actual lived experience of ageing (see, for example, Keller *et al.*, 1989). The Finnish study was an exploratory qualitative study with 20 older people, a small sub-set from a larger longitudinal project, who were interviewed at the ages of 80, 85 and 90 years. The concept of 'the boundary conditions' emerged as a key concept in understanding the ageing experience:

> Deteriorating health, deteriorating sense perception (particularly eyesight and hearing), frailty, pain, impaired memory, mobility problems and loss of human relations (particularly the loss of spouse through death), were the vulnerability factors that, either on their own or together, formed the boundary conditions for experienced ageing.
>
> (Heikkinnen, 2000: 469)

Whereas it was evident that at the age of 80 years most were not living an old-age existence, by 85 years the new life narratives were about change and decline, in particular bodily change. Walking had become a bit more awkward, feet heavy, and participants were troubled by a nagging sense of insecurity and of not having control over their life. Days had to be structured more and more according to physical needs, which replaced earlier interests. By the age of 85 bodiliness had become a critical concern. From these interviews, it becomes easier to understand how bodily continuity is essential to perceiving other forms of continuity such as a sense of continuous self (Becker, 1998; Oeberg, 1996).

In the absence of established criteria for assessing functional age – a project to which much research endeavour has been devoted, but with equivocal results demonstrating rather the multifaceted character of ageing changes – 85 years seems to offer a pragmatic criterion for deciding which studies to review pertaining to the psychology of advanced old age. In the remainder of this chapter and the next we will therefore only consider studies either of people over the age of 85, or special populations with significant levels of disability and/or frailty such as residential and nursing home residents.

Is there a developmental psychology of late life?

Although there seem to be some criteria for distinguishing those who have reached advanced old age and these changes can be represented in ordinary experience, it is still necessary to ask whether psychological differences are associated with this transition to advanced old age? For if there is no evidence of differences then the supposed distinction between the third and fourth age is perhaps misplaced. Is the bodily change experienced of greater import than, say, the changes in physical prowess in the twenties, thirties and forties, which oblige athletes and sportsmen/women to cease from serious professional competition?

There is no doubt that some psychological changes occur, particularly in cognition. Cognitive decline is one of the best-researched areas of the psychology of ageing. Although not the subject of this book, the perceived reality of mental decline is an important context for studying adaptation and development in late life. Cognitive ageing is a complex phenomenon, with changes tending to be more pronounced in some functions than others, and uniform decline being rare. The evidence from longitudinal studies is that by the age of 75 most measures show some average decline, but there are some individuals who still show little or no decline in most functions even at the age of 80 (Schaie, 1996). One of the most interesting areas of current debate is the relationship between 'normal' cognitive decline with age and dementia. For example, does continued mental exercise slow down the progress, or at least the effects it might have on everyday life, of disease processes in the brain?

Also self-esteem shows decline in later life, but the trajectory is very different from that, for example, of a cognitive function such as memory. Global self-esteem, in western populations at least, tends to show two periods of marked decline during the course of the life-span: during adolescence and during late life (Brown, 1998; Ranzijn et al., 1998; Robins et al., 2002). In between these times, self-esteem consolidates, so that those in the earlier stages of ageing often show peak levels of self-esteem (Dittmann-Kohli, 1990). In fact, of all psychological variables, self-esteem is the one on which differences between the young-old and the old-old are maximised. This supports the distinction that Atchley draws between the influences of ageing and of frailty on the self.

Care needs to be taken, however, in interpreting late-life decline in self-esteem. In the first place far from every very old person shows such decline. Moreover, as Robins and colleagues (2002) acknowledge, developmental theories of ageing such as those discussed in Chapter 2 imply a 'diminished need for self-promotion and self-aggrandizement which might artificially boost reports of self-esteem earlier in life' (Robins et al., 2002: 431). Thus decline in self-esteem at the end of life may not necessarily mean lowered emotional health, but simply a more modest, balanced and ultimately truthful view of the self.

The Berlin Aging Study provides the most detailed recent evidence on a large range of psychological indicators into advanced old age. By means of profile analysis Smith and Baltes (1997) compared very old Berliners (85 years and over) with younger older people (65 to 84 years) on intellectual functioning, self and personality characteristics, and social relationships. Proportionately many more of the over-85s (75 per cent) belonged to cluster groups with less desirable profiles (with high scores on one or more of neuroticism, loneliness, external control, and cognitive impairment) than did the younger group (31 per cent).

In general the groups in which the younger-old were represented reported significantly higher subjective well-being. But the relationship was by no means clear-cut. It is of particular interest that two of the apparently most dysfunctional cluster groups reported average levels of well-being. These included predominantly very old people who were markedly cognitively impaired and either had perceptions of high external control (i.e. believing that the actions of other people determined what happened to them) or high 'social aloneness' (i.e. perceiving themselves as neither belonging to a social group nor having other people to rely on). Yet these groups appeared reasonably happy both with their life circumstances and with their own company. These findings already suggest caution in assuming that the undoubted social, physical and cognitive losses of late life inevitably result in lowered states of well-being. There is no reason why there should not be processes at work, perhaps similar to those at earlier stages of life, perhaps qualitatively different, which allow very old people to combat losses of independence, contacts and mental ability. At least, as the Berlin Aging Study authors point out, they show that high levels of cognitive functioning, internal control and social embeddedness are not essential to well-being.

Despite the considerable evidence for a negative effect of impairment, chronic illness and other losses upon psychological well-being in later life (Erdal and Zautra, 1995; Prince *et al.*, 1997; Zeiss *et al.*, 1996), studies also support the view that many very old people adapt well to disability and loss. Advanced age itself is not associated with increased depression. In fact, Blazer *et al.* (1991) found a negative correlation between age and depression when confounding factors such as functional disability, income and cognitive impairment were controlled. Similarly, Halpert and Zimmerman (1986) showed that old-old adults in their sample reported less depression, anxiety and nervousness than young-old individuals. These and other studies, including the Berlin Aging Study (Smith and Baltes, 1999) and the Swedish twins study (Haynie *et al.*, 2001), support the view that very old people adapt to disability, and that they are in fact less depressed and anxious than one might expect when one takes the greater prevalence of disability and loss into account.

These findings strongly suggest that there is a developmental process of adaptation at work, underlying the emergence of this resiliency, which allows the very old to accept loss more easily (see also Aldwin *et al.*, 1996; Brandtstädter and Greve, 1994; Staudinger *et al.*, 1995). This is not to say that all very old people achieve a high level of serenity. Variation is the most evident fact about ageing through until death. Swedish studies (Femia *et al.*, 2001) demonstrate the role of subjective health, depression and social integration in influencing disability severity independently of impairment. There are compensatory mechanisms at work, but not all very old people benefit from them. As Poon concludes from his review of profiles of the oldest old, the diversities must reflect 'the simple fact that there are many paths to living beyond the average life span' (2005). The resiliency of the human spirit that so many persons demonstrate in old age has still to be understood.

The psychology of institutional care

This resiliency of late life was first demonstrated in the unlikely setting of institutions for elderly people. The general tenor of British as well as American literature on old age homes has been to focus on their negative features, originating in their historical precursors in the Elizabethan Poor Law and the 'Dickensian' workhouse. Unlike the continental European countries, Britain broke with the older, more charitable tradition of religious-based, especially monastic-based, care for the old and infirm. It was not until the latter part of the twentieth century, after the pioneering investigations of sociologists (Townsend, 1962) and workers within the welfare services (Robb, 1967), that determined efforts were made to improve the character of institutional care.

It is important to bear in mind this historical and cultural context when interpreting these first studies into the psychology of late life carried out in US homes for the elderly. These studies focused in particular on maintenance of the self (Lieberman and Tobin, 1983) and the influence of subjective control (Langer, 1983; 1989). The institutionalised aged provided a readily available and captive set of participants with whom ingenious psychological studies could be carried out. In the USA there was only one form of institution, the nursing home (as opposed to distinct provisions of residential care, nursing home and hospital long-stay ward place in Britain and other countries). There was also rising social concern in the USA about quality of life in these institutions (Vladeck, 1980). Regimes were clinical, physical care poor and mortality rates high. Institutional care symbolised for most Americans one of the most dreaded outcomes of the ageing process.

In a set of detailed studies, Lieberman and Tobin (1983) examined how elderly people in the United States adapted to the stress of relocation to nursing homes. The studies demonstrated the remarkable stability of self-image that many older people maintained across these transitions, but this was often achieved by changing the basis on which the self was constructed. Rather than relying on incidents from their current interpersonal interactions to confirm their image of self, people in these situations of loss and change also gave many examples from their past lives as well as reiterating general statements of conviction about themselves and their lives. They even seemed prepared to forego present reality altogether and use evidence based on wishes and distortions to maintain self-consistency.

Such behaviour might appear disturbing at first acquaintance, as when an elderly resident referred to a picture taken 50 years ago as if it was a picture of herself today. But this illustration serves to emphasise the importance of the achievement of a coherent life story in late life. To an older person, identities are persistent. She or he is not the frail, impaired person you see, but the sum – an integrated sum – of a long series of life experiences and events, of which the last may be of relatively little importance.

Other features noted about the very old by these researchers included a mythicising of the past, a dramatisation in which the important people and events became 'bigger and better'. The greater vividness, the recall of feelings of love and devotion from parents and others, created a sense of specialness. In a quite different context, Kaufman (1987) has also illustrated how older persons transform present experience in ways that conform to the important themes of their lives. It is the theme, for example, of being the loved mother of a united family, that provides the persistent sense of meaning even when the reality fails to match it.

In other ways, though, very old people appeared to show a truer awareness, particularly of their own feelings. Destructive and antisocial feelings were admitted without the embarrassment and defensive explanations that might have been elicited earlier in life. According to Tobin (1991) this was because even previously unwelcomed motives can be useful for self-definition in the face of the losses of old age; they affirm who one is and has been. Coherence and wholeness can be and are achieved, Tobin argues, even by those 'whose reminiscence is, unfortunately, filled with vivid and, most likely, accurate memories of losses and deprivation' (1991: 12). The studies of relocation to institutions show that it is the elderly people who are prepared to be more assertive and combative in defining their own interests who survive longer. Passivity – including accepting how others define one – leads to earlier decline and death.

Lieberman and Tobin (1983) pointed to the analogies between maintenance of sense of self and of physical survival – it can be that desperate a matter. Many older people find it difficult to acknowledge change. For example, a changing appearance can be hard for a woman to bear if she has always prided herself on her appearance. The same applies to a man who has always emphasised his physical strength, which he now sees declining. Evidence of change – whether from mirrors, photographs or individual comparisons – is therefore resisted. Sometimes extreme strategies are used to maintain the old sense of self, which can appear strange and illogical to observers. Often, these involve myths that exaggerate and dramatise certain personal qualities – myths of being in control of circumstances when one is not, myths of self-constancy that deny change, and the blurring of the boundaries between past and present. People may reiterate behaviour that points to their own importance – for example, regularly writing to one's elected representative in parliament to complain about problems encountered in the residential home!

Tobin (1991; 1999) has elaborated further on the behaviours people may use to maintain the self in advanced old age, including making the past vivid, and distortion of both past and present. The material cited provides an important learning exercise for staff working in care settings (Tobin, 1989). Sometimes the distortion of past or present reality will become too extreme and diminish the possibility of successful adaptation, but generally a great deal of bending of reality is acceptable, and indeed in certain difficult circumstances may seem almost essential to survival. For example, an elderly man who had always insisted that he would not accept relocation to an institution, but would rather die first, in fact flourished in the home in which he was eventually placed. He had persuaded himself that he had been invited to live there in order to keep an eye on the other residents, to make sure that they behaved well and that their needs were properly catered for. Thus he had a role in the home, a reason for being there.

In a separate set of studies on US institutional care Langer and Rodin (Langer and Rodin, 1976; Rodin and Langer, 1977, Rodin *et al.*, 1985) highlighted the importance of the experience of being in control of daily life. Control has become an important subject in general health psychology, with clear evidence of the benefits for recovery and well-being of the patient of having some control over the administration of treatment. However, it is also significant that the value of a subjective sense of control was first demonstrated in the field of elderly care. Those residents of nursing homes who felt – truly or falsely did not seem to matter so much – that they had a say over their daily activities fared better emotionally and cognitively than those who felt life was determined for them. The studies involved manipulating variables such as staff instructions and behaviour. Even taking minor responsibilities (e.g. for the care of a plant) was associated with more favourable outcomes. Similar findings have been found by other investigators (Baltes and Baltes, 1986).

Although these studies were not conducted primarily to investigate the psychology of advanced old age, Rodin, Timko and Harris (1985) did suggest that older adults may be particularly vulnerable to the negative consequences of low perceived control. This suggestion is supported in a recent study conducted by Menec and Chipperfield (1997) to investigate whether perceived control takes on a particularly important role in the older age groups. Their results suggest that perceived control over health moderates the effects of functional impairment on perceived health, but only in those over the age of 80. In this group a high sense of control also reduced hospitalisation and mortality in those with relatively little functional impairment.

Other studies, too, support the finding that feeling in control provides a buffer against the detrimental consequences of disability (e.g. Krause, 1988; Roberts *et al.*, 1994). As Menec and Chipperfield note, the classification into age groups that they employed was based on sample size consideration. They do not indicate that there is anything particularly critical about the age of 80. It is only through further research that such phenomena can better be tied down to factors in the ageing process itself (see also Smith *et al.*, 2000).

Subsequent research has provided a more nuanced view of the contribution of control to well-being (Moos, 1981; Reich and Zautra, 1990). There is an optimum level of subjective control for a particular individual in a particular situation. In most environments we operate below optimum; but exceeding that level can also be counter-productive, provoking anxiety and consequent underperformance. This type of 'U'-shaped performance function can be seen in other areas of psychogerontology. For example, studies of social support show limits to the beneficial effects of assistance provided to older people. Social support beyond a certain level may actually exacerbate the noxious impact of stress (Krause, 1995a). Older adults may be able to increase their coping skills if they are encouraged to confront stressful situations without the undue involvement of others.

It is also apparent that in high-constraint environments that cannot be changed, elderly people with an external locus of control appear better adjusted (Cicirelli, 1987; Felton and Kahana, 1974). Also Smith and Baltes (1997) have shown that high belief in control by others can co-exist with average levels of well-being in cognitively impaired elderly people. These findings illustrate the value of 'person–environment congruence' theory, where well-being is a function of matching between environmental characteristics and a person's needs (see Lawton, 1980; Parmalee and Lawton, 1990). In the following chapter we will illustrate recent studies on the significance of self-determination for elderly people residing in institutions. Lack of autonomy and control remain very important issues in the transition to residential care (Hughes *et al.*, 2001; Reed and Payton, 1996; Reed *et al.*, 2003). Modern societies need to find more effective ways of involving older people in decision-making about their future that does not overwhelm them but succeeds in enhancing their control and hence their sense of belonging.

The self in late life: accommodation and self-transcendence

The study of the self came to take prominence in gerontology in the early post-war years. Maintenance of self-esteem was seen as crucial to morale, but threatened by the losses of ageing (Schwartz, 1975). The important role of social labelling in contributing to decline in functioning via damage to the sense of self was highlighted in the so-called 'social breakdown' theory of ageing (Kuypers and Bengtson, 1973). Only over time did it come to be accepted that self-esteem did not normally decline, at least in the early stages of ageing (Bengtson *et al.*, 1985), and that the crucial difference came with the onset of frailty (Atchley, 1991). Now we are beginning to appreciate better how even in circumstances of considerable loss and dependency many very old people maintain a positive self-image. How do they manage it?

Because of the striking and surprising character of many of the findings about adjustment to institutional care settings, they have come to take a prominent place in thinking about the psychology of late life in general, and preservation of the self in particular. However, as only a minority of even very old people live in institutions, it is important to study more representative samples. As already mentioned, there is a problem with data on long-term survivors from most longitudinal studies of ageing, as they are often the elderly elite, those who have had the stamina, goodwill and morale to meet the investigators' demands. Hence the recent interest in studying and following over time samples of the very old, including centenarians (Poon *et al.*, 1992; Martin *et al.*, 2000).

Evidence so far from such studies provides a highly contrasting picture. They confirm that some average loss of morale and self-esteem does occur in the eighties and nineties, but there is a wide variation in outcome, and successful coping patterns emerge that are quite distinct from those described in the institutional studies. For example, the San Francisco studies of the over-85s indicate that acceptance of change is normal among the very old, as well as disengagement from potentially bothersome or stressful roles and relationships (Johnson and Barer, 1997). Contrary to findings on the younger-old, the oldest-old appear to gain benefit from giving up some control. Living in the present, one day at a time, is a favoured mode of life, and new emotional attachments are avoided. The sense of aloneness resulting from multiple bereavements is counter-balanced by the very old's special status as long-term survivors.

Cultural differences are also evident in the way long life is evaluated, African-Americans tending to see their long lives most positively, attributing to them religious and supernatural significance. But in both black and white members of the sample change is accepted more readily than might be imagined, not only in the outside world but also in the self. People convey the sense of having lived beyond their old lives and selves.

The qualitative material collected in the course of this study is particularly telling. It illustrates how the very old ignore bothersome events: 'I put a frame around my life and only see what I want to see.' The bonds of reciprocity are loosened: 'Life gets easier all the time because people don't expect much of me.' There is increased detachment both from the present ('More things are beyond my control, so I just roll with the waves') and the past ('I have no regrets about [events in] the past because I've just forgotten them') (Johnson and Barer, 1992: 359–61). The overall finding that disengagement is adaptive in those with frailty and failing powers runs counter to the earlier institutional literature, which emphasises assertiveness and control.

Compatible with these observations is one of the first theories to emerge on late-life adjustment. As discussed in Chapter 4 one major approach to understanding successful development during ageing is examining processes of maximising gains and minimising losses. Such processes as selection, optimisation and compensation can help maintain role and function into late life. But the positive balance becomes increasingly more difficult to achieve in late life. For example, practice in compensating for cognitive decline becomes less efficacious with advanced age (Baltes, 1997). According to Brandtstädter, it is then that accommodation comes into its own as a mode of adjustment (Brandtstädter and Greve, 1994). To refer back to the illustration we gave in Chapter 4, how does an ageing pianist, who may have adapted to ageing changes experienced so far on the basis of selection, optimisation and compensation, know when he or she should cease playing in public? Concentrating on a limited repertoire and finding strategies to compensate for failing capacity may be successful for a limited period, but there may come a time when public performance would reveal an embarrassing lack of judgement with regard to one's continuing pianistic ability.

Brandtstädter's two-stage model of coping with ageing has similarities with Atchley's two stages mentioned earlier, but it is more constructive about the transition to older age. As we noted in Chapter 4, Brandtstädter views the self as a protective and dynamic system, comprising 'immunising' (e.g. denial, selective attention and reinterpretation of evidence), 'assimilative' (e.g. self-correction and compensation, selection of enhancing environments and self-verification), and 'accommodative' processes (e.g. rearrangement of priorities, devaluation of blocked goals, rescaling of self-evaluative criteria and construction of palliative meanings).

Immunising processes are well illustrated in the earlier US studies on relocation of elderly people to institutions in the 1960s and 1970s already cited. These demonstrated how powerful is the ability of some older people to manipulate perceived reality in self-threatening situations – for example, to reinterpret circumstances in favourable ways and to intermingle evidence from the past and present (Lieberman and Tobin, 1983). They present a picture of extreme and sometimes bizarre manoeuvres, of denial and illusion, which older people can use to preserve their previous sense of self. However, it would be misleading to overemphasise such processes. They are more likely to be characteristic of people in settings where they have had little or no time to adapt to change.

The most common response to challenge is assimilation, and this appears as true of older people as of younger. Many older people fight long and hard to keep desired aspects of themselves alive through preventative, corrective and compensatory activities. Assimilation is a key element stressed in the Baltes and Baltes (1990) model of successful ageing as 'selective optimisation with compensation'. Empirical study supports an association between these processes and well-being (Freund and Baltes, 1998). Selection, optimisation and compensation are also clearly evident ways of coping in younger older adults adapting to chronic disability (Gignac et al., 2000). But while assimilative processes rightly predominate in younger old age, Brandtstädter and Greve (1994) argue that they are subject to a law of diminishing returns. There comes a time when it is best to switch to the accommodative mode, to accept change, to disengage from blocked commitments and to adjust aspirations to what is feasible. This transition from assimilative to accommodative modes of coping may be marked by feelings of helplessness and depression, but accommodation itself should not be confounded with depression. According to Brandtstädter and Greve, it is the failure to accommodate that more often marks depression.

Brandtstädter's model is more optimistic than Atchley's in that the accommodative processes of later old age are neither devalued nor seen as difficult to realise. This is consistent with other theoretical positions on adaptation to ageing, especially the changing value given to previously important life goals. Even dependency itself can be reinterpreted positively (Baltes et al., 1991). Processes of (re)interpretation are common to much contemporary thinking about the self in later life (Dittmann-Kohli, 1990; Kaufman, 1987). While control over external events may be relinquished, control over meaning remains important. Although one can acknowledge its special place in late life, it is important to recognise that accommodative coping also plays an important role in maintaining a positive life perspective among younger people living with disability (Schmitz et al., 1996).

Research within both the stress and coping paradigm, as well as control theory support this model. The old-old are more likely to find ways of avoiding problems and accepting difficulties that they cannot avoid (Aldwin et al., 1996). A similar argument to Brandtstädter's is presented by Heckhausen and Schulz (1993), that the increasing constraints with ageing on the exercise of primary control are compensated by a heightened investment in secondary control strategies such as disengagement and positive reappraisal. Recent longitudinal studies of the very old living in the community have already been cited (e.g. Johnson and Barer, 1997). The emphasis on the concept of disengagement in this literature contrasts strongly with the 'survival of the fittest' emphasis of earlier research on institutional living.

Nevertheless both Brandtstädter and Atchley note that societal pressure often works against such psychological adaptation in late life. Striving to maintain the goals of younger life is admired in our society and, as a result, may be conducive to enhancing self-esteem in the short term. In the long term, of course, death intervenes. Some people may never incur severe disability in their lives, but may die suddenly or after a short illness. Both assimilation and accommodation are valuable in the course of ageing, and skill is required in judging when one or the other is appropriate. While the correct balance may seem difficult to define, we know that most elderly

people are capable of finding an acceptable solution for themselves, otherwise their self-esteem would not remain so high. The ability to discern
which goals are of lasting importance and to accept which may have to be
relinquished links with the concept of wisdom (Ardelt, 1997) discussed in
Chapter 3.

Not unrelated is the growing emphasis on the importance of self-
transcendence in late life. We referred in Chapter 5 to the growing research
literature on spirituality and ageing. Although there have, up to now, been
more studies carried out in this field on younger older people, it can be
argued that the culmination of processes of self-transcendence occur in late
life. Sherman and Webb (1994), for example, discuss the self as process in
late-life reminiscence, with a developing emphasis on being and belonging
rather than having. In research comparing community-residing and institutionalised older adults, Fry has demonstrated that the pattern of associations between religious involvement, spirituality and well-being was
stronger for the institutionalised elders (Fry, 2000). In a recent study of
older people living in sheltered housing we have also produced evidence
that the influence of spiritual belief on well-being is stronger at higher levels
of frailty (Kirby, Coleman and Daley, 2004).

Self-transcendence is easier spoken about than achieved in an acquisitive
and individualistic culture such as that of the USA or UK. Still relevant to
discussions on the self in late life is Alfred Adler's pioneering approach to
those with feelings of inferiority and inadequacy (Adler, 1927; see also
Brink, 1979). Adler recognised that concerns about sense of worth, competence and efficacy are bound to resurface in later life as one loses physical
power and social influence over others. His solution for both older and
younger people was to look beyond self-assertion and towards '*gemein-
schaftsgefuhl*' ('social interest'), working with others for a common good that
transcends self-interest.

In studies of self-evaluation an important distinction can be made
between judgements of competence and judgements of value. It is possible
for someone to accept declining competence while maintaining that life has
not lost any of its meaning or value. A key concept in this context is 'commitment'. Even if a person feels their own contribution is minimal or non-
existent, to feel committed to a cause, whether religious, ideological or
political, or simply to one's family or community, gives reason for living, if
only to continue to bear witness to that cause. As we saw in Chapter 5,
researchers in gerontology are giving more consideration to the role of belief
systems in adaptation to the inevitable losses and changes associated with
ageing, to the development of what Sherman has referred to as 'psychophi-
losophy', a way of thinking about life that actually influences one's daily
experience (Sherman, 1981).

Thus in principle another approach to good quality of life in residential
care would be to place less emphasis on individuality, while stressing the

importance of the community, shared tasks and 'team spirit'. It is significant that some of the most successful examples of community day centres recorded in the literature are of this kind. Hazan's classic ethnographic study of a Jewish day centre in North London analysed how it had evolved to meet the needs of its members by eschewing personal reminiscing and individual concerns outside the centre, while emphasising group activities and care (Hazan, 1980). Although it is hard to imagine such an establishment functioning in this way nowadays, the centre clearly satisfied the psychological and social needs of most of its attenders, many of whom had been disappointed in their families, and welcomed the new 'family' they had entered. Jerrome's studies on day centres in Brighton, England, have also emphasised the benefits of identification with others achieved through repetitive ceremonies and assertion of strong in-group values (Jerrome, 1988; 1992). We agree with Baltes (1997) that a major problem for ageing people in modern society is that cultural support has failed to keep up with increases in the numbers of the very old. Religious institutions in particular have not addressed the present and future challenges of a rapidly ageing population. We will examine recent examples of research on the self in late life in the next chapter.

Dementia: the negation of development?

The onset of physical disability, suddenly as in stroke, or more gradually as with osteoarthritis, is one form of entrance to late life. A quite different pathway is through dementia. The many disabling consequences arising from mental frailty make dementia the major health problem of later life in modern western society. It is the most age-related of all the disabling conditions affecting older people. The rate of dementia changes with age in a strikingly consistent manner. According to a theoretical model derived from 22 studies, the age-specific prevalence rate approximately doubles every five years, from an average rate of 5.6 per cent at 75–79, to 10.5 per cent at 80–84 and 39 per cent in the first half of the tenth decade (Black *et al.*, 1990). A summary of eight European studies showed an increase of prevalence rate from 40 per cent to 70 per cent between the ages of 90 and 95 (Hofman *et al.*, 1991). It is not clear whether the rate continues to increase in centenarians. But certainly, with many more people surviving into their nineties, the overall prevalence is increasing. Dementia has now become the major reason for receiving institutional care, and a challenge to the physically frail who need to be cared for in the same environment.

Unfortunately, dementia has until recently been a neglected condition, not only in terms of quality of provision but also of research into its nature, cause and treatment. Research effort has not been comparable to that in the fields of heart disease and cancer, but is now expanding fast (Woods, 2005).

The role of psychologists in dementia has also been limited, until recently almost exclusively focused on developing appropriate cognitive tests for use in its detection. Nevertheless this remains a very important task. For example, it may be difficult to distinguish superficially the reactions of an elderly person who is depressed from one who is demented. Procedures that provide a profile of an individual's mental abilities help in making a more confident diagnosis. However, psychological interest in dementia has recently broadened to include the development and evaluation of different types of therapeutic intervention. Perhaps most important of all recent developments has been psychologists' contribution to understanding what it means to be demented (Woods, 2001).

With greater publicity and openness about dementia – including, notably, ex-US President Ronald Reagan's admission that he was suffering from Alzheimer's disease – there is now much greater curiosity about the condition. This has extended to the sufferer's own experience of becoming and being demented. In addition, family caregivers' accounts have become important material for books and, in the case of John Bayley's writings about his wife, the philosopher Iris Murdoch, popular film as well (Bayley, 1998). There is much in this field to challenge developmental psychologists. Considerable imagination is required to appreciate the impact of crumbling powers of memory and identification upon the individual's feelings of security. A life-span developmental approach, too, can be valuable in understanding an individual's behaviour and the cues to which he or she responds as a consequence of habits established earlier in life. There is also the possibility that a study of psychological factors, motivational and affective as well as cognitive, will eventually contribute in significant ways to a total picture of the aetiology and process of dementing illnesses. If this seems implausible, one should ask oneself why psychology should be relevant to understanding the origins of heart disease and cancer, and not a condition that affects the brain.

Much has been contributed by British psychologists to this new wave of thinking about dementia (Downs, 1997). In particular the late Tom Kitwood had already started, in the 1980s, to argue for a radical rethinking of our understanding of dementia, to give more attention to internal psychological factors, such as personal reactions to the stress of finding oneself mentally frail, as well as external social circumstances, including the quality of family care (Kitwood, 1997; Kitwood and Bredin, 1992). However, these issues are relatively neglected topics for research. The biomedical model remains dominant. In part, this may be because the consequences of considering dementia as something for which we are each partly responsible has too drastic implications for the way we treat people with the condition. It is far easier to accept dementia as a disease over which we have as yet no control, but in the future hope to master by pharmaceutical means. In neglecting psychosocial factors, however, we may be missing important lines of enquiry into the disturbing ways in which dementia ends so many people's lives.

It is possible to distinguish between a 'strong' (causation) versus 'weak' (exacerbation) hypothesis about the role of psychosocial factors in the aetiology of dementia. Kitwood in his early writings (Kitwood, 1988) speculated on the kinds of personality factor that could be involved, such as difficulty in acknowledging personal vulnerability and in appraising one's emotional states. A more likely hypothesis, perhaps, is that personality factors determine the types of coping responses individuals display at the first signs of mental frailty. Some of these reactions, such as learned helplessness (Seligman, 1975), may provoke further decline, over and above that which the actual neurological damage warrants. Kitwood drew attention not only to the role of personality in affecting behavioural symptoms in dementia alongside neurological impairment, but also to factors in individual biography, social psychology and physical health (Kitwood, 1993). Personality, of course, may also influence the rate of mental impairment in later life by its influence on styles of life, including mental exercise, which may protect against dementia.

It might be thought that dementia is incompatible with considerations of development – that it is, in fact, its very antithesis. But this view deserves challenging. Of course one would wish for there to be some cure for the neurological disease processes that seemingly underlie the memory and other dysfunctions of dementia. This does not mean, however, that other types of development – in personal relationships, for example – may not occur in the presence of these losses and perhaps even because of them. In the remaining sections of this chapter we will consider briefly the concepts necessary for building a developmental psychology of dementia, relating first to the psychological changes that are most commonly observed in this condition, second to the subjective experience of becoming demented, and third to the emotional and other responses that dementia calls forth, not only in the dementia sufferer but also the caregiver.

Cognitive and personality change in dementia

There are many types of dementia, including those brought on by brain injuries, tumours, toxic states and infections. There appear to be two prevalent physical associates of the dementia we call Alzheimer's disease: the development in the brain of clumps of protein fragment called amyloid, known as plaques, as well as the deterioration of the brain's blood vessels leading to their obstruction. However, we do not yet know to what extent the formation of amyloid is a cause of dementia rather than a by-product of a more fundamental process. The occurrence of multiple small strokes, which the person may not be aware of, and the resulting death of brain cells, is more understandable as a cause of cognitive decline.

It is important to note that dementia is unlike heart disease, cancer and other physical diseases in that it is not, strictly speaking, a disease but a behavioural syndrome. Its severity cannot yet be defined in terms of brain pathology. It is sometimes assumed that levels of mental disability resulting from dementia can be explained in terms of observable pathology of the brain. But post-mortem studies show that the states of the brains of some demented people – for example, the number of plaques – are well within the range of those of mentally well-preserved individuals, whereas some people become demented with comparatively little accompanying neuropathology. Of course, it could be that with improved understanding of the disease at the biochemical as well as physiological level a better correlation would be found between biological markers and actual impairment.

At present dementia is more appropriately considered a psychological condition, and defined as an acquired progressive global deterioration of mental functioning. This is by necessity a rather broad definition. In practice, dementia is usually characterised in terms of cognitive change, especially memory and learning disturbance. However, personality change is also an important aspect of the disease (and one emphasised by Alois Alzheimer, who first identified the condition), with sufferers behaving in ways uncharacteristic of their former selves. Dementia illustrates well the difficulty of distinguishing in practice personality from cognition, for a person's abilities also define and limit their characteristic ways of behaving.

Issues concerning the correct identification of dementia remain important for psychology and will become even more so if ways are found of treating dementia effectively, whether to reverse the condition or at least to slow its further progression. More refined methods will be needed to detect dementia in its early stages and to measure change over time. For example, the most evident early signs of dementia are impairment of memory for recent events, name-finding difficulties and slowing of responses. But even very healthy people complain sometimes of similar problems. Moreover, the increased variability between people's abilities with age makes the detection of a threshold level for early onset of dementia very difficult to achieve. There is a danger of overdiagnosing dementia in persons of limited intelligence or poor education. Actual tests of performance are required, which also take account of the time needed to perform a task as well as accuracy. One can foresee the increasing application of computerised mental testing.

A more helpful criterion for dementia than memory loss is the loss of automatic intelligence. Dementia means that the person's ability to apply the intelligence they have acquired during life in the automatic way to which they have been accustomed is becoming less effective. Normally we do not have to think about who we are, where we are, what we are doing and what we are going to do next. We operate automatically and as a result of this, we can function efficiently. When we decide to do something, we simply activate strategies and procedures – whether for driving a car, keeping up with a conversation, or even eating one's food and dressing oneself – that rely upon the things that, once upon a time, we did learn to do. Even well-learned procedures are lost by persons in advanced states of dementia. As a result they can also lose a sense of where they are in the world and what they are doing. It is the loss of the past self that most sharply distinguishes dementia from other severe memory disorders resulting from neurological injury, where a person loses the ability to learn new information, but retains earlier memories (Miller and Morris, 1993).

Demented people also show failure of what is called schematic memory, which automatically allows us to make sense of new experiences, and to recognise and put new objects and experiences in the right categories. Early signs of dementia are often indications of loss of previous reference schemes – for example, forgetting that you can now buy a carton of milk at most general stores not only a bottle of milk from the dairy. A related idea is the distinction between automatic and effortable memory (Hasher and Zacks, 1979). Some forms of information we acquire automatically without having to think about it (for example, where you sat when you last went to the cinema), for others we require some considerable mental exertion in order to acquire it reliably (what, for example, was the title of the film). The former kind of automatic encoding is by and large age-invariant, whereas performance on learning tasks declines with age.

The difference between normal ageing and ageing with dementia is that there is also a breakdown in the automatic encoding of information; this is more disruptive because a greater proportion of our life relies upon automatic encoding than purposeful learning. The important point to realise is that dementia would be nothing like the social problem it is, and it would not strike at the core of the self, if it only concerned new information. An older person could live reasonably well with the experience of the long years already built up. But dementia attacks the sense of self already achieved, as well as the possibility of building a new self.

Whether dementia inevitably involves some form of personality change is a matter for debate. Clearly there are cases where damage – for example, to the frontal lobes of the brain – produces a very definite personality change characterised by carefreeness and disinhibition, even though memory may be relatively unimpaired. A profile of personality trait change is also observable at a more general level in dementia. Studies in which relatives/carers have been asked to use the 'big five' scales to rate the personality of their demented caree before and after the development of the disease show systematic changes both in the USA and the UK (Siegler *et al.*, 1994; Williams *et al.*, 1995), namely declines in 'conscientiousness' and 'extraversion', and increase in 'neuroticism'. These contrast strongly with the only minor changes observed during normal ageing (small decreases in neuroticism and extraversion being most often observed) (Costa and McCrae, 1997).

But it can be argued that this type of change in crude personality markers is less important than the preservation of more individualising characteristics such as a person's special interests, attitudes and styles of behaviour, and even more the sense of oneself as a person with a continuous story over time (McAdams, 1990; 1993). With the appropriate care, much can be done to keep these higher levels of personality alive. It also needs to be borne in mind that the experience of dementia may produce changes in relating to others, which may actually be perceived positively. For example, as some spouses note, dementia may lead to an acknowledgement of dependency in a previously distant individual, which strengthens rather than weakens the marital bond.

Understanding the experience of dementia

As well as objectively studying change in behaviour it is equally important to attempt to understand the subjective experience of dementia. Demented people should not be dismissed as outside the range of normal human consideration. It is still common to hear comments made about elderly people with dementia that imply a lack of sensitivity to their needs as human beings to be understood, respected and loved. People scoring low on mental test scores tend to be excluded from consumer studies, an increasingly important part of contemporary health and social services provision, yet with effort and imagination their reactions to the way they are treated can be gauged (Sutton, 2004). Issues in the developmental psychology of ageing referred to in previous chapters, such as coming to terms with the past, with both personal losses and social change, apply just as much to demented elderly people. Adjustment may be exacerbated (or in some cases made easier) by their condition, but those suffering from dementia face similar issues to 'ordinary' elderly people – for example, needing reassurance, a feeling of being wanted, and reconciliation for past wrongs done by or to them.

For any person involved in dementia care it is important to try to appreciate the implications of being demented. This is not easy. It is hard to appreciate what it is like to suffer from relatively simple handicaps such as blindness and deafness, let alone a set of disabilities as complex as those resulting from dementia. What is it like to hear people talking but to be unable to make sense of what they are saying? Or to realise that someone is angry but not to be able to understand why? The lack of understanding shown by demented people and their difficulties in communicating their own needs require that those who try to help them should use their own powers of imagination and empathy to help bridge the gap in understanding. It is a proper concern of psychology not only to describe a person's behaviour patterns, but also to conceptualise the view (or lack of view) of the world that may underlie them.

It is insufficient to characterise dementia purely in terms of cognitive failure. Its impact is more global, more terrifying. It has been described in terms of loss of 'personhood' or 'self' (Gilleard, 1984). Whereas the amnesic person suffering brain trauma and the person with a learning difficulty still retain a self and a grasp on reality, the onslaught the dementing person faces eventually takes away the basis for a sense of personal integrity unless properly supported.

Dementing persons present their broken-ness clearly to us, but, as Kitwood has so eloquently written in theorising about dementia care, we are all damaged, frail and vulnerable. The only difference between 'us' and 'them' is that whereas 'they' are more likely to admit their problems, we hide and defend ours. Kitwood, along with others, has recognised that the key to improving dementia care is the concept of the 'person':

> The core of our position is that personhood should be viewed as essentially social: it refers to the human being in relation to others. But also, it carries essentially ethical connotations: to be a person is to have a certain status, to be worthy of respect.
>
> (Kitwood and Bredin, 1992: 275)

Relationship is central to this conception of personhood. This also has theological roots, which define a person in terms of relationship to other persons and ultimately to God, who in the Christian tradition is understood to be a Trinity constituting a community of mutual love (Coleman and Mills, 2001).

Kitwood refers to Martin Buber's *I and Thou* ([1923] 1937), which contrasts two ways of being in the world, two ways of forming a relationship, the first being purely instrumental, the second involving commitment. To be a person is to be related to in the second sense, to be addressed as 'Thou'. At the other extreme is the 'I–It' mode of relating. Kitwood argued that modernity, as a product of western reason and logic, had brought with it a distancing and objectification in human relationships (Kitwood, 1997; Wilson, 1999). The consequences for treatment of madness, the institutions that were built to confine those who offended against rationality and good order, have been recorded by Foucault (1967). Dementing people have suffered especially from this approach of isolating and analysing people as separate individuals rather than as persons in relationship.

The American psychologist Steven Sabat (Sabat, 2001; Sabat and Harré, 1992) distinguishes between different conceptions of selfhood that are affected by dementia. Whereas loss of 'social self' is greatly influenced by others' behaviour towards the person with dementia, 'personal self' is usually preserved until the late stages of dementia and is demonstrated by the use of first-person indexicals. When we refer to loss of self in dementia we refer principally to the social self, and articulation of this self depends crucially on the two-way process of communication. The problem is also other people's failure to understand the increasingly fragmented and fragile cues the dementia sufferer expresses. As a result the social self can no longer be sustained. Sabat introduces the concept of social 'positioning':

> Technically a 'position' is defined by a certain set of rights, duties and obligations as a speaker. Each episode of everyday life can be seen as the development of a 'story-line'. ... So if the Alzheimer's Disease sufferer's position as a self cannot be brought into being, a story line may be followed out antithetical to the intentions of the sufferer when his or her actions are interpreted by the other person without reference to the presentational cues indicative of a certain self, presented by the sufferer. And in these different interpretations there is considerable possibility for social misunderstanding of the meaning of the A.D. sufferer's behaviour.
>
> (Sabat and Harré, 1992: 453)

Thus the fundamental cause of loss of social self is to be found in the character of the social interactions and the interpretations that follow in the wake of the difficulties in communication. 'The ultimate result of such a situation is the fencing off of the sufferer so that no adequate self can be constructed' (Sabat, 2001: 459). Others have also taken the research line of analysing speech and communication as a way of revealing the demented person's vulnerability to personal demotion. Small *et al.* (1998), for example, videotaped nursing staff–resident interactions, and analysed use of personal pronouns, proper nouns, interpersonal conflicts and discursive positioning. They observed decline in 'self' indexicals and discuss how changes to institutional policy could prevent this process occurring. Close observation and discussion with people in the early stages of dementia show that they have some insight and awareness of what is happening to them (Froggatt, 1988). The continuing absence of effective biomedical solutions makes the need for psychological support even more pressing.

Dementia and emotions

It is not surprising that emotional reactions of depression, worry and frustration should be very much in evidence in the early stages of dementia. However, psychologists and other professionals have tended to concentrate on cognition in the assessment and care of people with dementia. Yet their emotions remain intact longer, and through emotions we can continue to make contact. Dementia care is much more about responding to emotions and maintaining a sense of well-being than it is about preserving cognitive function.

The study of emotions has been neglected in psychology (Oatley, 1989; Oatley and Jenkins, 1996). There is a vast imbalance of literature in favour of the study of cognitive processes. Yet emotions are an important and essential part of what make us human. Western civilisation, from Aristotle through to Aquinas and the philosophers of the seventeenth- and eighteenth-century Enlightenment, have defined humans in terms of their reasoning and thinking component. Feelings tended to be regarded as part of the lower order. Even Darwin, who might have been expected to have provided a fresh impetus to the study of the functions of the emotions, tended to look down on emotional expressions as vestiges of patterns of action that once were useful but were no longer so. He gave support to an attitude already strong in western culture that emotions were suspect, sub-vertors of reason and scarcely to be approved of in adult humans. The end result is the twentieth-century vision of future humans and aliens as super-reasoning but emotionless beings.

It has taken a different, more respectful, attitude to human and animal emotions, stimulated especially by the work of ethologists, to realise that emotions are centrally important in human and animal behaviour. Emotions are our way of responding to situations where we are not sure how we should respond. They are so because humans, as well as animals, are not automata. They often find themselves in situations where they lack appropriate patterns of behaviour, when they are not fully adapted to an environment that has changed or when no habit or instinct fits a situation. Emotions are important at such junctures because they prompt us towards certain types of action when perhaps we should do something but lack already established modes of action. Joy, sorrow, anger, anxiety are essential parts of life.

According to this view (Oatley, 1989), emotions happen when certain events affect our goals. All our various emotions can be understood as based on just a few distinctive mental states that go with readiness for action, and that each is set off when we evaluate an event in relation to our goals. Thus the primary emotions (and their corresponding moods in brackets) appear to be: happiness (contentment) at the achievement of goals and solving problems as they arise; sadness (depression) at the loss of a goal or a par-ticular avenue leading towards it; anger (aggression) at the frustration of a plan to reach a goal; fear (anxiety) because of a conflict between goals, including the important goal of self-preservation; disgust (aversion) at per-ceiving something (or someone) to be harmful.

Whereas emotions arise suddenly, and last for seconds or minutes, moods are emotional states that may be more vague, and they can last for hours or days. The distinction between emotions and moods is like that between two types of muscular activity: contractions, which change the pattern of a limb, and muscle tone, which maintains a posture. Discrete emotions are concerned with changing a situation, and moods with maintaining it. Negative emotions in particular have the function of interrupting ongoing behaviour, but in turn through the production of mood states create new patterns of behaviour or thought, concentrating the attention, ensuring that we think about making sense of what has happened, constructing new plans about what to do about it, and perhaps modifying our goals in relation to the new events.

In short, emotions help us to act in a world that can be known only imperfectly. Where something has not gone as expected, a change in readiness to act may be followed by a longer-lasting mental preoccupation in which we can concentrate on reprogramming the way we think about our lives – for example, the turning-in on self and greater reflection produced by sadness, the capacity for vigorous action produced by anger, the restless searching that results from anxiety. Only when these reactions get out of hand and become pathological do we have problems. Whether or not this view of emotions has lasting value, it has undoubtedly had the beneficial effect of creating greater respect for the human capacity to react emotionally, and to understand disturbance of emotional reactions, where emotions are over- or under-expressed.

This line of thinking has particularly important implications for dementia. Precisely because the world to a confused person is likely to appear less certain, one would expect people suffering from a dementing condition to be more emotional. Unexpected things will happen more often. There will be sadness over losing things, anger at being frustrated in achieving aims, and fear and anxiety because of uncertainty over what might happen. (Perhaps also disgust as a result both of the increased incidence of accidental mistakes and false perceptions of the outside world.) There will also be more expressions of joy as problems are solved and familiar faces recognised. It is also probable that emotions will be expressed more extremely, and that resulting moods will be more prolonged. These tendencies, however, will be countered by forgetfulness, a boon to many sores.

Professional staff and carers need education and training in handling these different states, and many helpful books have been produced that tackle these issues, from Mace and Rabins' cleverly titled *The 36-Hour Day* onwards (Mace and Rabins, 1985; Stokes, 1996). Important principles in responding to sadness and despondency include the provision of opportunity for activity, in particular successful activity, and contact with familiar and friendly others. Angry or violent behaviour needs to be treated as a catastrophic reaction, to be responded to calmly and if possible by removing the persons from the circumstances that are upsetting them. Very often, anger is a reaction to a situation and the actions of others that have been misunderstood, and this needs to be appreciated by the caregiver.

Anxiety and nervousness are major problems – as the earlier-cited studies on personality traits indicated, ratings of 'neuroticism' or 'affectivity' increase markedly in dementia – and do not subside easily, which is why staff often have recourse to sedative medication. While some anxiety and nervousness may result from changes within the brain, a lot may arise from real feelings of loss and tension. It is noteworthy that even severely demented people remain sensitive to the moods of the people around them. If there is tension in the household, no matter how well attempts are made to conceal it, the dementing person may recognise and respond in kind.

Sometimes the actual feeling may become dissociated from its origin. So a person may become sad and worried about losing something. Later reassurance that it has been found may not seem to help. The mood state has been triggered by a feeling that something has been lost, but it is not so easy to remove the feeling because the person cannot now remember what it was that was lost. Different sensations of loss – the wristwatch is lost, time is lost, memory is lost – may merge to produce a longer-lasting state of anxiety. Calmness, gentleness and reassurance communicate best, and sometimes the opportunity to do something constructive can dislodge the mood state.

A very important principle, therefore, which should guide dementia care, is respect for emotions. Their very presence is a sign of continuing vitality. Both their expression and the type of responses they elicit from care staff have been used to develop systems of monitoring quality of dementia care within institutions, such as 'dementia care mapping' (Brooker *et al.*, 1998; Kitwood, 1997). The field of dementia care has become at last a dynamic one (Woods, 2001). In the next chapter we will examine research on one approach that draws specifically on a developmental theory, originating in studies of child deprivation but now applied to issues throughout the lifespan: John Bowlby's theory of attachment relationships. Relationships are the key to quality of life in ageing, and especially in dementia. Yet late life, and even more so with dementia, is the time of the greatest loss of established relationships.

7 Current research on development and adaptation in advanced old age

As in Chapters 3 and 5 we have selected three topics to illustrate current research on the psychology of development and adaptation in advanced old age. Because of the relative neglect of late life by psychologists, there is less research material to choose from than in previous chapters. However, our first chosen topic illustrates what has been a major theme in the psychogerontological literature since the 1960s: preservation of the self in later life. There has been a wealth of studies carried out on the subject, but relatively few on the very old. We examine how recent researchers have begun to study self-management in representative samples of people over the age of 85 years.

As we saw in the previous chapter the psychology of institutional care was also one of the first research fields to be developed in the study of ageing. Our examination of recent research in this area focuses on some of the burgeoning literature on person–environment congruence, choice and self-determination, all central themes in present-day residential care practice. It takes account of the pioneering work on the effects of manipulating perception of control in institutional care settings (Langer, 1983; Rodin, 1986), but focuses on recent developments in the study of self-determination in institutional care based on a needs model of motivation (Deci and Ryan, 2000). It also considers other recent literature on identifying and changing key psychological features of the institutional environment.

The third topic also deals with issues relating to caregiving, but more specifically directed to dementia. It examines the recent application of attachment theory to improving the quality of care of mentally infirm elderly people. Although most of the research carried out so far in this particular field has focused on care within institutions, the general principles are applicable as well to care provided within family settings. All three themes we have chosen have a clear developmental aspect to them: the changing dynamics of self and identity with ageing, the continued need for self-determination despite growing constraints on its use, and the preservation of attachment relationships in a world where the dead greatly outnumber the living. What they all have in common is the necessity of loving support from the world around. But this is true of development throughout life. We do not grow in isolation.

Sources of continuity of the self in late life

As discussed in the previous chapter, literature and theory development on the psychology of ageing has focused on the self, in particular on maintenance and change in self-conceptions. The centrality of the concept of the self is common to many topics in the social and behavioural sciences (George, 1998). Those who emphasised the dangers of decrease in self-esteem in older people admitted to institutions (Lieberman and Tobin, 1983) and the association between loss of self-esteem and depression (Busse and Reckless, 1961) were emphasising common themes in the psychological and sociological literature. However, the emphasis given to these subjects in gerontology has been misleading in certain respects. Only a minority of older people enter institutional care even at advanced ages. Nor does depression appear to be a special problem of late life; indeed, as noted in the previous chapter, there is evidence that the propensity to depression may decrease in late life. Too much emphasis has been placed on loss of self in later life and not enough on self-enhancement (George, 1998).

Nevertheless, maintenance of the self still seems a critical subject in the developmental study of advanced old age. The types of changes commonly associated with late life – ill-health, bereavement, loss of role – are regularly associated with loss of self-esteem and depression earlier in life. So if the self is maintained better in such circumstances in later life it would suggest that there are developmental processes at work. The kinds of health changes involved can greatly diminish a person's previous lifestyle. We know from work on younger stroke victims (Becker, 1993) how they often experience a temporary loss of self as they question whether their old selves still exist. Impaired mobility and sensory deficits also lead to a decline in contact, including telephone contact, with family and friends (Johnson and Barer, 1997). Moves from familiar homes and neighbourhoods that have become part of self-representations after many years' residence can also lead to the dislocation of self. All these factors we might assume will lead to perception of loss of identity and loss of control.

The major theories of adaptation of the self in later life discussed in the last chapter emphasise either the lack of adaptability of the old (Atchley, 1991) or the different types of adaptation, in particular disengagement, required in late life (Brandtstädter and Greve, 1994). Both therefore suggest major changes in self-management, but until we have properly documented empirical evidence, any assumption that assimilation, for example, becomes less important and/or effective as people age is unjustified. To consider progress in understanding the self in late life, we have decided to examine studies that have attempted to investigate representative samples of older people, and have sought not only to assess self-conception in later life but also to get behind positive and/or negative expression of self to the underlying processes at work.

Evidence for stability of core and self descriptors

The first study we have chosen to highlight is that by Troll and Skaff (1997). This draws on a longitudinal study of very old people carried out in the San Francisco area of the United States. Their approach to the issue of continuity of self was to examine the responses of very old individuals to questions about how they may have changed or remained the same during the course of ageing. The study is unusual in two respects. First, it draws not on fixed answers to test items but on analysis of the person's discourse in response to questioning about continuity of the self. In this the authors follow the call of noted researchers such as Neugarten, Breytspraak and Atchley, to carry out more descriptive work on self-description in late life. As Breytspraak in her pioneering study of the self in old age stressed: 'If we are interested in how people go about interpreting and making sense of themselves as they age, we must start with their interpretations, not with an investigator's attempt to preconceive and measure the dimensions assumed to be relevant' (Breytspraak, 1984: 121).

Second, rather than examining self-conceptions alone, they take the bold step of attempting to assess awareness of the perceiving self, William James' 'I', as well as the perceived self or 'me' (James, 1890). Whereas the objective self corresponds to later psychologists' use of the self-concept (i.e. individuals' descriptions of themselves), it is the subjective or phenomenological self that does the perceiving, interpreting or evaluating. The latter has been largely neglected in studies of ageing. Although it is assumed that the subjective self is more resilient than the perceived objective self, it is change in the former that is most threatening to a person's sense of identity. This issue has been recognised in studies of dementia, as noted in the previous chapter.

Most of the participants in Troll's study were identified from public voting records, with about one-fifth added via a snowball technique. Letters of invitation were followed by telephone calls. These were used not only to identify those willing to participate but also those competent enough to respond to in-depth personal interview. Those with signs of marked cognitive failure (i.e. who were unable to recall their date of birth, address and telephone number) were excluded. This might be thought an unnecessary exclusion, but is typical of much research on ageing, which unfortunately neglects the views of those with dementia only because these views are more difficult to gather and interpret (Sutton, 2004).

A relatively small number, 21 per cent of those judged competent, declined to participate. The participants were interviewed on two occasions 30 months apart. Complete data were collected on 144 persons initially and 90 on the second occasion. Three-quarters of the original sample were women with an age range of 85 to 103 years, and about one-third were over 90 years. The average age for men was 88 and for women 89 years. All lived in the community; roughly half (64 per cent of the women and 45 per cent of the men) lived alone. Whereas half of the men were still married, only one-tenth of the women were. About two-thirds, slightly more men than women, had living children, but only just over half (55 per cent) had a child living in the area. One-third had children who had died before them. Three-quarters of the sample (82 per cent of the men and 71 per cent of the women) perceived themselves to be in good or excellent health. Whereas 66 per cent of the men had no disabilities, only 19 per cent of the women were without disabilities.

These statistics are themselves instructive. The gender differences, including the different disability levels between the sexes, are consistent with other studies. Perhaps more surprising is the loss of contact with children. This illustrates the potential greater isolation of the oldest old. Two and a half years later, 19 per cent of the original respondents had died, 9 per cent had become too impaired mentally or physically to continue and 11 per cent declined to participate, had moved or could not be located. These figures, together with the initial selection criteria, public voting records and absence of marked cognitive decline, need to be taken into account in discussing the results. It is particularly important to note that the study did not include some of the most frail people of advanced age.

The results are striking for the evidence they provide on stability of self. Participants were encouraged to speak freely about their lives, and what they said was recorded verbatim. Questions about self-continuity were incorporated into the interview. At the initial interview participants were asked, 'In what ways have you always been the same?' and 'In what ways have you changed over the years?' On the follow-up visit, after they had described their average day, participants were asked, 'Do you feel that you are the same person as you were a year ago?' Although clearly attempting to assess the strength of the subjective self, the 'oddness' of asking such a question, which directly challenges a person's sense of continuity, needs to be considered.

Both the 'I' and 'me' aspects of the self were scored on a three-point scale. Ratings of continuity of the subjective self were based on evidence as to whether individuals still considered themselves to be the same person they had always been. Thus answers such as 'I didn't change, I'm still the same person' and 'I've always been the same, about everything' were given ratings of '3', whereas 'Maybe I've changed, but the fundamental me is the same' was given a '2'. Imagined responses such as 'The person I used to be is no longer there' and 'I feel I've changed into a different person' would have been given ratings of '1', but in fact no one answered in this way. Almost three-quarters (74 per cent) of the 144 participants were rated as thinking they were essentially the same person. One-fifth (18 per cent) thought they might have changed somewhat, and the responses of fewer than one-tenth (8 per cent) were too ambiguous to be coded.

Therefore the evidence for perception of continuity of a subjective feeling of self appears very strong. Consistent with the studies on dementia reported in the previous chapter, even the most cognitively deteriorated persons included used the pronoun 'I' with assurance. However, it is important to remember that more severely mentally infirm people were excluded and no qualitative analysis was conducted on the 'ambiguous' material that could not readily be coded. It is arguable that a more sophisticated approach is necessary for investigating such a profound but also subtle phenomenon as loss of sense of self.

By contrast, two-thirds (68 per cent) of those whose responses were analysed identified some change in attributes, and one-tenth (9 per cent) thought there had been major change. Less than a quarter (22 per cent) could name no characteristics on which they thought they had changed. No significant relation was found between disruptive events experienced during the months leading up to the interview and the sense of continuity expressed. The authors note that the major changes in self characteristics, which the persons themselves commented on, such as widowhood, had often occurred earlier in life. Although the results support the consensus emerging in the literature, that older people show considerable resilience in defending their sense of self, the combination of exclusions from the study as well as from data analysis, together with drop-out rates and death, mean that it can only be considered a pilot study into this important issue. Obtaining representative samples is a very important aspect of research methodology in psychology and perhaps nowhere more so than in the study of late life.

Differences in self-definition between the younger-old and the older-old

A more sophisticated study, comparing self-definition in the younger-old and older-old has been reported by Alexandra Freund and Jacqui Smith (1999). It draws on the Berlin Aging Study, which we mentioned in Chapter 6. In the previous chapter we referred to the emphasis its director, Paul Baltes, has placed on studying adaptations in the fourth age. The study on self-descriptions draws on data from the first observation of the longitudinal study with a carefully stratified sample divided into six age/cohort groups from 70 to 103 years, with equal numbers of men and women. The samples for comparing the younger-old (70–84 years) and the older-old (85–103 years) are relatively large, comprising 258 people in each group.

The authors emphasise that their study is not simply about self-description but self-definition, by which they mean 'that part of self-related knowledge that contains attributes crucial for the definition of oneself. It involves the subjectively most important characteristics to which individuals feel committed and which subjectively distinguish their own person from that of others' (Freund and Smith, 1999: 55). It includes core goals, values and interests, as well as personal characteristics and behaviour. In agreement with Troll and Skaff they note that not only have few previous studies considered the very old but that they have used mostly domain-overarching measures of global self-esteem (Bengtson *et al.*, 1985). As a result they reveal little or nothing about the changing nature of the self with age.

Of particular interest in Freund and Smith's study is the attempt to derive and test hypotheses about how the self might change in late life. As we have stressed throughout this book, theory development and empirical work in the study of ageing need to be more closely attuned to one another. Theory is often developed without consideration for its subsequent testing, and data collection carried out without consideration of the theoretical context within which it can be interpreted. Freund and Smith identify a wide range of propositions relating to the self in late life, all derived from theory relating to relevant topics: life review, family relationships, body image, financial concerns, personal interests and hobbies, outdoor activities, and health and activities of daily living. Some of the propositions date from literature published 30 years and more before. That many of them have remained untested for so long is itself testimony to the neglect of the study of late life.

Drawing hypotheses from Erikson's writings and those who have followed his arguments about the developmental task of integrity vs despair (see Chapters 2 and 3), we might deduce the proposition that the older people become, the greater is the measure of integration they should have achieved between the different aspects of their self-definition. We might also expect very old adults in comparison to their younger counterparts to show a more marked tendency to make judgements on their life as a whole.

Carstensen's socio-emotional selectivity theory (Carstensen, 1991; Lang and Carstensen, 1994), referred to in Chapter 4, would suggest that the family represents a more important part of older people's self-definition as they become increasingly selective with regard to social partners towards the end of their lives. As old friends die, only family members provide the same emotional significance. But, with bereavement and geographical separation, many older people will in fact have lost family roles and obligations as well as long-standing professional ones. Therefore, as Waterman and Archer (1990) have argued, there is increased room for personal interests and hobbies, at least those that can be conducted indoors. Outdoor activities, by contrast, are more likely to decline as a result of increasing problems with mobility (Manton *et al.*, 1995).

Both body image and financial concerns should also be less important in advanced old age, because physical decline and the approach of death should lead to transcendence of the importance previously attributed to good looks and material belongings (Peck, 1968). Also limited pensions mean that little improvement is possible on the financial front. Much more prominent considerations are likely to be health and everyday competence because of the increasing threat that their decline poses to independent living (Atchley, 1991). It has been known, for example, that older adults report more 'possible selves' in the realm of health than young people (Hooker, 1992).

On the basis of these considerations, Freund and Smith developed a category system for coding responses to the open question 'Who am I?' Participants were asked to generate ten answers to the question, and these were then taped and transcribed verbatim. Having been segmented into meaningful idea units, these were then coded as reflecting one of 24 content categories; this was done by two independent raters using a computer-based randomised procedure in order to avoid context effects. The researchers were able to demonstrate a high level of agreement between the two raters. Statements that included an explicit evaluation (e.g. 'I am a very good cook', or 'It's so sad that I cannot get around in the city any more') were coded as positive or negative depending on the words used.

Both the old and very old participants expressed more positive than negative evaluations, but with declining positive and increasing negative evaluations in the very old. It is striking, however, that there are more similarities than differences in the category profiles of the two groups. Only five of the twenty-four categories revealed statistically significant age-related differences. In regard to the hypotheses already mentioned, considerations of health, competence and daily living routines emerged as stronger than expected in the very old group. They also indicated fewer outdoor activities, but fewer interests and hobbies at home as well. Evidence for completed life review, and for increased expression of religious/existential attitudes was only minimally present. Perhaps most surprising of all, the findings on family relationships were quite contrary to Carstensen's socio-emotional selectivity theory. The very old mentioned their families significantly less. This could not be explained by changes in marital status with age, for the widowed, divorced and single participants mentioned their families as much as married people.

Overall, the results suggest that an activity-oriented lifestyle is the central theme in both the younger-old and the older-old. Hobbies and interests, social participation and daily living routines are principal sources of self-definition. However, health does become a more important aspect of self-definition in advanced old age (Dittmann-Kohli, 2001), and the declining number of positive self-descriptions is consistent with observations on loss of self-esteem in late life (Robins et al., 2002).

Although a more detailed analysis of changes in the self with advanced age than the previously discussed study of Troll and Skaff, it is important to draw attention to the limitations of the methodology used in this research. Not only is the self defined in terms of fixed characteristics, rather than dynamically in narrative terms (McAdams, 1993), there is also no attempt to look at the complexity of relationships between the characteristics that make up the self and to identify more central aspects of self-definition. Nevertheless, the Berlin Aging Study provides the most substantial and representative data set on advanced old age yet available.

The same authors have gone on to analyse differences in possible selves among the same participants (Smith and Freund, 2002). Again their findings show that interindividual differences outweigh age-related differences, and that also the oldest old display active, achievement-oriented future selves. The sharp differences suggested by theory on increased disengagement with advanced age are not evident in the Berlin study.

Changing sources of self-esteem with age

We consider now the results of a longitudinal study of ageing carried out in Southampton, England (Coleman, 1984; Coleman, Ivani-Chalian and Robinson, 1993; 1998; 1999), which assessed key themes in participants' self-descriptions over time. The data offers points of comparison with the Berlin Aging Study, albeit on a much smaller sample of participants.

Self-description was a major focus of data collection at each of eight observation points over 20 years. Common to each assessment was the administration of a scale of bipolar self-esteem ascriptions, designed to elicit not only positive and negative self-ascriptions but also propositions illustrating the ascription. Thus participants were asked to provide an example for why they felt 'useful' or 'useless'. Their answers were coded in terms of categories that reflected the major domains of sources of identity in later life: family relationships; other interpersonal relationships; health and independence; interest and hobby activities; inner self beliefs; external quality of life; work and other formal roles. Indices of both self-esteem and sources of self-esteem have shown a significant measure of stability over periods as long as 13 years (Coleman, Ivani-Chalian and Robinson, 1993). At different points in the study other forms of self-description were collected. These included open responses to sentence stems about the self (Dittmann-Kohli, 1990) and to a short questionnaire on 'life strengths' adapted from Kivnick's operationalisation of Erikson's eight life tasks (Kivnick, 1991).

By the time of the last data analysis point, the surviving participants had all passed the age of 85 years, so it was possible to compare responses over time from earlier to later old age. Both cross-sectional and longitudinal analysis showed a small but significant drop in the number of positive self-esteem ascriptions as the age of the cohort groups passed 80 years, consistent with theory on the greater difficulty of maintaining self-esteem in advanced old age (Atchley, 1991). However, the mean decline in self-esteem is relatively small and masks the very varied trajectories people displayed over the 20 years, including stability of high (and low) self-esteem, gradual loss of self-esteem, precipitous decline of self-esteem, and loss of self-esteem followed by recovery (Coleman *et al.*, 1999). In certain cases it is possible to observe relatively long alternating cycles of diminishing and increasing self-esteem. Drawing attention to neglected phenomena is one of the most useful products of individual longitudinal case analysis.

Of particular interest in the Southampton data are the changes in illustrative self-descriptions as the average age of the sample passed beyond 80 years (Coleman, Ivani-Chalian and Robinson, 1993). A comparison of those interviewed in both 1977–78 (average age 71.0 years) and 1990–91 (average age 83.8 years) showed that reference to interest and hobby activities had moved from fourth to first place in frequency of mention. The order had otherwise remained the same, with health and independence the next most frequently mentioned source, followed by family, interpersonal relationships and inner beliefs. The importance of activities to people in the mid-old age group was also shown by the fact that numbers of hobbies and interests, different types of journey outside the home, and perception of oneself as an active person, assessed at the initial observation, predicted maintained self-esteem ten years later. This study's findings, therefore, support the hypothesis that activity is important to the maintenance of well-being in later life (Morgan and Bath, 1998), and that descriptions of activity become more salient parts of the self as people age.

Subsequent analysis of the same sample, however, suggests that this may be only a temporary effect, and not necessarily characteristic of the very old (Coleman *et al.*, 1998). The predominant identity theme emphasised by the 27 survivors interviewed five years later, when they had all reached 83 years and had an average age of 87.8 years, was neither activities nor health and independence, but family relationships. Although a study on a small number of people, the data it draws on are rich. The investigators were able to construct detailed case analyses on each individual, drawing on a considerable range of data including interview transcripts as well as questionnaire instruments. These analyses examined the changing sources of each person's identity over time, and concluded with a rank ordering of the present three most important themes in their lives, drawing on the same seven general categories used from the outset of the study. These conclusions were checked with the participants themselves.

Far from declining as a source of self-esteem, family had become central to the identity of this small sample of very old survivors. Interestingly, this finding applied as much to the men as to the women, despite the former's earlier strong work identity. Analysis is proceeding on the data relating to all participants in the study who reached the age of 80 years to see if it supports the hypothesis, emerging from our last study, that self-descriptions in late life tend to emphasise or re-emphasise family links. Often, links are (re)discovered, that were not apparent previously, with children or more distant relatives such as nephews and nieces. Whereas work roles decline as a source of self-description with age, family links, although gravely affected by bereavements, tend to be preserved. Most people appear to adjust to the end of their working life, but not to loss of their family. Indeed older people may seek long and hard to recover family connections that may have become weaker as the result of pressures from other roles and activities. Although the presence of a wide range of interpersonal contacts appears most beneficial to continued well-being in the earlier stages of ageing (Coleman, Ivani-Chalian and Robinson, 1993), family emerges as more important in the long run. This study therefore suggests a view of family relationships much more complementary to Carstensen's theoretical position than the Berlin Aging Study reports.

However, like the Berlin study, the Southampton study does not support the drawing of any sharp theoretical divide between appropriate modes of adaptation for different chronological stages of later life (Coleman *et al.*, 1999). Assimilation rather than accommodation was evident in 90 year olds in the period preceding their death. For example, 'Mrs Darby', at the age of 97, was still seeking ways of maintaining her relational self, through social contact and work for charity. She found social clubs to attend most days of the week, and fought obstacles that stood in the way of her busy social life. She wrote to the local council, complaining about uneven paving stones in the local streets and about the speed of traffic outside the sheltered housing complex where she lived. Right up to her death she maintained a high level of vital activity. As Brandtstädter has pointed out, the level of energy the individual is capable of is more decisive than chronological age in determining the need for disengagement.

Studies on person–environment congruence in institutional settings

The studies on continuity of the self reported in the previous section indicate relatively minor changes with advanced age. But the samples studied have been selected on the basis of chronological age, which evidently functions only as a very crude marker for whether people have yet entered the 'fourth age'. Defined at 80 or 85 years, or even higher, there will always be people above and below the criterion age who do not show equivalent levels of biological decline. The validity of measures of concepts such as frailty, which may provide more unambiguous criteria for defining late life status (see Chapter 6), is not yet sufficiently well established.

We can probably learn more about the psychology of late life by focusing on those who are receiving care from welfare services, their family or others, and thus are highly likely to have become disabled and/or frail. Unfortunately there is still relatively little literature on the psychology of those being cared for in their own homes. Most studies in this area focus on people receiving care in institutional settings. As we saw in the previous chapter there is a long tradition of developmental psychological research (e.g. Lieberman and Tobin, 1983), which has drawn attention to the remarkable adjustments some elderly residents show in very difficult circumstances.

Some of the earliest studies on the psychology of control were also carried out in American nursing homes (Langer, 1983). These demonstrated the dramatic results of manipulating residents' sense of control over their lives on their activity levels, cognitive functioning and general well-being. The effects were surprisingly large, and the study of control has subsequently become a major topic in general health psychology. Taking account of individual differences in need for control has led to better tuning of effort. Some individuals are made anxious by having too much control over their daily lives. Enhancing their sense of control is therefore counter-productive. This demonstrates the importance of the principle of person–environment congruence, in particular to enhancing quality of life in residential settings. The 'average' resident is an imaginary construct. Although one can expect all those living within a single institution to be infirm, their degree of frailty will differ and this will affect their ability and motivation to carry out different tasks.

Residents will also vary in the way they like to be treated, whether to be left as far as possible to their own devices or to be closely monitored. These preferences will relate to their own personality and family background. Psychologists have attempted to formulate models to explain optimum environmental fit. For example, the competence-press model (Lawton and Nahemow, 1973) predicts an inverse relationship between persons' level of competence and the demands of their environment in determining relative well-being. In the following sections, we will consider recent examples of research that takes these ideas further in investigating institutional care. It is important to stress that older people can also demonstrate capacity for development in care environments. Indeed, among the most remarkable lessons older people provide to younger members of the population is their ability to maintain their identity and sense of existential meaning and well-being in diminished circumstances.

Need for autonomy in residential settings

One of the most striking recent conceptual advances in the study of human motivation has been the elaboration of human need provided by Deci and Ryan (2000). This gives new impetus to research by specifying 'competence', 'relatedness' and 'autonomy' as three needs essential to goal-related activity. The authors' fundamental postulate is that humans are 'active, growth-oriented organisms who are naturally inclined toward the development of an organized coherence among the elements of their psychological makeup and between themselves and the social world' (2000: 262). As might be expected, they provide evidence for this model from research on human development. However, they cite relatively little from gerontology.

This is a common failing of research in personality and social psychology. Theoreticians have been insufficiently interested in applications to ageing (Coleman, 2000). It is particularly surprising, however, that motivation and needs theorists have not given more attention to older people. The experience of ageing can and does place harsh limitations on needs satisfaction and it therefore becomes an ideal time to investigate the nature of these needs. As we have seen, theory on adaptation in late life emphasises the value of modifying goals, but as Deci and Ryan's theory implies, this flexibility is limited by the persistent character of the underlying psychological needs.

Dialogue between general psychological theory and psychogerontological research is essential. It is not only theoreticians in mainstream psychology that have been remiss. Gerontologists, too, have failed to keep up with developments in theory and research that are often highly applicable to their particular fields of study. Fortunately this is one area where there have already been some interesting applications. In particular, O'Connor and Vallerand (1994) have applied Deci and Ryan's self-determination theory to nursing home residents in Canada. They have investigated whether the experience of autonomy in behaviour has a beneficial effect on residents' well-being.

It is necessary first, however, to distinguish the concept of autonomy from that of control. So far we have emphasised the importance of a sense of control for the experience of ageing. Autonomy is a subtly but significantly different concept. The literature on locus of control and learned helplessness focuses on the perception of contingency between the person's own behaviours and observable outcomes, whereas self-determination refers to the experience of freedom in initiating one's behaviour. Control does not ensure self-determination, and self-determination does not ensure control. The central notion in self-determination is the experience of choice and not mere perception of control over outcomes. Deci and Ryan (2000) describe four types of behaviour that vary along a continuum of self-determination. 'Intrinsically motivated' behaviour is carried out for the pleasure and satisfaction derived from the performance. 'Extrinsically motivated but self-determined' behaviour is performed to receive some benefit or avoid some ill, but not because the activity is intrinsically rewarding. 'Extrinsically motivated non-self-determined' behaviour, on the other hand, is externally determined. Finally, 'amotivated' behaviour lacks any sense of awareness of contingency between behaviour and outcomes.

O'Connor and Vallerand (1994) use the example of physical exercise to indicate the differences between the four categories. The 'intrinsically motivated' person exercises for the pleasure and satisfaction derived from the activity. 'Self-determined extrinsic' persons exercise to receive benefits or avoid ills; although they do not exercise for its own sake, their behaviour is still purposeful and self-directed. The 'non-self-determined extrinsic' person exercises because others – for example, a doctor – tell them to do so; the behaviour is still purposeful, but directed by others. The 'amotivated' are unaware of any contingency between their behaviour and desirable outcomes. They do not have, or have lost, a sense of purpose or expectation of reward. They do not know why they exercise. Unless they (re)discover motivation to exercise they are not likely to continue for long.

The benefits for psychological adjustment of the more self-determined forms of motivation have been demonstrated in a number of different areas, but surprisingly little work has been done on older people. O'Connor and Vallerand's research work, therefore, is of particular significance. It uses a measure of elderly motivational style, which they developed on the basis of Deci and Ryan's work. Their initial study tested whether person–environment congruence is as important in the area of self-motivation as is control.

Developing a questionnaire or other instrument to measure a construct or set of constructs is an essential part of translating theoretical ideas into testable hypotheses. It is worth examining how Vallerand and O'Connor translated Deci and Ryan's ideas into a questionnaire applicable to the situation of elderly people. Their first step was to identify areas of life that the literature showed to be important at this stage of life. They then had elderly people from nursing homes, hospitals, private residences, and low-cost public housing rate the importance of the 23 domains they had identified. Six domains emerged as the most important for both men and women, and for individuals living in different settings: health, religion, biological needs, interpersonal relations, current events and recreation.

They then asked both elderly persons and nursing home staff to nominate important situations within each of the life domains. A variety of situations were identified, and for each domain the two most commonly nominated situations were selected for inclusion as questions in the final questionnaire (e.g. 'Why do you go to church?'), as well as general questions for each domain (e.g. 'In general, why do you practise your religion?'). Thus three questions were chosen for each domain, making an instrument of 18 items in total. For each question participants made four ratings corresponding to the four forms of motivation: (i) 'I don't know, I don't see what it does for me' (amotivation); (ii) 'Because I am supposed to do it' (non-self-determined extrinsic motivation); (iii) 'I choose to do it for my own good' (self-determined extrinsic motivation); (iv) 'For the pleasure of doing it' (intrinsic motivation). Responses were provided on a seven-point Likert scale ranging from 'strongly disagree' (1) to 'strongly agree' (7). O'Connor and Vallerand report extensive testing and strong psychometric properties for this instrument.

In their study of intermediate care nursing homes in Montreal, O'Connor and Vallerand (1994) identified 11 homes on a random basis from available lists. The homes varied in size from 39 to 247 residents. Considerable care was taken to interview a representative sample in each home. The investigators excluded those who were judged too mentally or physically frail to participate (15 per cent of residents), but interviewed about 10 per cent of the remaining residents. A total of 80 per cent of those approached agreed to be interviewed, providing a sample of 129 persons (111 women and 18 men), ranging in age from 65 to 96 (mean 80.5) years. Participants had been residents of the homes for an average of 3.8 years.

Interestingly, the four kinds of motivational style displayed no significant correlations with age or physical health. All indices of motivational style correlated strongly with indices of psychological adjustment (which comprised self-esteem, depression, life satisfaction, existential meaning in life) – intrinsic motivation and self-determined extrinsic motivation positively, non-self-determined extrinsic motivation and amotivation negatively.

Assessment of the nursing home environment was an important part of this project. This was based on interviews with both the head nurse and administrator regarding the rules and treatment of residents. An elaborate description of the rules in each nursing home was then written, focusing on how much choice residents had regarding their daily activities, the extent to which the nursing home staff took responsibility for residents' personal care, and the degree to which the staff encouraged or discouraged personal initiative. Three psychologists, who were highly familiar with self-determination theory, independently read the written descriptions and rated the degree of self-determination provided by each home on each of these dimensions. Since the intraclass correlations were high, mean self-determination scores for each home could be computed.

As expected, residents in high self-determination nursing homes tended to score higher on self-determined motivation. Much more interesting, however, was the finding of interaction effects with motivational styles. There was a tendency for low self-determined motivation individuals to report better psychological adjustment in low self-determination nursing homes than in high self-determination nursing homes, and for high self-determined motivation individuals to report better psychological adjustment in high self-determination nursing homes than in low self-determination nursing homes. This is another powerful demonstration of person–environment congruence. One cannot expect all elderly nursing home residents to benefit from high levels of autonomy. But O'Connor and Vallerand suggest the interesting hypothesis that long-term adjustment is better served by an environment that provides opportunities for autonomy that are always slightly greater than one's initial level of self-determined motivation.

Identifying and fostering developmental features of the institutional care environment

Research such as O'Connor and Vallerand's suggests ways in which the features of the institutional environment could be changed in order to enhance the adaptation of residents. This is the rationale for much current research on institutional care. Thinking of these issues in terms of the developmental perspective on later life put forward by Paul Baltes (Baltes, 1997), we can appreciate better how the prolongation of ageing that has become a feature of modern societies lacks the appropriate cultural and environmental support. The incorporation and enhancement of aged members in earlier societies was made possible by cultural developments. But the further societal adjustments now required by a much larger, longer-living and frailer elderly population have not yet been initiated. This applies at the macro level – in the appropriate adaptation of new technology suitable for elderly people's use, for example – and at the micro level of care environments.

How can care environments be matched more closely to the psychological adaptations of their older residents? A number of different strategies are being pursued in this area. One is to assess the characteristics of residents and to examine associations with well-being. At the crudest level of assessment, at population level, one can take prolongation of life within the institution as a sign of good adjustment. Earlier studies on institutional care documented the very high mortality rates observed (Lieberman and Tobin, 1983). Depression and low self-esteem have been found to be predictors of mortality in nursing home residents, along with perceived control and activity level, also when controlled against physical health (O'Connor and Vallerand, 1998).

A more sophisticated approach is to assess relevant dimensions in the institutions themselves. There is a long tradition of work in this field (Lemke and Moos, 1980). A good recent example is Mitchell and Kemp's study of quality of life in a large number of Californian assisted-living homes (Mitchell and Kemp, 2000). They employed well-established scales to assess staff's rating of facility characteristics including resident control, and residents' ratings of the environment including aspects such as cohesion, conflict, independence and resident influence (Moos and Lemke, 1992). The cohesion sub-scale, for example, measured how helpful and supportive staff members were towards residents, and how involved and supportive residents were with each other. The results demonstrated that a more home-like and warm environment with a less conflictual setting, as rated by the residents, were main factors influencing contentment, along with both family and social involvement. Organisational or facility variables appeared to be much less important than social cohesion as perceived by the residents.

These studies provide helpful information on institutional care at the more macro level, but do not necessarily reveal the staff skills required to enhance adaptation and quality of life. At a more micro level, it is possible to examine interactions between staff and residents. One has first to identify the key aspects of interaction that may enhance residential living and find valid means of assessment. Thus O'Connor and Rigby (1996) carried out an intriguing study on 'baby talk', which is a common feature of staff behaviour in care settings, often commented on critically by observers but rarely examined for its impact on residents. A particular strength of this study is that not only did it assess staff behaviour but also the personality characteristics and needs of residents. In so doing it provided another test of the importance of person–environment congruence.

The elderly resident's need for succourance was found to be associated with perceptions of warmth in baby talk, whereas the younger age of the resident and a higher level of functional health were associated with negative perceptions of being 'talked down to'. Significant interactions were evident, suggesting the harmful effect of receiving baby talk on self-esteem for those who perceived it negatively. The opposite result was found for those with positive perceptions of baby talk. It would be interesting to confirm these findings in a longitudinal study.

However, the best test of the influence of environmental and staff behaviour characteristics is to attempt to change them in a positive direction and to see whether the desired effects occur. Some of the best examples of this mode of research evaluation are provided by the late Margret Baltes' programme of research on German nursing homes. As mentioned earlier, control theory is one theory arising from gerontological research to have influenced general psychology. As Margret Baltes has shown, it has a very direct relation to practice, as professional carers tend to 'prefer' elderly people who give up self-control and become more easy to 'manage' (Baltes *et al.*, 1991). This is because encouraging self-control and individual participation can often be more costly in terms of staff time.

The premise of Baltes' work, that autonomy is a key factor in the well-being of elderly residents of institutions, is in line with Deci and Ryan's theoretical emphasis on autonomy as a basic human need at all stages of life. If this is so, designing institutions or altering them in ways that facilitate independence, despite frailty, should enhance well-being. But, a complication in carrying out a simple test of this hypothesis, which Baltes observed (Baltes, 1988), is that there is a countervailing factor at work. A pattern of dependency script operates in institutions, whereby dependent behaviour is most likely to result in staff providing social contact and attention. These are usually highly valued by most residents and, in learning theory terms, function as 'rewards'.

In an intervention to alter this pattern of staff behaviour, Baltes, Neumann and Zank (1994) developed a training programme that involved confronting staff with their own videotaped interactions. They were told the aim was to improve their interactions and communications with all residents. To assess the effects on residents, the researchers needed to develop careful assessment of the elderly people's behaviours. They differentiated between independent and dependent self-care behaviours, and among constructively engaged, destructively engaged, and non-engaged behaviours. The intervention produced an increase in independence-supportive behaviours and a decrease in dependence supportive-behaviours in the experimental group of staff who received the intervention, as opposed to a control group who did not. Impressively, the same study also demonstrated an increase in independent behaviours among residents after the intervention period. Further research was indicated to identify the most effective parts of the training package.

This important line of research strongly suggests that it is possible to design institutional environments that are both stimulating and protective. To quote Margret Baltes,

> if staff behavior is tailored to the individual competence level of elderly residents – that is, providing security and support only when and where truly needed and otherwise supporting autonomy and stimulation – the elderly residents can compensate for deficits with the help of staff but maintain and even optimize remaining competencies.
>
> (Baltes *et al.*, 1994: 186)

These and the other studies indicate that we can move towards a more person-sensitive system of care for people in the fourth age, where individual differences in needs for autonomy and support can be better catered for. If so, the research process will have proved to be an important element in this advance.

Dementia care and attachment

Our third and final topic also concerns improving quality of life in institutions, but focuses on the most vulnerable of residents: those suffering from dementia or mental frailty. As noted in the previous chapter, dementia poses particularly difficult challenges to care services. More attention is now being given to the needs of dementia sufferers. There is greater appreciation of their intrinsic worth and potential, but the legacy of insensitive care, especially within institutions, weighs heavily.

Tom Kitwood has provided a revealing analysis of why dementia care can be so poor (Kitwood, 1993; 1997; Kitwood and Bredin, 1992). There is a loss of intersubjective insight. Caregivers may no longer make the effort to understand what the other person is thinking or feeling, showing a disregard for the other that would be unthinkable in other professional or interpersonal circumstances. Mental infirmity – in a similar but far greater way than hearing impairment – disables the caregiver. It is a hindrance to getting on with the tasks one is required to do. This situation is made worse by the chronic 'busy-ness' of dementia care settings. The combination of pressure and insensitivity may lead to a loss of belief in the personhood of the person with dementia, together with all the rights and dignity that term implies. An unconscious fear of death, decay and dissolution keeps staff members at a psychological distance from what may have become in effect an object of care rather than another person like themselves.

Kitwood referred to a 'malignant social psychology', which may surround the person with dementia (Kitwood, 1997). A habitual way of responding to a person's confusion, distress and discomfort may develop that demeans or confuses them further. Examples of such behaviours are using tricks or lies to get persons to do what the caregiver wants, doing things for them that they are actually able to do for themselves, so as to complete tasks more quickly, and accusing a person or throwing back in their face something they did or didn't do in order to try to make them 'see sense'. Caring for someone with dementia can be highly stressful, but in such circumstances it is important always to bear in mind the cared-for person's needs. As stressed in the previous chapter, it is responding at the emotional level that is the key to high-quality care of someone who is mentally frail. Thus this may mean careful explanation and reassurance for someone who is saddened by a sense of loss and the disturbance of their normal environment, and calmness and support for someone frustrated by their inability to change their circumstances.

These are not easy tasks, and require training and support themselves. Even more demanding is the responsibility for maintaining 'personhood'. Ideally this requires a continued presence, seeking to understand the needs of the other and drawing out meaning from every communication. Kitwood has made an analogy with Winnicott's description of the 'good mother', one who makes sense of a child's gestures, who draws meaning from them wherever possible, and who does not dismiss or ignore them (Winnicott, 1965). In looking for and making meaning, the mother promotes the child's development. The ageing process leads ultimately towards dissolution, but that does not mean effort should not be made to preserve meaning where it can still be found. Care, even for the dying, is about life not death.

In this last section we focus on research and development work derived from another psychodynamic thinker, John Bowlby, whose attachment theory has been extended across the life-span from its origins in identifying the importance for children of providing them with a secure base early on in their development. Research has confirmed Bowlby's view that the patterns of secure and insecure attachment he described in young children are indeed acquired in early life rather than determined by one's genetic or biological make-up (O'Connor and Croft, 2001). These attachment patterns remain important at all stages of life, and have been studied for their influence – for example, in romantic and marital relationships (Crittenden, 1997; Hazan and Shaver, 1990), in bereavement (Archer, 1999; Day, 1993), and in the development of religious faith (Kirkpatrick, 1992).

Research on ageing and attachment is still very limited. We do know that perceived attachment to children provides the oldest old with one of the most significant buffers against loneliness (Long and Martin, 2000). However, at present we can only speculate whether the striking variation that we see among older people in their responses to loss – the ease or unease with which they are able to let people and things come and go from their lives – reflects early attachment styles.

Although not included in Bengtson, Burgess and Parrott's (1997) review of gerontological theory, we consider attachment theory to have great potential to link earlier and later life (see, for example, Coleman and Jerrome, 1999; McAdams et al., 1997). It is within the dementia care field that it has made its first notable impact on psychogerontology, by illuminating a hitherto neglected area of human experience.

Dementia, attachment and the Strange Situation

In our own research on older people's needs we have been concerned to balance discussion of issues of empowerment, control and achievement with those of love, friendship and relationship. This duality of motivation runs through psychology (McAdams, 1990). Although 'agentic' motivation receives considerable emphasis because of the fear of loss of control that may accompany ageing – and has been the focus of much of the research we have already discussed in this and the previous chapter – this should not lead us to minimise the importance of 'communion' motivation. As other theories of ageing have stressed (for example, Carstensen's socio-emotional selectivity theory, as described in Chapter 4), maintenance of relationship to those remaining in the world around becomes a critical issue in the wake of the bereavements of late life. Not everyone is able to achieve the transcendent relationships to humankind that theorists such as Erikson and Tornstam refer to. For the demented person there is the added loss of the ability to learn and recognise new relationships.

Bowlby first identified the significance of childhood attachment behaviour in explaining the persisting distress experienced by infants when they were separated from their primary caregivers for long periods of time (Bowlby, 1969; 1973; 1980). As a consequence of this observation, Mary Ainsworth developed the so-called 'Strange Situation' to study styles of attachment in young children (Ainsworth et al., 1971). Bere Miesen, a clinical psychogerontologist in the Netherlands, was the first to recognise the relevance of attachment theory to dementia care. He became increasingly aware that much of a dementing person's behaviour reflected feelings of insecurity as a consequence of diminishing cognitive capacities. Miesen took the initiative to contact Bowlby about the relationship of attachment to ageing, and their resulting interview was subsequently published (Bowlby, 1986).

For Miesen, attachment theory became the key that unlocked much of the behaviour of demented people that caregivers typically find puzzling and disturbing (Miesen, 1992; 1998). Emphasising that we need to see situations through the eyes of the person who experiences them, Miesen has suggested that the experience of becoming demented is rather like entering

Ainsworth's Strange Situation. Behaviours such as crying, clinging and calling out represent attachment behaviors in elderly people with dementia. The constant request and searching for parents, which becomes more common as the illness progresses, can be seen partly as a reflection of the greater clarity of the more distant past, but more helpfully as a search for security and comfort in an increasingly uncertain world, a response to feeling 'unsafe'. Seen this way it is much easier for caregivers to appreciate how elderly people eventually fall back on their deepest memories of security in attachment to their families, as the more recent past gradually fades from view. Miesen has even gone so far as to suggest that if we knew enough in detail about a person's attachment history, we would be able to predict the course their dementia will take as they progressively lose contact with successive stages of their life.

Miesen developed an intriguing method for testing his theory (Miesen, 1992). He had noticed that 'parent fixation', as he described it, was associated with certain types of behaviour on the nursing home ward during family visits. So he adapted Ainsworth's Strange Situation into what he described as a 'Standard Visiting Procedure' to analyse elderly people's behaviour in relation to their family before and after the latter left. He observed that participants expressed themselves towards family members through different forms of attachment behaviour such as touching, crying and calling. Those with lower levels of cognitive functioning behaved differently – for example, being more inclined to touch other people they knew. When family members left, those with higher cognitive functioning called after them. Lower cognitive-functioning participants had apparently more difficulty keeping family members in mind and called more after their deceased parents. There was also a longitudinal element to Miesen's research. As dementia became more pronounced and participants could no longer recognise their caregivers, so they called more on their parents than they had done before. This strongly suggests that 'parent fixation' substitutes for attachment to caregivers after the latter are no longer recognisable.

Although this research and the techniques of observation on which it relies clearly require replication in other settings to see how generalisable the findings are, it does appear to be an important set of observations with practical relevance for care.

Developing staff attitudes towards persons with dementia

Through his training programmes in the Netherlands, Miesen has had a significant impact on practice. Care staff are encouraged to see what it means to feel unsafe and insecure, and so to appreciate what demented persons are looking for. Miesen shows how important it is for caregivers to understand their own previous experience of attachment. The goals of training are thus both psychoeducational and psychotherapeutic. Participants become familiar with both the demented person's emotional needs and their own characteristic responses, which are modified in the course of the training. This reflects an important new trend in research on attachment behaviour, which is to attempt to understand better the caring motivation that underlies the response to attachment behaviours in the infant (Bell and Richard, 2000).

The biological basis for caregiving of adults appears less strong than for child care. That makes analysis of motivation to care more rather than less important. We know that mental frailty makes older people more unpopular to professional caregivers and it is important to understand precisely why this is so (Cooper and Coleman, 2001). Even where caregivers are more enthusiastic, questions can arise about quality of care. One of the concerns commonly expressed about even good dementia care settings is that professional caregivers may adopt an approach to care that turns elderly persons into dependent babies or young children. This approach may make caring easier for the caregiver because they are drawing on a fundamental 'instinct'. However, although preferable to the impersonal approach to care, there is danger in this attitude to care. Some elderly persons may like to be cosseted – perhaps a reflection of their attachment needs – but many may not, as we remarked earlier when discussing evaluation of 'baby talk'. Despite the undoubted parallels between elderly and child care, their phenomenological worlds are completely different.

Perhaps the biggest change in dementia care over the last ten years has been the emphasis on understanding better the experience of the elderly person with dementia (Woods, 2001). Not only Miesen (1998), Kitwood (1997) and Sabat (2001), but also others (e.g. Bender and Cheston, 1997; Solomon and Szwarbo, 1992) have drawn attention to the strong, often negative, emotions of grief, anger, fear and even terror that are commonly seen in dementia care settings. These can only be countered by understanding better the way the other person sees the world and their psychological needs. A succession of new initiatives have been taken to improve caregivers' understanding and response to dementia (Woods, 1996; 2005).

'Reality orientation' was the first such approach, developed to counteract the inclination of professional caregivers, particularly in large institutional settings, to ignore the people in their care – for example, as they passed by them in the corridor (see Holden and Woods, 1995). Rather, caregivers were encouraged to keep hospital patients and residents in regular contact with reality, by taking opportunities to remind them of their situation throughout the day. In the most current approaches to care for people with dementia this has been superseded by a more sensitive approach to interaction that takes less account of external reality and more account of the person's own experienced reality. The carer attempts to 'validate' thoughts and feelings important to the older person's present sense of identity (Bleathman and Morton, 1988; Feil, 1992).

Much more research is needed on these new approaches to dementia care. There is, for example, still a lack of appropriate controlled studies into the beneficial effects of reminiscence work with mentally frail elderly people, despite many recorded initiatives (Gibson, 1994; Lowenthal and Marrazzo, 1990; Mills and Coleman, 1994; Spector et al., 1998; Woods and McKiernan, 1995).

Probably the most useful research to date on caregiving for people with dementia, which takes a genuinely developmental approach to older people's capacities, is in detailed, often case-based, accounts of innovative interventions. Thus Mills (1997) has shown that it is still possible, for those sufficiently well acquainted with the dementing person, to hear the story he or she tells about her life, fragmented though it may be. Memories from the distant past may become more vivid with the loss of more recent memories. Memories that are coloured by emotion are particularly important for care-givers to identify. Positive memories, which can enhance feelings of identity, can be stimulated by selective recall, but even for memories that are still disturbing, psychotherapeutic work may be possible. Much patience and sensitivity may be required, but the benefits are rewarding and are a useful antidote to an overly pessimistic view of dementia as a time of regression. Also, as Cheston (1996) has shown, group psychotherapy has a definite place in dementia care.

In Southampton we have developed a similar training course to that of Bere Miesen and are also evaluating its outcome (Coleman and Jerrome, 1999; Meade et al., 1998; Mills et al., 1999). The Attachment Awareness and Dementia Care Course focuses on both skills and feelings, and combines informative teaching about psychological theory and research with attention to personal and group dynamics. However, adhering closely to the theoretical principle of attachment as well as the experiential learning mode produces particular challenges. The expression of emotional difficulty around attachment affects both students and trainers. A high level of skill is required in working at both levels – creating shifts in knowledge and attitudes, and changing feelings. The firmness of the foundation – knowledge of the subject and understanding of the subject matter, clear organisation of material, good preparation and presentation, and communication skills – in combination with sensitive supervision of the trainers themselves kept our project going. Above all, though, it was the degree of our commitment to the theoretical principle of attachment that gave us the confidence to persist.

In the last two sections of this chapter we have focused on institutional care. We recognise, however, that much needs to be done, also from a developmental perspective, on family care. Because of its perceived greater intrusiveness, there has been little direct observation of family care for people with dementia, although research of this character is currently being undertaken from the University of Southampton. There has been some work carried out from an attachment perspective. For example, Magai and Cohen (1998) have demonstrated that caregiver burden is higher for caregivers of insecurely attached individuals. In an interesting qualitative analysis of interviews from a longitudinal study of spouses of persons with dementia in Norway, Ingebretsen and Solem (1998) have examined attachment patterns in the caregivers themselves and indicated some important outcomes that professional caregivers need to take into account in supporting families. For example, compulsive caregiving persons attend to their spouse beyond their needs, whereas spouses in anxious attachment often panic and try to fight back the symptoms of dementia.

Attachment theory has provided a much-needed boost to a developmental perspective on ageing, particularly in the last stage of life, which so far has been considered rather unimaginatively. It is a particularly good example of the enriching value of theory, providing new perspectives on phenomena thought to be well understood but in fact often simply observed without much understanding. Yet attachment theory is just one theoretical perspective, one of the very few theories that has been found to connect development across the life-span. Hopefully in the not too distant future there will be additional theoretical perspectives that will allow us to engage more creatively with the last phase of life.

Conclusion

8 Concluding thoughts and suggestions for further reading

As we stressed at the beginning, this book has been necessarily selective. We have tried to employ our selection to good effect by emphasising what we hope has seemed a coherent pathway through various studies on the experience of ageing. Both authors continue to have an interest in developmental psychology, and especially in attempts to produce a genuine life-span developmental approach to ageing. Such work is still rare, particularly in the UK.

Some notable specialists in the psychology of ageing – for example, Dennis Bromley – consider that attempts to link across the whole life-span from child development to ageing are premature (Bromley, 1990). The methodological and conceptual obstacles, at least in the short term, are too formidable: child development and ageing use distinctive concepts. Many consider that it is in the interest of ageing studies that psychogerontology is developed in isolation from child development. Certainly it is discouraging that attempts to build, for example, unified departments of life-span developmental psychology have broken down, and that psychogerontologists (or geropsychologists) by and large prefer to make links with sociologists and medical scientists rather than with their fellow psychologists. It is perhaps significant, too, that the last occasion a review of life-span psychology appeared in the *Annual Review of Psychology* was 17 years ago (Datan *et al.*, 1987), and it only considered adult development and ageing, and strongly emphasised links with sociology.

However, as we have emphasised at various points throughout this book, it is important that psychogerontology does strive to maintain links with all areas of psychology. It has to keep pace with the latest developments in neuroscience, and in cognitive and social psychology. We particularly wish to emphasise the value of continuing links with child psychology. As Maas pointed out more than 20 years ago, there has developed a curious 'childlessness' about gerontology (Maas, 1985), curious because of the connections people readily make between life at both ends of the life course, and because of the traditional importance of the older person as teacher to the young. Of course, older people should not be treated as children, but this does not rule out there being fruitful parallels in understanding psychological development at different stages of life.

We have pointed to attachment theory, developed by Bowlby, Ainsworth and Crittenden, as a prime example of a theory originating in the study of childhood that has major implications for the whole of the life-span, not least for the last part. Perhaps there are other child development theories that could be mined in this way. The concept of attachment in itself offers rich possibilities, and can encourage further dialogue across the life-span. Why, for example, do some older people comparatively easily accept separation and loss, and others suffer greatly? Issues of relationship and loss are crucial to the study of ageing, so attachment has to be a central concept in understanding these differences.

Readers may have observed a tension between the theories discussed in Parts 1 and 2 of this book, between normative stage developmental theories and those that emphasise differential ageing, between those that postulate ideal models of ageing and those that argue for extreme plasticity, that ageing is what we make it. The last point of view is most strongly expressed by Paul Baltes:

> As was true for other age periods such as infancy and childhood, it takes a long evolutionary process and much technological investment before we will achieve the kind of differentiated culture of old age that is required to uncover the latent potential of old age and empower older persons to choose among a variety of opportunity structures.
>
> (Baltes, 1991: 851)

We respect both points of view. We greatly admire the efforts of Baltes and colleagues to direct more attention to the problems of late life, to develop a more positive attitude to correcting and compensating for the deficiencies of age. Cultural developments have lagged behind the realities of an ageing population. We have to direct more of our human ingenuity to solving the problems.

At the same time, the traditional developmental models do capture an essential respect for the qualities age may bring that we in western culture have somewhat lost. This recognition is reflected in this book in the growing interest in issues of wisdom, meaning and spirituality. The experience of ageing raises the great existential questions of life: 'Why do we live?' 'Why do we die?' A gerontology that neglects these issues misses something essential from discussions of quality of life and successful ageing. We have, therefore, kept such developmental models firmly in sight despite their current scientific unfashionability. We have also maintained the link between the experience of ageing and the mid-life transition as its gateway, as developed in the writings of Jung and Levinson.

We have also advocated multiple methodology. Of course, psychogerontology must develop as strong an expertise in quantitative research design and statistical analysis as other areas of psychology, but it must also make creative use of the range of qualitative methodologies available, from ethnography to case study analysis. In our selection of particular studies to highlight in Chapters 3, 5 and 7, we have tried to give some flavour of this variation in methodological approach, and hopefully of its symbiotic character.

In composing this book, we have also tried to convey some sense of the history of gerontology. It is a relatively recent history, mainly a product of the last half-century, but already a history worth celebrating. In the end everything is history. We all stand on what came before, and it is important to be aware of previous development or degeneration of ideas if we do not want to needlessly repeat fruitless ventures. A critical awareness of the past helps to make us more sensitive to current fashions and trends – for example, the current interest in 'productive ageing'. This appears to be largely motivated by the pending crisis of pension provision, especially within European countries but also elsewhere. This is not always made explicit. Psychologists, unlike sociologists, often have little appreciation of the social policy considerations that underlie funding of their research. Psychology is a social science as well as a biological or life science, and it must retain an important element of reflexive criticism as to the direction of its enquiries.

Other features we have sought to emphasise are the psychology of advanced old age and the importance of individual differences. We strongly agree that relatively more research effort needs to be addressed to the issues of late life, to the needs of the growing numbers of the very old. New methodologies are required, a more composite approach perhaps, employing both qualitative and quantitative elements. We cannot expect very old people to happily fill in long questionnaires or undergo laboratory tests. We need to observe and reflect more. Individual differences continue throughout life into very old age (Smith and Baltes, 1997: 469) and we need to understand their trajectories more. This requires longitudinal study, both large-scale surveys and detailed case reports.

For those who wish to become more acquainted with developmental psychogerontology, we would recommend that they follow up particular topics that have caught their attention while reading this book, making use of the references we have provided as starting points for exploration. For general reviews of developments in the psychology of ageing, we would recommend the *Handbooks* that have so far been produced regularly and edited by Birren and Schaie (1977; 1985; 1990; 1996; 2001) for reviews of key topics. The *Handbook of the Theories of Ageing* (Bengtson and Schaie, 1999) is another important text, and one that gives the interested reader a good feel for the multidisciplinary subject matter of gerontology. Note should also be made of the forthcoming *Handbook of Age and Ageing* (Johnson *et al.*, 2005).

As regards journals, we recommend acquaintance with the two major US journals: *Psychology and Aging*, produced by the American Psychological Association, and the *Journal of Gerontology: Psychological and Social Sciences*, produced by the Gerontological Society of America. Many major scientific studies in psychogerontology are first published in these journals. It is important, however, not to neglect the more qualitative and multidisciplinary journals in which exploratory studies and ideas are often aired for the first time and also critiqued. These include *Ageing and Society*, the *Journal of Aging Studies* and the *International Journal of Aging and Human Development*. Of course, one should not forget the general developmental psychology journals. Hopefully, life-span developmental psychology will revive and journals like *Human Development* and *Developmental Review* will have an important role in fostering connections across the life-span. Last but not least we recommend *The Gerontologist*, also produced by the Gerontological Society of America, as a journal that links research and practice. Some of the most lucid accounts of ideas and research developments in the field of ageing studies are given here. Such a journal is an admirable advertisement for a science that genuinely desires to be of service to humanity.

References

Achenbaum, W. A. and Bengtson, V. L. (1994) Re-engaging the disengagement theory of aging: on the history and assessment of theory development in gerontology. *The Gerontologist*, 34, 756–63.

Ackerman, S., Zuroff, D. C. and Moskowitz, D. S. (2000) Generativity in midlife and young adults: links to agency, communion and subjective well-being. *International Journal of Aging and Human Development*, 50, 17–41.

Adler, A. (1927) *The Practice and Theory of Individual Psychology*. New York: Harcourt Brace World.

Ahmadi Lewin, F. (2001) Gerotranscendence and different cultural settings. *Ageing and Society*, 21, 395–415.

Ainsworth, M. D. (1989) Attachments beyond infancy. *American Psychologist*, 44, 709–16.

Ainsworth, M. D. S., Bell, S. M. and Stayton, D. J. (1971) Individual differences in strange situation behaviour of one-year olds. In Schaffer, H. R. (ed.) *The Origins of Human Social Relations*. London: Academic Press.

Ainsworth, M. D. S., Blehar, M. C., Waters, E. and Wall, S. (1978) *Patterns of Attachment: Assessed in the Strange Situation and at Home*. Hillsdale, NJ: Lawrence Erlbaum.

Aldwin, C. M., Sutton, K. J., Chiara, G. and Spiro, A. (1996) Age differences in stress, coping and appraisal: findings from the Normative Aging Study. *Journal of Gerontology: Psychological Sciences*, 51B, P179–P188.

Alexander, B. B., Rubinstein, R. L., Goodman, M. and Luborsky, M. (1991) Generativity in cultural context: the self, death and immortality as experienced by older American women. *Ageing and Society*, 11(4), 417–42.

Allport, G. W. (1966) The religious context of prejudice. *Journal for the Scientific Study of Religion*, 5, 447–57.

Andersen, J. E. (1956) *Psychological Aspects of Aging*. Washington, DC: American Psychological Association.

Andrews, M. (1997) Life review in the context of acute social transition: the case of East Germany. *British Journal of Social Psychology*, 36, 273–90.

Antonucci, T. *et al.* (2001) Dynamics of social relationships in midlife. In Lachman, M. (ed.) *Handbook of Midlife Development*. Chichester: Wiley.

Archer, J. (1999) *The Nature of Grief. The Evolution and Psychology of Reactions to Loss*. London: Routledge.

Ardelt, M. (1997) Wisdom and life satisfaction in old age. *Journal of Gerontology: Psychological Sciences*, 52B, P15–P27.

Ardelt, M. (1998) Social crisis and individual growth: the long-term effect of the great depression. *Journal of Aging Studies*, 12(3), 291–314.

Ardelt, M. (2000a) Antecedents and effects of wisdom in old age: a longitudinal perspective on aging well. *Research on Aging*, 22(4), 360–94.

Ardelt, M. (2000b) Intellectual versus wisdom-related knowledge: the case for a different kind of learning in the later years of life. *Educational Gerontology*, 26, 771–89.

Ardelt, M. (2003) Empirical assessment of a three-dimensional wisdom scale. *Research on Aging*, 25(3), 275–324.

Arendt, T. and Jones, G. (1992) Clinicopathologic correlations and the brain-behaviour relationship in Alzheimer's disease. In Jones, G. M. and Miesen, B. M. (eds) *Caregiving in Dementia. Research and Applications.* London: Tavistock.

Arlin, P. K. (1990) Wisdom: the art of problem findings. In Sternberg, R. J. (ed.) *Wisdom: Its Nature, Origins and Development.* New York: Cambridge University Press, 230–43.

Atchley, R. (1997) Everyday mysticism: spiritual development in later adulthood. *Journal of Adult Development,* 4, 123–34.

Atchley, R. C. (1991) The influence of aging or frailty on perceptions and expressions of the self: theoretical and methodological issues. In Birren, J. E., Lubben, J. E., Rowe, J. C. and Deutchman, D. E. (eds) *The Concept and Measurement of Quality of Life in the Frail Elderly.* New York: Academic Press, 207–25.

Baltes, M. M. (1988) The etiology and maintenance of dependency in the elderly: three phases of operant research. *Behavior Therapy,* 19, 301–19.

Baltes, M. M. and Baltes, P. B. (1986) *The Psychology of Control and Aging.* Hillsdale, NJ: Lawrence Erlbaum.

Baltes, M. M. and Carstensen, L. L. (1996) The process of successful ageing. *Ageing and Society,* 16, 397–422.

Baltes, M. M., Neumann, E.-V. and Zank, S. (1994) Maintenance and rehabilitation of independence in old age: an intervention program for staff. *Psychology and Aging,* 9, 179–88.

Baltes, M. M., Wahl, H.-W. and Reichert, M. (1991) Institutions and successful aging for the elderly? *Annual Review of Gerontology and Geriatrics,* 11, 311–37.

Baltes, P. B. (1987) Theoretical propositions of life-span developmental psychology: on the dynamics between growth and decline. *Developmental Psychology,* 23: 611–26.

Baltes P. B. (1991) The many faces of human ageing: toward a psychological culture of old age. *Psychological Medicine,* 21, 837–54.

Baltes, P. B. (1993) The aging mind: potential and limits. *The Gerontologist,* 33(5), 580–94.

Baltes, P. B. (1997) On the incomplete architecture of human ontogeny: selection, optimization and compensation as foundation of developmental theory. *American Psychologist,* 52, 366–80.

Baltes, P. B. and Baltes, M. M. (1990) Psychological perspectives on successful aging: the model of selective optimization with compensation. In Baltes, P. B. and Baltes, M. M. (eds) *Successful Aging: Perspectives from the Behavioural Sciences.* Cambridge: Cambridge University Press, 1–34.

Baltes, P. B. and Mayer, K. U. (eds) (1999) *The Berlin Aging Study: Aging from 70 to 100.* Cambridge: Cambridge University Press.

Baltes, P. B. and Smith, J. (1990) Toward a psychology of wisdom and its ontogenesis. In Sternberg, R. J. (ed.) *Wisdom: Its Nature, Origins and Development.* New York: Cambridge University Press, 317–32.

Baltes, P. B. and Staudinger, U. M. (1993) The search for a psychology of wisdom. *Current Directions in Psychological Science,* 2(3), 75–80.

Baltes, P. B. and Staudinger, U. M. (2000) Wisdom: a meta-heuristic (pragmatic) to orchestrate mind and virtue towards excellence. *American Psychologist,* 55, 122–36.

Baltes, P. B., Reese, H. W. and Lipsitt, L. P. (1980) Life-span developmental psychology. *Annual Review of Psychology,* 31, 65–110.

Baltes, P. B., Smith, J. and Staudinger, U. M. (1992) Wisdom and successful aging. In T. B. Sonderegger (ed.) *Nebraska Symposium on Motivation,* 39, 123–67.

Baltes, P. B., Staudinger, U. M., Maercker, A. and Smith, J. (1995) People nominated as wise: a comparative study of wisdom-related knowledge. *Psychology and Aging,* 10, 155–66.

Bar-On, D. (1995) *Fear and Hope. Three Generations of the Holocaust.* Cambridge,

MA: Harvard University Press.

Bartholomew, K. (1990) Avoidance of intimacy: an attachment perspective. *Journal of Social and Personal Relationships*, 7, 147–78.

Bayley, J. (1998) *Iris: A Memoir of Iris Murdoch*. London: Duckworth.

Becker, G. (1993) Continuity after a stroke: implications of life-course disruption in old age. *The Gerontologist*, 33, 148–58.

Becker, G. (1998) *Disrupted Lives. How People Create Meaning in a Chaotic World*. Los Angeles: University of California Press.

Bell, D. C. and Richard, A. J. (2000) Caregiving: the forgotten element in attachment. *Psychological Inquiry*, 11, 69–83.

Bellah, R. N., Madsen, R., Sullivan, W. M., Swidler, A. and Tipton, S. M. (1991) *The Good Society*. New York: Alfred Knopf.

Bender, M. P. and Cheston, R. (1997) Inhabitants of a lost kingdom: a model of the subjective experiences of dementia. *Ageing and Society*, 17, 513–32.

Bengtson, V. L. and Schaie, K. W. (1999) *Handbook of Theories of Aging*. New York: Springer.

Bengtson, V. L., Burgess, E. O. and Parrott, T. M. (1997) Theory, explanation and a third generation of theoretical development in social gerontology. *Journal of Gerontology: Social Sciences*, 52B, S72–S88.

Bengtson, V. L., Reedy, M. N. and Gordon, C. (1985) Aging and self-conceptions: personality processes and social contexts. In Birren, J. E., Schaie, K. W. (eds) *Handbook of the Psychology of Aging* (2nd edn). New York: Van Nostrand Reinhold, 544–93.

Bernard, M. (1998) Backs to the future? Reflections on women, ageing and nursing. *Journal of Advanced Nursing*, 27, 633–40.

Biggs, S. (1993) *Understanding Ageing – Images, Attitudes and Professional Practice*. Buckingham: Open University Press.

Biggs, S. (1997) Choosing not to be old? Masks, bodies and identity management in later life. *Ageing and Society*, 17(5), 533–53.

Biggs, S. (1999) *The Mature Imagination*. Buckingham: Open University Press.

Biggs, S. (2005) Psychodynamic approaches to the life-course and ageing. In Johnson, M., Bengtson, V. L., Coleman, P. G. and Kirkwood, T. (eds) *Cambridge Handbook of Age and Ageing*. Cambridge: Cambridge University Press (in press).

Birren, J. E. and Deutchman, D. E. (1991) *Guiding Autobiography Groups for Older Adults: Exploring the Fabric of Life*. Baltimore, MD: Johns Hopkins University Press.

Birren, J. E and Fisher, L. M. (1990) The elements of wisdom: overview and integration. In Sternberg, R. J. (ed.), *Wisdom: Its Nature, Origins and Development*. New York: Cambridge University Press, 317–32.

Birren, J. E. and Schaie, K. W. (eds) (1977) *Handbook of the Psychology of Aging*. New York: Van Nostrand Reinhold.

Birren, J. E. and Schaie, K. W. (eds) (1985) *Handbook of the Psychology of Aging* (2nd edn). New York: Van Nostrand Reinhold.

Birren, J. E. and Schaie, K. W. (eds) (1990) *Handbook of the Psychology of Aging* (3rd edn). San Diego: Academic Press.

Birren, J. E. and Schaie, K. W. (eds) (1996) *Handbook of the Psychology of Aging* (4th edn). San Diego: Academic Press.

Birren, J. E. and Schaie, K. W. (eds) (2001) *Handbook of Psychology of Aging* (5th edn). San Diego: Academic Press.

Birren, J. E. and Schroots, J. J. F. (1996) History, concepts and theory in the psychology of aging. In J. E. Birren and K. W. Schaie (eds), *Handbook of the Psychology of Aging* (4th edn). San Diego: Academic Press, 3–23.

Birren, J. E., Kenyon, G. M., Ruth, J.-E., Schroots, J. J. F. and Svensson, T. (eds) (1996) *Aging and Biography. Explorations in Adult Development*. New York:

Springer.

Black, S. E., Blessed, G., Edwardson, J. A. and Kay, D. W. K. (1990) Prevalence rates of dementia in an aging population: are low rates due to the use of insensitive instruments? *Age and Ageing*, 19, 84–90.

Blanchard-Fields, F. and Norris, L. (1995) The development of wisdom. In Kimble, M., McFadden, S., Ellor, J. and Seeber, J. (eds), *Aging, Spirituality and Religion. A Handbook*. Minneapolis, MN: Fortress Press, 102–18.

Blazer, D. G., Burchett, B., Service, C. and George, L. K. (1991) The association of age and depression among the elderly. An epidemiological exploration. *Journal of Gerontology: Medical Sciences*, 46, M210–M215.

Bleathman, C. and Morton, I. (1988) Validation therapy with the demented elderly. *Journal of Advanced Nursing*, 13, 511–14.

Bluck, S. and Alea, N. (2002) Exploring the functions of autobiographical memory: why do I remember the autumn? In Webster, J. D. and Haight, B. K. (eds) *Critical Advances in Reminiscence Work: From Theory to Application*. New York: Springer, 61–75.

Bluck, S. and Habermas, T. (2000) The life story schema. *Motivation and Emotion*, 121–47.

Bluck, S. and Levine, L. (1998) Reminiscence as autobiographical memory: a catalyst for reminiscence theory development. *Ageing and Society*, 18, 185–208.

Bornat, J. (ed.) (1994) *Reminiscence Reviewed: Perspectives, Evaluations, Achievements*. Buckingham: Open University Press.

Bowlby, J. (1969) *Attachment and Loss. Volume I, Attachment*. London: Hogarth Press.

Bowlby, J. (1973) *Attachment and Loss. Volume II, Anxiety and Anger*. London: Hogarth Press.

Bowlby, J. (1977) The making and breaking of affectional bonds. *British Journal of Psychiatry*, 130, 201–10.

Bowlby, J. (1979) Psychoanalysis as art and science. *International Review of Psychoanalysis*, 6, 3–14.

Bowlby, J. (1980) *Attachment and Loss. Volume III, Sadness and Depression*. London: Hogarth Press.

Bowlby, J. (1986) *Attachment, Life-span and Old Age*. Deventer, Netherlands: Van Loghum Slaterus.

Bowlby, J. (1988) *A Secure Base: Parent–Child Attachment and Healthy Human Development*. New York: Basic Books.

Bowling, A. (1987) Mortality after bereavement: a review of the literature on survival periods and factors affecting survival. *Social Science and Medicine*, 24, 117–24.

Brandtstädter, J. and Greve, W. (1994) The aging self: stabilizing and protective processes. *Developmental Review*, 14, 52–80.

Brandtstädter, J. and Rothermund, K. (1994) Self-precepts of control in middle and later adulthood: buffering loses by rescaling goals. *Psychology and Aging*, 9, 265–73.

Brandtstädter, J., Rothermund, K. and Schmitz, U. (1997) Coping resources in later life. *Revue Européennne de Psychologie Appliquée*, 47, 107–13.

Brandtstädter, J., Rothermund, K. and Schmitz, U. (1998) Maintaining self-integrity and efficacy through adulthood and later life: the adaptive functions of assimilative persistence and accommodative flexibility. In Heckhausen, J. and Dweck, C. S. (eds), *Motivation and Self-regulation across the Life-span*. Cambridge: Cambridge University Press, 365–421.

Brandtstädter, J., Wentura, D. and Greve, W. (1993) Adaptive resources of the aging self: outlines of an emergent perspective. *International Journal of Behavioral Development*, 16, 323–49.

Brewin, C. (1998) Intrusive memories, depression and PTSD. *The Psychologist*, 11,

281–3.

Breytspraak, L. (1984) *The Development of Self in Later Life*. Boston: Little, Brown.

Brink, T. L. (1979) *Geriatric Psychotherapy*. New York: Human Sciences Press.

Bromley, D. B. (1977) The psychological case-study. *Personality Description in Ordinary Language*. London: Wiley, Chapter 8.

Bromley, D. B. (1986) *The Case-study Method in Psychology and Related Disciplines*. Chichester: Wiley.

Bromley, D. B. (1990) *Behavioural Gerontology: Central Issues in the Psychology of Ageing*. Wiley, Chichester.

Brooker, D., Foster, N., Banner, A., Payne, M. and Jackson, L. (1998) The efficacy of Dementia Care Mapping as an audit tool: report of a 3-year British NHS evaluation. *Aging and Mental Health*, 2, 60–70.

Brown, J. D. (1998) *The Self*. New York: McGraw-Hill.

Browning, D. S. (1975) *Generative Man: Psychoanalytic Perspectives*. New York: Dell.

Bruce, E. (1998) How can we measure spiritual well-being? *Journal of Dementia Care*, May/June, 16–17.

Bruner, J. S. (1986) *Actual Minds, Possible Worlds*. Cambridge, MA: Harvard University Press.

Buber, M. ([1923], 1937) *I and Thou*. Edinburgh: Clark.

Burnside, I. M. (1996) Reminiscence. In Birren, J. E. (ed.) *Encyclopedia of Gerontology. Age, Aging and the Aged*. Vol. 2. San Diego: Academic Press, 399–406.

Burrow, J. A. (1986) *The Ages of Man: A Study in Medieval Writing and Thought*. Oxford: Clarendon Press.

Busse, E. and Reckless, J. (1961) Psychiatric management of the aged. *Journal of the American Medical Association*, 175, 645–8.

Busse, E. W. (1985) Normal aging: the Duke longitudinal studies. In Bergener, M., Ermini, M. and Staheline, H. B. (eds) *Thresholds in Aging*. New York: Academic Press, 215–29.

Butler, R. N. (1963) The life review: an interpretation of reminiscence in the aged. *Psychiatry*, 26, 65–76.

Campbell, A. J. and Buchner, D. M. (1997) Unstable disability and the fluctuations of frailty. *Age and Ageing*, 26, 315–18.

Cappeliez, P. and O'Rourke, N. (2002) Personality traits and existential concerns as predictors of the functions of reminiscence in older adults. *Journal of Gerontology: Psychological Sciences*, 57B, P116–P123.

Carr, D., House, J. S., Kessler, R. C., Nesse, R. M., Sonnega, J. and Wortman, C. (2000) Marital quality and psychological adjustment to widowhood among older adults: a longitudinal analysis. *Journal of Gerontology: Social Sciences*, 55B (4), S197–S207.

Carstensen, L. L. (1991) Selectivity theory: social activity in life-span context. *Annual Review of Gerontology and Geriatrics*, 11, 195–217.

Carstensen, L. L., Gottman, J. M. and Levenson, R. W. (1995) Emotional behavior in long-term marriage. *Psychology and Aging*, 10, 140–9.

Carstensen, L. L., Isaacowitz, D. M. and Charles, S. T. (1999) Taking time seriously: a theory of socioemotional selectivity. *American Psychologist*, 54, 165–81.

Carver, C. S. and Scheier, M. F. (1998) *On the Self-regulation of Behavior*. New York: Cambridge University Press.

Chandler, M. J and Holliday, S. (1990) Wisdom in a post-apocalyptic age. In Sternberg, R. J. (ed.), *Wisdom: Its Nature, Origins and Development*. New York: Cambridge University Press.

Chatters, L. M. and Taylor, R. J. (1994) Religious involvement among older African Americans. In Levin, J. S. (ed.) *Religion in Aging and Health: Theoretical Foundations and Methodological Frontiers*. Thousand Oaks, CA: Sage.

Cheston, R. (1996) Stories and metaphors: talking about the past in a psychotherapy group for people with dementia. *Ageing and Society*, 16, 579–602.

Chinen, A. B. (1989) *In the Ever After: Fairy Tales and the Second Half of Life.* Wilmette, IL: Chiron Publications.

Cicirelli, V. G. (1987) Locus of control and patient role adjustment of the elderly in acute-care hospitals. *Psychology and Aging*, 2, 138–43.

Clayton, V. P. and Birren, J. E. (1980) The development of wisdom across the life-span: A re-examination of an ancient topic. In Baltes, P. B. and Brim, O. G., *Life-span Development and Behavior*, Vol. 3. New York: Academic Press, 103–35.

Cohen, B. B. (1991) Holocaust survivors and the crisis of aging. *Journal of Contemporary Human Services*, 226–32.

Cole, T. R. (1984) Aging, meaning and well-being: musings of a cultural historian. *International Journal of Aging and Human Development*, 19, 329–36.

Cole, T. R. (1992) *Voices and Visions: Toward a Critical Gerontology.* New York: Springer.

Cole, T. R., Van Tassel, D. D. and Kastenbaum, R. (eds) (1992) *Handbook of the Humanities and Aging.* New York: Springer.

Coleman, P. G. (1974) Measuring reminiscence characteristics from conversation as adaptive features of old age. *International Journal of Aging and Human Development*, 5, 281–94.

Coleman, P. G. (1984) Assessing self-esteem and its sources in elderly people. *Ageing and Society*, 4, 117–35.

Coleman, P. G. (1986) *Ageing and Reminiscence Processes: Social and Clinical Implications.* Chichester: Wiley.

Coleman, P. G. (1999) Creating a life story: the task of reconciliation. *The Gerontologist*, 39, 133–9.

Coleman, P. G. (2000) Aging and the satisfaction of psychological needs. *Psychological Inquiry*, 11, 291–3.

Coleman, P. G. (2002) Doing case study research in psychology. In Jamieson, A. and Victor, C. R. (eds) *Researching Ageing and Later Life.* Buckingham: Open University Press, 135–54.

Coleman, P. G. and Jerrome, D. (1999) Applying theories of aging to gerontological practice through teaching and research. In Bengtson, V. L. and Schaie, K. W. (eds) *Handbook of Theories of Aging.* New York: Springer, 379–95.

Coleman, P. G. and McCulloch, A. W. (1990) Societal change, values and social support: exploratory studies into adjustment in late life. *Journal of Aging Studies*, 4, 321–32.

Coleman, P. G. and Mills, M. A. (1997) Listening to war memories in late life depression and dementia. In Hunt, L., Marshall, M. and Rowlands, C. (eds) *Past Trauma in Late Life: European Perspectives on Therapeutic Work with Older People.* London: Jessica Kingsley.

Coleman, P. G. and Mills, M. A. (2001) Philosophical and spiritual perspectives. In Cantley, C. (ed.) *Handbook of Dementia Care.* Buckingham: Open University Press, 62–76.

Coleman, P. G., Aubin, A., Ivani-Chalian, C., Robinson, M. and Briggs, R. (1993b) Predictors of depressive symptoms and low self-esteem in a follow-up study of elderly people over ten years. *International Journal of Geriatric Psychiatry*, 8, 343–9.

Coleman, P. G., Bond, J. and Peace, S. (1993) Ageing in the twentieth century. In Bond, J., Coleman, P. G. and Peace, S. (eds) *Ageing in Society: An Introduction to Social Gerontology* (2nd edn). London: Sage, 1–18.

Coleman, P. G., Hautamäki, A. and Podolskij, A. (2002) Trauma, reconciliation and generativity: the stories told by European war veterans. In Webster, J. D. and Haight, B. K. (eds) *Critical Advances in Reminiscence Work: From Theory to Application.* New York: Springer, 218–32.

Coleman, P. G., Ivani-Chalian, C. and Robinson, M. (1993) Self-esteem and its sources: stability and change in later life. *Ageing and Society*, 13, 171–92.

Coleman, P. G., Ivani-Chalian, C. and Robinson, M. (1998) The story continues: persistence of life themes in old age. *Ageing and Society*, 18, 389–419.

Coleman, P. G., Ivani-Chalian, C. and Robinson, M. (1999) Self and identity in advanced old age: validation of theory through longitudinal case analysis. *Journal of Personality*, 69, 819–48.

Coleman, P. G., Ivani-Chalian, C. and Robinson, M. (2004) Religious attitudes among British older people: stability and change in a 20 year longitudinal study. *Ageing and Society*, 24 (in press).

Coleman, P. G., McKiernan, F., Mills, M. and Speck, P. (2002) Spiritual belief and quality of life: the experience of older bereaved spouses. *Quality in Ageing – Policy, Practice and Research*, 3, 20–6.

Cooper, S. A. and Coleman, P. G. (2001) Caring for the older person: an exploration of perceptions using personal construct theory. *Age and Ageing*, 30, 399–402.

Costa, P. T. Jr and McCrae, R. R. (1994) Set like plaster? Evidence for the stability of adult personality. In Heatherton, T. F. and Weinberger, J. L. (eds) *Can Personality Change?* Washington, DC: American Psychological Association, 21–40.

Costa, P. T. Jr and McCrae, R. R. (1997) Longitudinal stability of adult personality. In Hogan, R., Johnson, J. A. and Briggs, S. R. (eds) *Handbook of Personality Psychology*. New York: Academic Press, 69–290.

Coupland, N. and Coupland, J. (2003) Discourse, identity and aging. In Nussbaum, J. F. and Coupland, J. (eds) *Handbook of Communication and Aging Research* (2nd edn). Mahwah, NJ: Lawrence Erlbaum (in press).

Craik, F. and Byrd, M. (1982) Aging and cognitive deficits: the role of attentional resources. In Craik, F. and Tehub, S. (eds) *Aging and Cognitive Processes*. New York: Plenum Press, 191–211.

Crittenden, P. M. (1995) Attachment and risk for psychopathology: the early years. *Journal of Developmental and Behavioral Pediatrics: Supplemental issue on Developmental Delay and Psychopathology in Young Children*, 16, S12–S16.

Crittenden, P. M. (1997) The effect of early relationship experiences on relationships in adulthood. In Duck, S. (ed.) *Handbook of Personal Relationships* (2nd edn). Chichester: Wiley, 99–119.

Crittenden, P. M. (1999) *Adult Attachment Interview Coding Manual*. Unpublished manual available from the author.

Crittenden, P. M. (2000) A dynamic-maturational approach to continuity and change in pattern of attachment. In Crittenden, P. M. and Claussen, A. H. (eds), *The Organization of Attachment Relationships: Maturation, Culture and Context*. New York: Cambridge University Press, 343–57.

Crittenden, P. M. (2002) *Adult Attachment Interview Coding Manual*. Unpublished manual available from the author.

Crowther, M. R., Parker, M. W., Achenbaum, W. A., Larimore, W. L. and Koenig, H. G. (2002) Rowe and Kahn's model of successful aging revisited: positive spirituality – the forgotten factor. *The Gerontologist*, 42, 613–20.

Csikszentmihalyi, M. (1990) *Flow: The Psychology of Optimal Experience*. New York: Harper & Row.

Csikszentmihalyi, M. and Rathunde, K. (1990) The psychology of wisdom: an evolutionary interpretation. In Sternberg, R. J. (ed.) *Wisdom: Its Nature, Origins and Development*. New York: Cambridge University Press.

Cumming, E. and Henry, W. (1961) *Growing Old: The Process of Disengagement*. New York: Basic Books.

Dannefer, D. (1988) Differential gerontology and the stratified life course: conceptual and methodological issues. In Maddox, G. L. and Lawton, M. P. (eds) *Annual*

Review of Gerontology and Geriatrics. Volume 8. Varieties of Ageing. New York: Springer, 3–36.

Dannefer, D. and Perlmutter, M. (1990) Development as a multidimensional process: individual and social constituents. *Human Development*, 33, 108–37.

Datan, N., Rodeheaver, D. and Hughes, F. (1987) Adult development and aging. *Annual Review of Psychology*, 38, 153–80.

Davie, G. (2002) *Europe: The Exceptional Case. Parameters of Faith in the Modern World.* London: Darton, Longman & Todd.

Davie, G. and Vincent, J. (1998) Religion and old age. Progress report. *Ageing and Society*, 18, 101–10.

Davies, S. (1997) The long-term psychological effects of World War Two. Implications for working clinically with older people. *The Psychologist*, 10, 364–7.

Day, P. R. (1993) Loss and bereavement and later life. In Day, P. R. (ed.) *Perspectives on Later Life.* London: Whiting & Birch, 100–18.

De Vries, S. (1995) *Strength Of Spirit: Pioneering Women of Achievement from First Fleet to Federation.* Australia: Millennium Books.

Deci, E. L. and Ryan, R. M. (2000) The 'what' and 'why' of goal pursuits: human needs and the self-determination of behaviour. *Psychological Inquiry*, 11, 227–68.

Dershimer, R. A. (1990) *Counseling the Bereaved.* New York: Pergamon Press.

De St Aubin, E. and McAdams, D. P. (1995) The relations of generative concern and generative action to personality traits, satisfaction/happiness with life and ego development. *Journal of Adult Development*, 2, 99–112.

Diener, E., Suh, E. M., Lucas, R. E. and Smith, H. L. (1999) Subjective well-being: three decades of progress. *Psychological Bulletin*, 125, 276–302.

Dietz, B. (1990) The relationship of aging to self-esteem: the reflective effects of maturation and role accumulation. *International Journal of Aging and Human Development*, 43, 249–66.

Disch, R. (ed.) (1988) *Twenty-five Years of the Life Review: Theoretical and Practical Considerations.* New York: Haworth Press.

Dittmann-Kohli, F. (1990) The construction of meaning in old age: possibilities and constraints. *Ageing and Society*, 10, 279–94.

Dittmann-Kohli, F. (2001) Selbst- und Lebensvorstellungen in der zweiten Lebenshaälfte: Ergebnisse aus dem Alters-Survey. In Dittmann-Kohli, F., Bode, C. and Westerhof, G. J. (eds) *Die Zweite Lebenshälfte – Psychologische Perspektiven Ergebnisse des Alters-Survey.* Stuttgart: Kohlhammer, 549–84.

Dixon, R. A. and Baltes, P. B. (1986) Toward life-span research on the functions and pragmatics of intelligence. In Sternberg, R. J. and Wagner, R. K. (eds) *Practical Intelligence: Origins of Competence in the Everyday World.* New York: Cambridge University Press, 203–35.

Downs, M. (1997) The emergence of the person in dementia research. *Ageing and Society*, 17, 597–607.

Drew, L. and Smith, P. K. (1999) The impact of parental separation/divorce on grandparent–grandchild relationships. *International Journal of Aging and Human Development*, 48, 191–216.

Eagly, A. H. and Chaiken, S. (1993) *The Psychology of Attitudes.* Harcourt Brace Jovanovich College Publishers.

Edel, L. (1985) *Henry James: A Life.* New York: Harper & Row.

Ellison, C. G. (1994) Religion, the life stress paradigm and the study of depression. In Levin, J. S. (ed.) *Religion in Aging and Health.* Thousand Oaks, CA: Sage, 78–121.

Erdal, K. J. and Zautra, A. J. (1995) Psychological impact of illness downturns: a comparison of new and chronic conditions. *Psychology and Aging*, 10, 570–7.

Erikson, E. H. (1950) *Childhood and Society.* New York: Norton.

Erikson, E. H. (1963) *Childhood and Society* (revised edition). Harmondsworth:

Penguin.

Erikson, E. H. (1978) Reflections on Dr. Borg's life cycle. In Erikson, E. H. (ed.) *Adulthood*. New York: Norton.

Erikson, E. H., Erikson, J. M. and Kivnick, H. Q. (1986) *Vital Involvement in Old Age. The Experience of Old Age in Our Time*. New York: Norton.

Featherstone, M. and Hepworth, M. (1991) The mask of ageing and the postmodern lifecourse. In Featherstone, M. and Hepworth, M. and Turner, B. S. (eds) *The Body: Social Processes and Cultural Theory*. London: Sage.

Feil, N. (1992) Validation therapy with late-onset dementia populations. In Jones, G. M. M. and Miesen, B. M. L. (eds) *Care-giving in Dementia. Research and Applications*. London: Routledge, 199–218.

Felton, B. and Kahana, E. (1974) Adjustment and situationally bound locus of control among institutionalized aged. *Journal of Gerontology*, 29, 295–301.

Femia, E. E., Zarit, S. H. and Johansson, B. (2001) The disablement process in very late life: a study of the oldest-old in Sweden. *Journal of Gerontology: Psychological Sciences*, 56B, P12–P23.

Fielden, M. A. (1990) Reminiscence as a therapeutic intervention with sheltered housing residents: a comparative study. *British Journal of Social Work*, 20, 21–44.

Fischer, D. H. (1978) *Growing Old in America*. New York: Oxford University Press.

Folkman, S., Lazarus, R. S., Pimley, S. and Novacek, J. (1987) Age differences in stress and coping processes. *Psychology and Aging*, 2, 171–84.

Foucault, M. (1967) *Madness and Civilization*. London: Tavistock.

Frankl, V. E. (1964) *Man's Search for Meaning*. London: Hodder & Stoughton.

Freden, L. (1982) *Psychosocial Aspects of Depression: No Way Out?* Chichester: Wiley.

Freedman, V. A. and Martin, L. G. (2000) The contribution of chronic conditions to aggregate changes in old-age functioning. *American Journal of Public Health*, 90, 1755–60.

Freeman, M. (1997) Death, narrative integrity and the radical challenge of self-understanding: a reading of Tolstoy's 'Death of Ivan Ilych'. *Ageing and Society*, 17, 373–98.

Freeman, M. and Robinson, R. E. (1990) The development within: an alternative approach to the study of lives. *New Ideas In Psychology*, 8, 53–72.

Freund, A. M. and Baltes, P. B. (1998) Selection, optimization and compensation as strategies of life management: correlations with subjective indicators of successful aging. *Psychology and Aging*, 13, 531–43.

Freund, A. M. and Baltes P. B. (1999) Selection, optimization and compensation as strategies of life management: correction to Freund and Baltes (1999). *Psychology and Aging*, 14, 700–2.

Freund, A. M. and Baltes P. B. (2000) The orchestration of selection, optimization and compensation: an action-theoretical conceptualization of a theory of developmental regulation. In Perrig, W. J. and Grob, A. (eds) *Control of Human Behavior, Mental Processes and Consciousness*. Mahwah, NJ: Lawrence Erlbaum, 35–58.

Freund, A. M and Baltes, P. B. (2002) Life management strategies of selection, optimization and compensation: measurement by self-report and construct validity. *Journal of Personality and Social Psychology*, 82(4), 642–62.

Freund, A. M. and Smith, J. (1999) Content and function of the self-definition in old and very old age. *Journal of Gerontology: Psychological Sciences*, 54B, P55–P67.

Froggatt, A. (1988) Self-awareness in early dementia. In Gearing, B., Johnson, M. and Heller, T. (eds) *Mental Health Problems in Old Age: A Reader*. Chichester: Wiley, 131–6.

Fry, P. M. (1991) Individual differences in reminiscence among older adults: predictors of frequency and pleasantness ratings of reminiscence activity. *International Journal of Aging and Human Development*, 33, 311–26.

Fry, P. S. (1998) Spousal loss in later life: a 1-year follow-up of perceived changes in life meaning and psychosocial functioning following bereavement. *Journal of Personal and Interpersonal Loss*, 3, 369–91.

Fry, P. S. (2000) Religious involvement, spirituality and personal meaning for life: existential predictors of psychological wellbeing in community-residing and institutional care elders. *Aging and Mental Health*, 4, 375–87.

Fry, P. S. (2001) The unique contribution of key existential factors to the prediction of psychological well-being of older adults following spousal loss. *The Gerontologist*, 41, 69–81.

Fung, H. H., Carstensen, L. L. and Lutz, A. M. (1999) The influence of time on social preferences: Implications for life-span development. *Psychology and Aging*, 14, 595–604.

Gamino, L., Easterling, L., Stirman, L. and Sewell, K. (2000) Grief adjustment as influenced by funeral participation and occurrence of adverse funeral events. *Omega*, 41(2), 79–92.

Garliski, J. (1975) *Fighting Auschwitz: The Resistance Movement in the Concentration Camp*. London: Orbis Books.

Gatz, M. and Karel, M. J. (1993) Individual change in perceived control over 20 years. *International Journal of Behavioral Development*, 16, 305–22.

George, L. K. (1998) Self and identity in later life: protecting and enhancing the self. *Journal of Aging and Identity*, 3, 133–52.

George, L. K., Larson, D. B., Koenig, H. G. and McCullough, M. E. (2000) Spirituality and health: what we know, what we need to know. *Journal of Social and Clinical Psychology*, 19, 102–16.

Gergen, K. J. and Gergen, M. M. (1988) Narrative and the self as relationship. In L. Berkowitz (ed.) *Advances in Experimental Social Psychology*, Vol. 21. New York: Academic Press.

Gething, L., Fethney, J., McKee, K., Goff, M., Churchward, M. and Matthews, S. (2002) Knowledge, stereotyping and attitudes towards self-ageing. *Australasian Journal on Ageing*, 21(2), 74–79.

Gibson, F. (1994) What can reminiscence contribute to people with dementia? In Bornat, J. (ed.) *Reminiscence Reviewed: Perspectives, Evaluations and Achievements*. Buckingham: Open University Press, 46–60.

Gignac, M. A. M., Cott, C. and Badley, E. M. (2000) Adaptation to chronic illness and disability and its relationship to perceptions of independence and dependence. *Journal of Gerontology: Psychological Sciences*, 55B, P362–P372.

Gilleard, C. J. (1984) *Living with Dementia*. London: Croom Helm.

Goldberg, D. (1978) *Manual of the General Health Questionnaire*. Slough: NFER-Nelson.

Golde, P. and Kogan N. (1959) A sentence completion procedure for assessing attitudes toward old people. *Journal of Gerontology*, 14, 355–63.

Goldman, N., Korenman, S. and Weinstein, R. (1995) Marital status and health among the elderly. *Social Science and Medicine*, 40 (12), 1717–30.

Gould, R. L. (1978) *Transformations: Growth and Change in Adult Life*. New York: Simon & Schuster.

Greenwald, A. (1980) The totalitarian ego: fabrication and revision of personal history. *American Psychologist*, 35, 603–18.

Groves, T. and Pennell, I. (1995) *The Consumer Guide to Mental Health*. HarperCollins Publishers.

Gutmann, D. (1987) *Reclaimed Powers: Towards a New Psychology of Men and Women in Later Life*. New York: Basic Books (2nd edn, 1994).

Gutmann, D. L. (1997) *The Human Elder in Nature, Culture and Society*. Boulder, CO: Westview Press.

Habermas, T. and Bluck, S. (2000) Getting a life: the emergence of the life story in adolescence. *Psychological Bulletin*, 126, 748–69.

Haight, B. K. (1988) The therapeutic role of a structured life review process in homebound elderly subjects. *Journal of Gerontology*, 43, 40–4.

Haight, B. K. (1991) Reminiscing: the state of the art as a basis for practice. *International Journal of Aging and Human Development*, 33, 1–32.

Haight, B. K. (1992) Long-term effects of a structured life review process. *Journal of Gerontology*, 47, 312–15.

Haight, B. K. and Hendrix, S. (1995) An integrated review of reminiscence. In Haight, B. K. and Webster, J. D. (eds) *The Art and Science of Reminiscing. Theory, Research, Methods and Applications.* Washington, DC: Taylor & Francis, 3–21.

Haight, B. K., Coleman, P. G. and Lord, K. (1995) The linchpins of a successful life review: structure, evaluation and individuality. In Haight, B. K. and Webster, J. D. (eds) *The Art and Science of Reminiscing. Theory, Research, Methods and Applications.* Washington, DC: Taylor & Francis, 179–92.

Haight, B. K., Michel, Y. and Hendrix, S. (2000) The extended effects of the life review in nursing home residents. *International Journal of Aging and Human Development*, 50, 151–68.

Halpert, B. P. and Zimmerman, M. K. (1986) The health status of the 'old-old': a reconsideration. *Social Science and Medicine*, 22, 893–9.

Hamerman, D. (1999) Toward an understanding of frailty. *Annals of Internal Medicine*, 130, 945–50.

Hasher, L. and Zacks, T. T. (1979) Automatic and effortful processes in memory. *Journal of Experimental Psychology: General*, 108, 356–88.

Hass, A. (1990) *In the Shadow of the Holocaust.* New York: Cornell University Press.

Hassan, J. (1997) From victim to survivor. The possibility of healing in ageing survivors of the Nazi holocaust. In Hunt, L., Marshall, M. and Rowlings, C. (eds) *Past Trauma in Late Life: European Perspectives on Therapeutic Work with Older People.* London: Jessica Kingsley, 122–35.

Hautamäki, A. and Coleman, P. G. (2001) Explanation for low prevalence of PTSD among older Finnish war veterans: social solidarity and continued significance given to wartime sufferings. *Aging and Mental Health*, 5, 165–74.

Havighurst, R. J. (1972) *Developmental Tasks and Education* (3rd edn). New York: David McKay (first published 1948).

Havighurst, R. J. and Albrecht, R. (1953) *Older People.* New York: Longman.

Haynie, D. A., Berg, S., Johansson, B., Gatz, M. and Zarit, S. H. (2001) Symptoms of depression in the oldest old: a longitudinal study. *Journal of Gerontology: Psychological Sciences*, 56B, P111–P118.

Hazan, C. and Shaver, P. R. (1990) Love and work: an attachment-theoretical perspective. *Journal of Personality and Social Psychology*, 59, 270–80.

Hazan, H. (1980) *The Limbo People. A Study of the Constitution of the Time Universe among the Aged.* London: Routledge.

Hazan, H. (1984) Religion in an old age home: symbolic adaptation as a survival strategy. *Ageing and Society*, 4, 137–56.

Heckhausen, J. (1997) Developmental regulation across adulthood: primary and secondary control of age-related challenges. *Developmental Psychology*, 33, 176–87.

Heckhausen, J. (1999) *Developmental Regulation in Adulthood: Age-Normative and Sociostructural Constraints as Adaptive Challenges.* New York: Cambridge University Press.

Heckhausen, J. (2005) Psychological approaches to human development. In Johnson, M., Bengtson, V. L., Coleman, P. G. and Kirkwood, T. (eds) *Cambridge Handbook of Age and Ageing.* Cambridge: Cambridge University Press (in press).

Heckhausen, J. and Schulz, R. (1993) Optimisation by selection and compensation: balancing primary and secondary control in life-span development. *International*

Journal of Behavioral Development, 16, 287–303.

Heckhausen, J. and Schulz, R. (1995) A life-span theory of control. *Psychological Bulletin*, 102, 284–304.

Heckhausen, J., Dixon, R. A. and Baltes, P. B. (1989) Gains and losses in development throughout adulthood as perceived by different adult age groups. *Developmental Psychology*, 25, 109–21.

Heckhausen, J., Wrosch, C. and Fleeson, W. (2001) Developmental regulation before and after a developmental deadline: the sample case of 'biological clock' for child-bearing. *Psychology and Aging*, 16, 400–13.

Heelas, P. (1998) *Religion, Modernity and Postmodernity*. Oxford: Blackwell.

Heikkinnen, R.-L. (2000) Ageing in an autobiographical context. *Ageing and Society*, 20, 467–83.

Helson, R. and Moane, G. (1987) Personality change in women from college to midlife. *Journal of Personality and Social Psychology*, 53, 176–86.

Helson, R. and Wink, P. (1992) Personality change in women from the early 40s to the early 50s. *Psychology and Aging*, 7(1), 46–55.

Hendrix, S. and Haight, B. K. (2002) A continued review of reminiscence. In Webster, J. D. and Haight, B. K. (eds) *Critical Advances in Reminiscence Work. From Theory to Application*. New York: Springer, 3–29.

Henry, J. P. (1988) The archetypes of power and intimacy. In Birren, J. E. and Bengtson, V. L. (eds) *Emergent Theories of Aging*. New York: Springer, 269–98.

Hinde, R. A. (1999) *Why Gods Persist. A Scientific Approach to Religion*. London: Routledge.

Hofman, A., Rocca, W., Brayne, C., Breteler, M. B. B., Clarke, M., Cooper, B., Copeland, J. R. M., Dartigues, J. F., Da Silva Droux, A., Hagnell, D., Heeran, T. J., Endegal, K., Jonker, C., Lindesay, J., Lobo, A., Mann, A. H., Molsa, P. K., Morgan, K., O'Connor, D. W., Sulkava, R., Kay, D. W. K. and Amaducci, L. (1991) The prevalence of dementia in Europe: a collaborative study of 1980–1990 findings. *International Journal of Epidemiology*, 20, 736–48.

Holden, U. P. and Woods, R. T. (1995) *Positive Approaches to Dementia Care*. Edinburgh: Churchill Livingstone.

Holliday, S. G. and Chandler, M. J. (1986) *Wisdom: Explorations in Adult Competence*. Basel: Karger.

Hooker, K. (1992) Possible selves and perceived health in older adults and college students. *Journal of Gerontology: Psychological Sciences*, 47, P85–P95.

Hopton, J. L. and Hunt, S. M. (1996) Housing conditions and mental health in a disadvantaged area in Scotland. *Journal of Epidemiology and Community Health*, 50(1), 56–61.

Horowitz, M. J., Wilner, N. and Alwarez, W. (1979) Impact of event scale: a measure of subjective distress. *Psychosomatic Medicine*, 41, 207–18.

Howse, K. (1999) *Religion and Spirituality in Later Life: A Review*. London: Centre for Policy on Ageing.

Hughes, M., Mayes, D. and Le Riche, P. (2001) Decision-making and moving into long-term care. *Generations Review*, 11(2), 10–14.

Hunt, L., Marshall, M. and Rowlings, C. (eds) (1997) *Past Trauma in Late Life: European Perspectives on Therapeutic Work with Older People*. London: Jessica Kingsley.

Hunt, N. (1997) Trauma of war. Long-term psychological effects of war in World War Two veterans. *The Psychologist*, 10, 357–60.

Hunt, N. and Robbins, I. (2001a) World War II veterans, social support and veterans' associations. *Aging and Mental Health*, 5, 175–82.

Hunt, N. and Robbins, I. (2001b) The long-term consequences of war: the experience of World War II. *Aging and Mental Health*, 5, 183–90.

Ingebretsen, R. and Solem, P. E. (1998) Spouses of persons with dementia: attachment, loss and coping. *Norwegian Journal of Epidemiology*, 8, 149–56.

James, W. (1890) *The Principles of Psychology*. Cambridge, MA: Harvard University Press.

Jason, L. A., Reichler, A., King, C., Madsen, D., Camacho, J. and Marchese, W. (2003) The measurement of wisdom: a preliminary effort. *Journal of Community Psychology*, 585–98.

Jerram, J. L. and Coleman, P. G. (1999) The big five personality traits and reporting of health problems and health behaviour in old age. *British Journal of Health Psychology*, 4, 181–92.

Jerrome, D. (1988) 'That's what it's all about': old people's organizations as a context for aging. *Journal of Aging Studies*, 2, 71–81.

Jerrome, D. (1992) *Good Company: An Anthropological Study of Old People in Groups*. Edinburgh: Edinburgh University Press.

Johnson, C. L. and Barer, B. M. (1992) Patterns of engagement and disengagement among the oldest old. *Journal of Aging Studies*, 6, 351–64.

Johnson, C. L. and Barer, B. M. (1997) *Life beyond 85 Years: The Aura of Survivorship*. New York: Springer.

Johnson, M., Bengtson, V. L., Coleman, P. G. and Kirkwood, T. (eds) *Handbook of Age and Ageing*. Cambridge: Cambridge University Press (in press).

Jonson, H. and Magnusson, J. A. (2001) A new age of old age? Gerotranscendence and the re-enchantment of aging. *Journal of Aging Studies*, 15, 317–31.

Jung, C. G. (1938) *Psychology and Religion*. New Haven, CT: Yale University Press.

Jung, C. G. (1972) The transcendent function. In Read, H., Fordham, M., Adler, G. and McGuire, W. (eds), *The Structure and Dynamics of the Psyche: Volume 8. The Collected Works of C. G. Jung* (2nd edn). London: Routledge and Kegan Paul.

Kalish, R. A. and Reynolds, D. K. (1976) *Death and Ethnicity: A Psychocultural Study*. Los Angeles: University of California Press.

Kaminsky, M. (ed.) (1984) *The Uses of Reminiscence: New Ways of Working with Older Adults*. New York: Haworth Press.

Kastenbaum, R. J. (1984) When aging begins: a lifespan developmental approach. *Research on Aging*, 6, 105–17.

Kaufman, S. R. (1987) *The Ageless Self: Sources of Meaning in Late Life*. Madison: University of Wisconsin Press, 1987.

Keller, B. (2002) Personal identity and social discontinuity: on memories of the 'war generation' in former West Germany. In Webster, J. D. and Haight, B. K. (eds) *Critical Advances in Reminiscence Work: From Theory to Application*. New York: Springer, 165–79.

Keller, M. L., Leventhal, E. A. and Larson, B. (1989) Aging: the lived experience. *International Journal of Aging and Human Development*, 29, 67–82.

Kenyon, G. M. and Randall, W. L. (1997) *Restorying our Lives: Personal Growth through Autobiographical Reflection*. Westport, CT: Praeger.

Keyes, C. L. M. and Ryff, C. (1998) Generativity in adult lives; social structural contours and quality of life consequences. In McAdams, D. P. and de St Aubin, E. (eds) *Generativity and Adult Development: How and Why We Care for the Next Generation*. Washington, DC: American Psychological Association, 227–63.

King, M., Speck, P. and Thomas, A. (1999) The effect of spiritual beliefs on outcome from illness. *Social Science and Medicine*, 48, 1291–9.

Kirby, S. E., Coleman, P. G. and Daley, D. (2004) Spirituality and well-being in frail and non-frail older adults. *Journal of Gerontology: Psychological Sciences*, 59B (in press).

Kirkpatrick, L. A. (1992) An attachment-theory approach to the psychology of religion. *International Journal for the Psychology of Religion*, 2, 3–28.

Kitwood, T. (1988) The contribution of psychology to the understanding of senile dementia. In Gearing, B., Johnson, M. and Heller, T. (eds) *Mental Health Problems in Old Age: A Reader*. Chichester: Wiley, 123–30.

Kitwood, T. (1993) Towards a theory of dementia care: the interpersonal process. *Ageing and Society*, 13, 51–67.

Kitwood, T. (1996) A dialectical framework for dementia. In Woods, R. T. (ed.) *Handbook of the Clinical Psychology of Ageing*. Chichester: Wiley, 267–82.

Kitwood, T. (1997) *Dementia Reconsidered: The Person Comes First*. Buckingham: Open University Press.

Kitwood, T. and Bredin, K. (1992) Towards a theory of dementia care: personhood and well-being. *Ageing and Society*, 12, 269–87.

Kivnick, H. Q. (1991) *Living with Care, Caring for Life: The Inventory of Life Strengths*. Minneapolis: University of Minnesota.

Koenig, H. G. (1993) Religion and aging. *Reviews in Clinical Gerontology*, 3, 195–203.

Koenig, H. G. (2001) Religion and medicine III: developing a theoretical model. *International Journal of Psychiatry in Medicine*, 31, 199–216.

Koenig, H. G., George, L. K. and Siegler, I. C. (1988) The use of religion and other emotion-regulating coping strategies among older adults. *The Gerontologist*, 28, 303–10.

Kogan, N. (1961) Attitudes toward old people: the development of a scale and an examination of correlates. *Journal of Abnormal and Social Psychology*, 62, 616–22.

Kotre, J. (1984) *Outliving the Self: Generativity and the Interpretation of Lives*. Baltimore: Johns Hopkins University Press.

Kotre, J. (1996) *Outliving the Self: How we Live on in Future Generations*. New York: Norton.

Kramarow, E., Lentzer, H., Rooks, R., Weeks, J. and Saydah, S. (1999) *Health and Aging Chart Book, Health, United States*. Hyattsville, MD: National Center for Health Statistics.

Kramer, D. A. (1990) Conceptualizing wisdom: the primacy of affect-cognition relations. In Sternberg, R. J. (ed.), *Wisdom: Its Nature, Origins and Development*. New York: Cambridge University Press, 279–313.

Kramer, D. A. (2000) Wisdom as a classical source of human strength: conceptualization and empirical inquiry. *Journal of Social and Clinical Psychology*, 19, 83–101.

Krause, N. (1988) Stressful life events and physician utilization. *Journal of Gerontology: Social Sciences*, 43, S53–S61.

Krause, N. (1995a) Assessing stress-buffering effects: a cautionary note. *Psychology and Aging*, 10, 518–26.

Krause, N. (1995b) Religiosity and self-esteem among older adults. *Journal of Gerontology: Psychological Sciences*, 50B, P236–P246.

Kruse, A. (1989) Coping with chronic disease and elder abuse, In Wolf, R. S. and Bergman, S. (eds) *Stress, Conflict and Abuse of the Elderly*. Jerusalem: JDC-Brookdale Institute of Gerontology and Adult Development.

Kruse, A. (1991) Caregivers coping with chronic disease, dying and death of an aged family member. *Reviews in Clinical Gerontology*, 1, 411–15.

Kruse, A. and Schmitt, E. (2000) *Wir haben uns als Deutsche gefuehlt. Lebensrueckblick und Lebenssituation juedischer Emigranten und Lagerhaeftlinge*. Darmstadt: Steinkopff Verlag.

Kruse, A., Schmitt, E., Coleman, P. G. and Re, S. (2003) On the significance of memories of war captivity and deliverance – a contribution to research on life span development and productivity in old age. Presentation at the Vth European Congress of Gerontology, Barcelona.

Kunzman, U., Little, T. D. and Smith, J. (2000) Is age-related stability of subjective well-being a paradox? Cross-sectional and longitudinal evidence from the Berlin Aging Study. *Psychology and Aging*, 15, 511–26.

Kuypers, J. and Bengtson, V. (1973) Competence and social breakdown: a social-psychological view of aging. *Human Development*, 16, 181–201.

Labouvie-Vief, G. (1990) Wisdom as integrated thought: historical and developmental perspectives. In Sternberg, R. J. (ed.), *Wisdom: Its Nature, Origins and Development*. New York: Cambridge University Press, 52–83.

Labouvie-Vief, G. (2005) The psychology of emotions and ageing. In Johnson, M., Bengtson, V. L., Coleman, P. G. and Kirkwood, T. (eds) *Cambridge Handbook of Age and Ageing*. Cambridge: Cambridge University Press (in press).

Labouvie-Vief, G. and Diehl, M. (2000) Cognitive complexity and cognitive-affective integration: related or separate domains of adult development. *Psychology and Aging*, 15 (3), 490–504.

Labouvie-Vief, G., Chiodo, L. M., Goguen, L. A., Diehl, M. and Orwoll, L. (1995) Representations of self across the life span. *Psychology and Aging*, 10, 404–15.

Lachman, M. E. and Weaver, S. L. (1998) Sociodemographic variations in the sense of control by domain: findings from the MacArthur studies of midlife. *Psychology and Aging*, 13, 553–62.

Lang, F. R. and Heckhausen, J. (2001) Perceived control over development and subjective well-being: differential benefits across adulthood. *Journal of Personality and Social Psychology*, 81(3), 509–23.

Lang, F. R. and Carstensen, L. L. (1994) Close emotional relationships in late life: further support for proactive aging in the social domain. *Psychology and Aging*, 9, 315–24.

Langer, E. (1983) *The Psychology of Control*. Beverly Hills: Sage.

Langer, E. J. (1989) Minding matters: the consequences of mindlessness–mindfulness. *Advances in Experimental Social Psychology*, 22, 137–73.

Langer, E. J. and Rodin, J. (1976) The effects of choice and enhanced personal responsibility for the aged: a field experiment in an institutional setting. *Journal of Personality and Social Psychology*, 34, 191–8.

Lasher, K. P. and Faulkender, P. J. (1993) Measurement of aging anxiety: development of the Anxiety About Aging Scale. *International Journal of Aging and Human Development*, 37(4), 247–59.

Laslett, P. (1989) *A Fresh Map of Life: The Emergence of the Third Age*. London: Weidenfeld & Nicolson.

Lawton, M. P. (1980) *Environment and Aging*. Belmont, CA: Brooks-Cole.

Lawton, M. P. and Nahemow, L. (1973) Ecology and the aging process. In Eisdorfer, C. and Lawton, M. P. (eds) *The Psychology of Adult Development and Aging*. Washington, DC: American Psychological Association, 464–88.

Lazarus, R. S. (1966) *Psychological Stress and the Coping Process*. New York: McGraw-Hill.

Lazarus, R. S. (1999) *Stress and Emotion: A New Synthesis*. New York: Springer.

Lazarus, R. S. and DeLongis, A. (1983) Psychological stress and coping in aging. *American Psychologist*, 38, 245–54.

Lazarus, R. S. and Folkman, S. (1984) *Stress, Appraisal and Coping*. New York: Springer.

Lee, G. R., DeMaris, A., Bavin, S. and Sullivan, R. (2001) Gender differences in the depressive effect of widowhood in later life. *Journal of Gerontology: Social Sciences*, 56(1), S56–S61.

Lemke, S. and Moos, R. (1980) Assessing the institutional policies of sheltered care settings. *Journal of Gerontology*, 35, 233–43.

Levin, J. S. (ed.) (1994a) *Religion in Aging and Health*. Thousand Oaks, CA: Sage.

Levin, J. S. (1994b) Religion and health: is there an association, is it valid and is it causal? *Social Science and Medicine*, 38, 1475–82.

Levin, J. S. (1995) Religion. In Maddox, G. L. (ed.) *The Encyclopedia of Aging* (2nd edn). New York: Springer, 799–802.

Levinson, D. J. (1977) The mid-life transition: a period in adult psychosocial development. *Psychiatry*, 40, 99–112.

Levinson, D. J. (1986) A conception of adult development. *American Psychologist*, 41, 3–13.

Levinson, D. J. (1996) *The Seasons of a Woman's Life*. New York: Ballantine Books.

Levinson, D. J., Darrow, D. N., Klein, E. B., Levinson, M. H., and McKee, J. B. (1978) *The Seasons of a Man's Life*. New York: Alfred A. Knopf.

Levy, B. R., Slade, M. D., Kunkel, S. and Kasl, S. V. (2002) Longevity increased by positive self-perceptions of aging. *Journal of Personality and Social Psychology*, 83(2), 261–70.

Lewis, C. N. (1971) Reminiscing and self-concept in old age. *Journal of Gerontology*, 26, 240–3.

Lieberman, M. A. and Tobin, S. S. (1983) *The Experience of Old Age. Stress, Coping and Survival*. New York: Basic Books.

Lindenberg, S. M. (1996) Continuities in the theory of social production functions. In Lindenberg, S. M. and Ganzeboom, H. B. G. (eds) *Verklarende Sociologie: Opstellen voor Reinhard Wippler* [Explanatory Sociology: Essays for Reinhard Wippler]. Amsterdam: Thesis Publishers, 169–84.

Litwin, H., (1999) Support network type and patterns of help-giving and receiving among older adults. *Journal of Social Service Research*, 24(3/4), 83–101.

Long, M. V. and Martin, P. (2000) Personality, relationship closeness and loneliness of oldest old adults and their children. *Journal of Gerontology: Psychological Sciences*, 55B, P311–P319.

Lowenthal, R. I. and Marrazzo, R. A. (1990) Milestoning: evoking memories for resocialization through group reminiscence. *The Gerontologist*, 30, 269–72.

Main, M., Kaplan, N. and Cassidy, J. (1985) Security in infancy, childhood and adulthood: a move to the level of representation. In Bretherton, I. and Waters, E. (eds) Growing points in attachment theory and research. *Monographs of the Society for Research in Child Development*, 50, 66–106.

Maas, H. S. (1985) The development of adult development: recollections and reflections. In Munnichs, J. M. A., Mussen, P., Olbrich, E. and Coleman, P. G. (eds) *Life-Span and Change in a Gerontological Perspective*. Orlando, FL: Academic Press, 161–75.

Maas, H. S. and Kuypers, J. A. (1974) *From Thirty to Seventy*. San Francisco: Jossey-Bass Publishers.

Mace, N. L. and Rabins, P. V. (1985) *The 36-Hour Day. Caring at Home for Confused Elderly People*. London: Age Concern England.

MacKinlay, E. (2001) *The Spiritual Dimension of Ageing*. London: Jessica Kingsley.

Maddox, G. L. (1987) Aging differently. *The Gerontologist*, 27, 557–64.

Magai, C. and Cohen, C. I. (1998) Attachment style and emotion regulation in dementia patients and their relation to caregiver burden. *Journal of Gerontology: Psychological Sciences*, 53B, P147–P154.

Maldonado, D. (1995) Religion and racial/ethnic minority elderly populations. In Kimble, M. A., McFadden, S. H., Ellor, J. W. and Seeber, J. L. (eds) *Aging, Spirituality and Religion: A Handbook*. Minneapolis, MN: Fortress Press.

Manton, K. G., Stallard, E. and Corder, L. (1995) Changes in morbidity and chronic disability in the U.S. elderly population: evidence from the 1982, 1984 and 1989 National Long Term Surveys. *Journal of Gerontology: Social Sciences*, 50B, S194–S204.

Marcoen, A. (1993) The search for meaning: some reflections from a psychogerontological perspective. *Ultimate Reality and Meaning – Interdisciplinary Studies in the Philosophy of Understanding*, 16, 228–40.

Marcoen, A. (2005) Religion, spirituality and older people. In Johnson, M., Bengtson, V. L., Coleman, P. G. and Kirkwood, T. (eds) *Cambridge Handbook of Age and Ageing*. Cambridge: Cambridge University Press (in press).

Markides, K. S. and Cooper, C. L. (eds) (1989) *Ageing, Stress and Health*.

Chichester: Wiley.

Markus, H. R. and Herzog, A. R. (1991) The role of the self-concept in aging. In Schaie, K. W. and Lawton, M. P. (eds) *Annual Review of Gerontology and Geriatrics.* Vol. 11. New York: Springer, 110–43.

Markus, H. R. and Nurius, P. (1986) Possible selves. *American Psychologist*, 41, 954–69.

Markus, H. R. and Wurf, E. (1987) The dynamic self-concept: a social psychological perspective. *Annual Review of Psychology*, 38, 299–337.

Marsiske, M., Delius, J., Maas, I., Lindenberger, U., Scherer, H. and Tesch-Römer, C. (1999) Sensory systems in old age. In Baltes, P. B. and Mayer, K. U. (eds) *The Berlin Aging Study. Aging from 70 to 100.* New York: Cambridge University Press, 360–83.

Marsiske, M., Lang, F. B., Baltes, P. B. and Baltes, M. M. (1995) Selective optimization with compensation: life-span perspectives on successful human development. In Dixon, R. and Bäckman, L. (eds) Compensating for Psychological Deficits and Declines: Managing Losses and Promoting Gains. Mahwah, NJ: Lawrence Erlbaum, 35–79.

Martin, P., Rott, C., Hagberg, B. and Morgan, K. (eds) (2000) *Centenarians: Autonomy versus Dependence in the Oldest Old.* New York: Springer.

McAdams, D. P. (1990) Unity and purpose in human lives: the emergence of identity as a life story. In Rabin, A. I., Zucker, R. A., Emmons, R. A. and Frank, S. (eds) *Studying Persons and Lives.* New York: Springer, 148–200.

McAdams, D. P. (1993) *Stories We Live By: Personal Myths and the Making of the Self.* New York: Morrow.

McAdams, D. P. (1995) What do we know when we know a person? *Journal of Personality*, 63, 365–96.

McAdams, D. P. and de St Aubin, E. (1992) A theory of generativity and its assessment through self-report, behavioral acts and narrative themes in autobiography. *Journal of Personality and Social Psychology*, 62, 6, 1003–15.

McAdams, D. P. and de St Aubin, E. (eds) (1998) *Generativity and Adult Development: Psychosocial Perspectives on Caring for and Contributing to the Next Generation.* Washington, DC: American Psychological Association Press.

McAdams, D. P., de St Aubin, E. and Logan, R. L. (1993) Generativity among young, midlife and older adults. *Psychology and Aging*, 8(2), 221–30.

McAdams, D. P., Diamond, A., de St Aubin, E. and Mansfield, E. (1997) Stories of commitment: the psychosocial construction of generative lives. *Journal of Personality and Social Psychology*, 72(3), 678–94.

McFadden, S. H. (1996a) Religion and spirituality. In Birren, J. E. (ed.) *Encyclopedia of Gerontology.* Vol. 2. San Diego: Academic Press, 387–97.

McFadden, S. H. (1996b) Religion, spirituality and aging. In Birren, J. E. and Schaie, K. W. (eds) *Handbook of the Psychology of Aging* (4th edn). San Diego: Academic Press, 162–77.

McFadden, S. H. (1999) Religion, personality and aging: a life span perspective. *Journal of Personality*, 67, 1081–104.

McFadden, S. H. and Levin, J. S. (1996) Religion, emotions and health. In Magai, C. and McFadden, S. H. (eds) *Handbook of Emotion, Adult Development and Aging.* San Diego: Academic Press, 349–65.

McKee, K. J., Wilson, F., Elford, H., Hinchliff, S., Bolton, G., Chung, M. C. and Goudie, F. (2003) Reminiscence: is living in the past good for wellbeing? *Nursing and Residential Care*, 5, 489–91.

McMahon, A. W. and Rhudick, P. J. (1967) Reminiscing: adaptational significance in the aged. In Levin, S. and Kahana, R. J. (eds) *Psychodynamic Studies on Aging. Creativity, Reminiscence and Dying.* New York: International Universities Press, 64–78.

Meacham, A., (1990) The loss of wisdom. In Sternberg, R. J. (ed.) *Wisdom: Its Nature, Origins and Development*. New York: Cambridge University Press, 181–214.

Meade, R., Coleman, P. G., Conroy, M. C., Jerrome, D. and Mills, M. (1998) Attachment, awareness and dementia care: the development of a research instrument. *Newsletter of the Psychologists' Special Interest Group Working with Older People*, 66, 39–43.

Menec, V. H. and Chipperfield, J. G. (1997) The interactive effect of perceived control and functional status on health and mortality among young-old and old-old adults. *Journal of Gerontology: Psychological Sciences*, 52B, P118–P126.

Mergler, N. L. and Goldstein, M. D. (1983) Why are there old people? Senescence as biological and cultural preparedness for the transmission of information. *Human Development*, 26, 72–90.

Merriam, S. B. (1993) Race, sex and age-group differences in the occurrences and uses of reminiscence. *Activities, Adaptation and Aging*, 18, 1–18.

Miesen, B. M. (1992) Attachment theory and dementia. In Jones, G. M. and Miesen, B. M. (eds) *Care-giving in Dementia. Research and Applications*. London: Tavistock, 38–56.

Miesen, B. M. (1998) *Dementia in Close-Up*. London: Routledge.

Miller, E. and Morris, R. (1993) *The Psychology of Dementia*. Chichester: Wiley.

Miller, W. R. and Thoresen, C. E. (2003) Spirituality, religion and health: an emerging research field. *American Psychologist*, 58, 24–35.

Mills, M. A. (1997) Narrative identity and dementia: a study of emotion and narrative in older people with dementia. *Ageing and Society*, 17, 673–98.

Mills, M. A. and Coleman, P. G. (1994) Nostalgic memories in dementia – a case study. *International Journal of Aging and Human Development*, 38, 121–37.

Mills, M. A., Coleman, P. G., Jerrome, D., Conroy, M. C., Meade, R., Miesen, B. M. (1999) Changing patterns of dementia care: the influence of attachment theory in staff training. In Bornat, J., Chamberlayne, P. and Chant, L. (eds) *Reminiscence: Practice, Skills and Settings*. London: School of Health and Social Welfare, Open University and Centre for Biography in Social Policy, University of East London, 15–20.

Minois, G. (1989) *History of Old Age from Antiquity to the Renaissance*. Chicago: University of Chicago Press (reissued by Polity Press, Cambridge).

Mitchell, J. M. and Kemp, B. J. (2000) Quality of life in assisted living homes: a multidimensional analysis. *Journal of Gerontology: Psychological Sciences*, 55B, P117–P127.

Moberg, D. O. (1968) Religiosity in old age. In Neugarten, B. L. (ed.) *Middle Age and Aging: A Reader in Social Psychology*. Chicago: University of Chicago Press, 497–508.

Moberg, D. O. (ed.) (2001) *Aging and Spirituality: Spiritual Dimensions of Aging Theory, Research, Practice and Policy*. New York: Haworth Press.

Montepare, J. M. (1996) Variations in adults' subjective ages in relation to birthday nearness, age awareness and attitudes toward aging. *Journal of Adult Development*, 3, 193–203.

Montepare, J. M. and Lachman, M. E. (1989) 'You're only as old as you feel': self-perceptions of age, fears of aging and life satisfaction from adolescence to old age. *Psychology and Aging*, 4, 73–8.

Montgomery, A., Barber, C. and McKee, P. (2002) A phenomenological study of wisdom in later life. *International Journal of Aging and Human Development*, 54(2), 139–57.

Moody, H. R. (1995) Ageing, meaning and the allocation of resources. *Ageing and Society*, 15, 163–84.

Moody, H. R. and Carroll, D. (1997) *The Five Stages of the Soul: Charting the Spiritual Passages that Shape Our Lives*. New York: Anchor Books.

Moos, R. H. (1981) Environmental choice and control in community care settings for older people. *Journal of Applied Social Psychology*, 11, 23–43.

Moos, R. H. and Lemke, S. (1992) *Sheltered Care Environment Scale Manual*. Palo Alto, CA: Stanford University Medical Centers.

Morgan, K. and Bath, P. A. (1998) Customary physical activity and psychological well-being: a longitudinal study. *Age and Ageing*, 27–S3, 35–40.

Munnichs, J. M. A. (1966) *Old Age and Finitude. A Contribution to Psychogerontology*. Basel: Karger.

Munnichs, J. M. A. (1992) Ageing: a kind of autobiography. *European Journal of Gerontology*, 1, 244–50.

Munnichs, J. M. A., Mussen, P., Olbrich, E. and Coleman, P. G. (eds) (1985) *Life-Span and Change in a Gerontological Perspective*. Orlando, FL: Academic Press.

Murphy, M. J. (1995) Methods for forecasting mortality and their performance. *Reviews in Clinical Gerontology*, 5, 217–27.

Murray, H. A. (1938) *Explorations in Personality*. New York: Oxford University Press.

Murray, H. A. (1943) *The Thematic Apperception Test: Manual*. Cambridge, MA: Harvard University Press.

Musick, M. A., Koenig, H. G., Hays, J. C. and Cohen, H. J. (1998) Religious activity and depression among community-dwelling elderly persons with cancer: the moderating effect of race. *Journal of Gerontology: Social Sciences*, 53B, S218–S227.

Neijmeyer, R. A. and Werth, J. L. (2005) The psychology of death. In Johnson, M., Bengtson, V. L., Coleman, P. G. and Kirkwood, T. (eds) *Cambridge Handbook of Age and Ageing*. Cambridge: Cambridge University Press (in press).

Neugarten, B. L. (1964) *Personality in Middle and Late Life*. New York: Atherton Press.

Neugarten, B. L. (1968) Adult personality: toward a psychology of the life cycle. In Neugarten, B. L. (ed.) *Middle Age and Ageing: A Reader in Social Psychology*. Chicago: University of Chicago Press, 137–47.

Neugarten, B. L. (1988) Personality and psychosocial patterns of aging. In Bergener, M., Ermini, M. and Stahelin, H. B. (eds) *Crossroads in Aging*. London: Academic Press, 205–18.

Neugarten, B. L. and Neugarten, D. A. (1987) The changing meanings of age in the aging society. In Pifer, A. and Bronte, L. (eds) *Our Aging Society: Paradox and Promise*. New York: Norton, 33–51.

Niederhoffer, K. G. and Pennebaker, J. W. (2002) Sharing one's story: on the benefits of writing or talking about emotional experience. In Snyder, C. R. and Lopez, S. J. (eds) *Handbook of Positive Psychology*. New York: Oxford University Press, 573–83.

Nourhashemi, F., Andrieu, S., Gillette-Guyonnet, S., Vellas, B., Albarede, J. L. and Grandjean, H. (2001) Instrumental activities of daily living as a potential marker of frailty: a study of 7364 community-dwelling elderly women (the EPIDOS Study). *Journal of Gerontology: Medical Sciences*, 56A, M448–M453.

O'Connor, B. P. and Rigby, H. (1996) Perceptions of baby talk, frequency of receiving baby talk and self-esteem among community and nursing home residents. *Psychology and Aging*, 11, 147–54.

O'Connor, B. P. and Vallerand, R. J. (1994) Motivation, self-determination and person-environment fit as predictors of psychological adjustment among nursing home residents. *Psychology and Aging*, 9, 189–94.

O'Connor, B. P. and Vallerand, R. J. (1998) Psychological adjustment variables as predictors of mortality among nursing home residents. *Psychology and Aging*, 13, 368–74.

O'Connor, T. G. and Croft, C. M. (2001) A twin study of attachment in preschool children. *Child Development*, 72, 1501–11.

O'Hanlon, A. (2002) Exploring, measuring and explaining negative attitudes to own future old age. University of Southampton: unpublished doctoral dissertation.

O'Hanlon, A. M., Camp, C. J. and Osofsky, H. J. (1993) Knowledge of and attitudes toward aging in young, middle-aged and older college students: a comparison of two measures of knowledge of aging. *Educational Gerontology*, 19, 753–66.

O'Hanlon, A. and Coleman, P. G. (2004). Attitudes towards ageing: adaptation, development and growth into later years. In Nussbaum, J. F. and Coupland, J. (eds) *Handbook of Communication and Aging Research* (2nd edn). Lawrence Erlbaum (in press).

Oatley, K. (1989) The importance of being emotional. *New Scientist*, 19 August, 33–6.

Oatley, K and Jenkins, J. M. (1996) *Understanding Emotions*. Oxford: Blackwell.

Öberg, P. (1996) The absent body: a social gerontological paradox. *Ageing and Society*, 16, 701–19.

Ochse, R. and Plug, C. (1996) Cross-cultural investigation of the validity of Erikson's theory of personality development. *Journal of Personality and Social Psychology*, 50(6), 1240–52.

Opinions About People (OAP) (1971) Ontario Welfare Council. In D. J. Mangen and W. A. Peterson (1982) *Research Instruments in Social Gerontology*. Minneapolis, MN: University of Minnesota, 556–61, 598–9.

Orwoll, L. and Perlmutter, M. (1990) The study of wise persons: integrating a personality perspective. In Sternberg, R. J. (ed.), *Wisdom: Its Nature, Origins and Development*. New York: Cambridge University Press, 160–77.

Palmore, E. (ed.) (1970) *Normal Aging I*. Durham, NC: Duke University Press.

Palmore, E. (ed.) (1974) *Normal Aging II*. Durham, NC: Duke University Press.

Palmore, E. (1977) Facts on aging: a short quiz. *The Gerontologist*, 17(4), 315–20.

Pargament, K. I. (1997) *The Psychology of Religion and Coping. Theory, Research, Practice*. New York: Guilford Press.

Pargament, K. I. (2002a) The bitter and the sweet: an evaluation of the costs and benefits of religiousness. *Psychological Inquiry*, 13, 168–81.

Pargament, K. I. (2002b) Is religion nothing but …? Explaining religion versus explaining religion away. *Psychological Enquiry*, 13, 239–44.

Pargament, K. I., Koenig, H. G. and Perez, L. M. (2000) The many methods of religious coping: development and initial validation of the RCOPE. *Journal of Clinical Psychology*, 56, 519–43.

Pargament, K. I., Smith, B. W., Koenig, H. G. and Perez, L. (1998) Patterns of positive and negative religious coping with major life stressors. *Journal for the Scientific Study of Religion*, 37, 710–24.

Pargament, K. I., Van Haitsma, K. and Ensing, D. S. (1995) When age meets adversity: religion and coping in the later years. In Kimble, M. A., McFadden, S. H., Ellor, J. W. and Seeber, J. J. (eds) *Aging, Spirituality and Religion: A Handbook*. Minneapolis, MN: Fortress Press, 47–67.

Parker, R. G. (1995) Reminiscence: a continuity theory framework. *The Gerontologist*, 35, 515–25.

Parmalee, P. W. and Lawton, M. P. (1990) The design of special environments for the aged. In Birren, J. E. and Schaie, K. W. (eds) *Handbook of the Psychology of Aging* (3rd edn). San Diego, CA: Academic Press, 465–89.

Pearlin, L. and McKean Skaff, M. (1996) Stress and the life course: a paradigmatic alliance. *The Gerontologist*, 36, 239–47.

Peck, R. (1968) Psychological developments in the second half of life. In Neugarten, B. L. (ed.) *Middle Age and Aging: A Reader in Social Psychology*. Chicago: University of Chicago Press, 88–92.

Peterson, B. E. and Stewart, A. J. (1990) Using personal and fictional documents to assess psychosocial development: a case study of Vera Brittain's generativity. *Psychology and Aging*, 5(3), 400–11.

Peterson, W. and Klohnen, E. (1995) Realization of generativity in two samples of women at midlife. *Psychology and Aging*, 10, 20–9.

Phillipson, C. and Walker, A. (eds) (1986) *Ageing and Social Policy. A Critical Assessment*. Aldershot: Gower.

Pomeroy, V. M., Conroy, M. C. and Coleman, P. G. (1997) Setting handicap goals with elderly people: a pilot study of the Life Strengths Interview. *Clinical Rehabilitation*, 11, 156–61.

Poon, L. W., Jang, Y., Reynolds, S. G. and McCarthy, E. (2005) Profiles of the oldest-old. In Johnson, M., Bengtson, V. L., Coleman, P. G. and Kirkwood, T. (eds) *Handbook of Age and Ageing*. Cambridge: Cambridge University Press (in press).

Poon, L. W., Sweaney, A. L., Clayton, G. M., Merriam, S. B., Martin, P., Pless, B. S., Johnson, M. A., Thielman, S. B. and Courtenay, B. C. (1992) The Georgia Centenarian Study. *International Journal of Aging and Human Development*, 34, 1–17.

Prince, M. J., Harwood, R. H., Blizard, R. A., Thomas, A. and Mann, A. H. (1997) Impairment, disability and handicap as risk factors for depression in old age. The Gospel Oak Project V. *Psychological Medicine*, 27, 311–21.

Prosser, J. and McArdle, P. (1996) The changing mental health of children and adolescents: evidence for a deterioration? *Psychological Medicine*, 26, 715–25.

Pruyser, P. W. (1975) Aging: downward, upward or forward? In Hiltner, S. (ed.) *Towards a Theology of Aging*. New York: Human Sciences Press, 102–18.

Quirouette, C. and Pushkar, D. (1999) Views of future aging among middle-aged, university educated women. *Canadian Journal on Aging*, 18 (2), 236–58.

Ram-Prasad, C. (1995) A classical Indian philosophical perspective on ageing and the meaning of life. *Ageing and Society*, 15, 1–36.

Randall, W. L. and Kenyon, G. M. (2001) *Ordinary Wisdom. Biographical Aging and the Journey of Life*. Westport, CT: Praeger.

Ranzijn, R., Keeves, J., Luszcz, M. and Feather, N. T. (1998) The role of self-perceived usefulness and competence in the self-esteem of elderly adults: confirmatory factor analyses of the Bachman revision of Rosenberg's Self-Esteem scale. *Journal of Gerontology: Psychological Sciences*, 33B, P96–P104.

Raphael, B., Middleton, W., Marinek, N. and Misso, V. (1993) Counselling and therapy of the bereaved. In Stroebe, M. S., Stroebe, W. and Hansson, R. O. (eds) *The Handbook of Bereavement: Theory, Research and Intervention*. New York: Cambridge University Press, 427–53.

Reed, J. and Payton, R. K. (1996) Constructing familiarity and managing the self: ways of adapting to life in nursing and residential homes for older people. *Ageing and Society*, 16, 543–60.

Reed, J., Cook, G., Sullivan, A. and Burridge, C. (2003) Making a move: care-home residents' experiences of relocation. *Ageing and Society*, 23, 225–41.

Reich, J. W. and Zautra, A. J. (1990) Dispositional control beliefs and the consequences of a control-enhancing intervention. *Journal of Gerontology*, 45, 46–51.

Reker, G. T. (1999) *Manual of the Life Attitude Profile* (revised edn). Peterborough, Ontario, Canada: Student Psychologists Press.

Reker, G. T. and Chamberlain, K. (2000) *Exploring Existential Meaning. Optimizing Human Development across the Life Span*. Thousand Oaks, CA: Sage.

Reker, G. T. and Wong, P. T. P. (1988) Aging as an individual process: toward a theory of personal meaning. In Birren, J. E. and Bengtson, V. L. (eds) *Emergent Theories of Aging*. New York: Springer, 214–46.

Riley, M. W. (1973) Aging and cohort succession: interpretations and misinterpretations. *Public Opinion Quarterly*, 37, 35–49.

Riley, M. W., Foner, A. and Riley, J. W. Jr (1999) The aging and society paradigm. In Bengtson, V. L. and Schaie, K. W. (eds) *Handbook of Theories of Aging*. New York: Springer, 327–43.

4

Robb, B. (1967) *Sans Everything – A Case to Answer*. London: Nelson.

Roberts, B. L., Dunkle, R., and Haug, M. (1994) Physical, psychological, and social resources as moderators of the relationship of stress to mental health of the very old. *Journal of Gerontology: Social Sciences*, 49, S35–S43.

Robins, W., Trzesniewski, K. H., Tracy, J. L., Gosling, S. D. and Potter, J. (2002) Global self-esteem across the life-span. *Psychology and Aging*, 17, 423–34.

Rodin, J. (1986) Aging and health: effects of the sense of control. *Science*, 233, 1271–6.

Rodin, J. and Langer, E. J. (1977) Long-term effects of a control-relevant intervention with the institutionalized aged. *Journal of Personality and Social Psychology*, 35, 897–902.

Rodin, J., Timko, C. and Harris, S. (1985) The construct of control: biological and psychosocial correlates. In Eisdorfer, C., Lawton, M. P. and Maddox, G. L. (eds) *Annual Review of Gerontology and Geriatrics*. Vol. 5. New York: Springer, 3–55.

Rosel, N. (1988) Clarification and application of Erik Erikson's eighth stage of man. *International Journal of Aging and Human Development*, 27, 11–23.

Rosencranz, H. A and McNevin, M. A. (1969) A factor analysis of attitudes toward the aged. *The Gerontologist*, 9, 55–9.

Rothbaum, F., Weisz, J. R. and Snyder, S. S. (1982) Changing the world and changing the self: a two-process model of perceived control. *Journal of Personality and Social Psychology*, 42, 5–37.

Rott, C. and Thomae, H. (1991) Coping in a longitudinal perspective: findings from the Bonn Longitudinal Study on Aging. *Journal of Cross-Cultural Gerontology*, 6, 23–40.

Rowe, J. W. and Kahn, R. L. (1998) *Successful Aging*. New York: Pantheon.

Runyan, W. M. (1984) *Life Histories and Psychobiography: Explorations in Theory and Method*. New York: Oxford University Press.

Runyan, W. M. (1997) The study of individual lives. In Hogan, R., Johnson, J. and Briggs, S. (eds) *Handbook of Personality Psychology*. San Diego: Academic Press, 41–69.

Ruth, J.-E. (1996) Personality. In Birren, J. E. (ed.) *Encyclopedia of Gerontology: Age, Aging and the Aged*. Vol. 2. San Diego: Academic Press, 281–94.

Ruth, J.-E. and Coleman, P. G. (1996) Personality and aging: coping and management of the self in later life. In Birren, J. E. and Schaie, K. W. (eds) *Handbook of the Psychology of Aging* (4th edn). San Diego: Academic Press, 308–22.

Ruth, J.-E. and Öberg, P. (1992) Expressions of aggression in the life stories of aged women. In Bjoerkqvist, K. and Niemelae, P. (eds) *Of Mice and Women: Aspects of Female Aggression*. San Diego: Academic Press, 133–46.

Ruth, J.-E. and Vilkko, A. (1996) Emotion in the construction of autobiography. In Magai, C. and McFadden, S. H. (eds) *Handbook of Emotion, Adult Development and Aging*. San Diego: Academic Press, 167–81.

Ruth, J.-E., Birren, J. E. and Polkinghorne, D. E. (1996) The projects of life reflected in autobiographies of old age. *Ageing and Society*, 16, 677–99.

Rutter, M. (1989) Age as an ambiguous variable in developmental research: some epidemiological considerations from developmental psychopathology. *International Journal of Behavioral Development*, 12(1), 1–34.

Ryff, C. D. (1991) Possible selves in adulthood and old age: a tale of shifting horizons. *Psychology and Aging*, 6, 286–95.

Ryff, C. D. (1995) Psychological well-being in adult life. *Current Directions in Psychological Science*, 4, 99–104.

Ryff, C. D. and Heinke, S. G. (1983) Subjective organisation of personality in adulthood and aging. *Journal of Personality and Social Psychology*, 44(4), 807–16.

Ryff, C. D. and Singer, B. (1998) The contours of positive human health. *Psychological Inquiry*, 9, 1–28.

Sabat, S. R. (2001) *The Experience of Alzheimer's Disease. Life through a Tangled Veil.* Malden, MA: Blackwell.

Sabat, S. R. and Harré, R. (1992) The construction and deconstruction of self in Alzheimer's Disease. *Ageing and Society*, 12, 443–61.

Sarbin, T. R. (1986) Narratology as a root metaphor in psychology. In Sarbin, T. R. (ed.) *Narrative Psychology: The Storied Nature of Human Conduct.* New York: Praeger.

Schaie, K. W. (1996) *Intellectual Development in Adulthood: The Seattle Longitudinal Study.* New York: Cambridge University Press.

Schmitz, U., Saile, H. and Nilges, P. (1996) Coping with chronic pain: flexible goal adjustment as an interactive buffer against pain-related distress. *Pain*, 67, 41–51.

Schoeni, R. F., Freedman, V. A. and Wallace, R. B. (2001) Persistent, consistent, widespread and robust: another look at recent trends in old-age disability. *Journal of Gerontology: Social Sciences*, 56B, S206–S218.

Schultz, R. and Heckhausen, J. (1996) A life span model of successful aging. *American Psychologist*, 51, 702–14.

Schulz, R. and Heckhausen, J. (1999) Aging, culture and control: setting a new research agenda. *Journal of Gerontology: Psychological Sciences*, 54B, P139–P145.

Schwartz, A. N. (1975) An observation on self-esteem as the linchpin of quality of life for the aged. *The Gerontologist*, 15, 470–2.

Sedikides, C., Wildschut, T. and Baden, D. (2003) Nostalgia: conceptual issues and existential functions. In Greenberg, J., Koole, S. L. and Pyszczynski, T. (eds) *Handbook of Experimental Existential Psychology.* New York: Guilford Press (in press).

Seligman, M. E. P. (1975) *Helplessness: On Depression, Development and Death.* San Francisco: Freeman.

Sherman, E. (1981) *Counseling the Aging: An Integrative Approach.* New York: Free Press.

Sherman, E. (1991) *Reminiscence and the Self in Old Age.* New York: Springer.

Sherman, E. and Webb, T. (1994) The self as process in late-life reminiscence: spiritual attributes. *Ageing and Society*, 14, 255–67.

Shock, N.W. (1977) System integration. In Finch, C. E. and Hayflick, L. (eds) *Handbook of the Biology of Aging.* New York: Van Nostrand Reinhold, 639–65.

Siegler, I. C., Dawson, D. V. and Welsh, K. A. (1994) Caregiver ratings of personality change in Alzheimer's Disease patients: a replication. *Psychology and Aging*, 9, 464–6.

Sloan, R. P., Bagiella, E. and Powell, T. (1999) Religion, spirituality and medicine. *The Lancet*, 353, 664–7.

Small, J. A., Geldart, K., Gutman, G. and Scott, M. A. C. (1998) The discourse of self in dementia. *Ageing and Society*, 18, 291–316.

Smith, J. and Baltes, P. B. (1997) Profiles of psychological functioning in the old and oldest old. *Psychology and Aging*, 12, 458–72.

Smith, J. and Baltes, P. B. (1999) Trends and profiles of psychological functioning in very old age. In Baltes, P. B. and Mayer, K. U. (eds) *The Berlin Aging Study: Aging from 70 to 100.* Cambridge: Cambridge University Press, 197–226.

Smith, J., Dixon, R. and Baltes, P. B. (1989) Expertise in life planning: a new research approach to investigating aspects of wisdom. In Commons, M. L., Sinnott, J. D., Richards, F. A. and Armon, C. (eds) *Beyond formal operations II: comparisons and applications of adolescent and adult developmental models.* New York: Praeger.

Smith, J. and Freund, A. M. (2002) The dynamics of possible selves in old age. *Journal of Gerontology: Psychological Sciences*, 57B, P492–P500.

Solomon, K. and Szwarbo, P. (1992) Psychotherapy for patients with dementia. In Morley, J. E., Coe, R. M., Strong, R. and Grossberg, G. T. (eds) *Memory Function and Aging-related Disorders.* New York: Springer.

Spector, A., Orrell, M., Davies, S. and Woods, B. (1998) *Reminiscence Therapy for Dementia.* Cochrane Database of Systematic Reviews, 4.

Staudinger, U. M. (1999) Older and wiser? Integrating results on the relationship between age and wisdom-related performance. *International Journal of Behavioral Development,* 23, 641–64.

Staudinger, U. M. (2005) Personality and aging. In Johnson, M., Bengtson, V. L., Coleman, P. G. and Kirkwood, T. (eds) *Cambridge Handbook of Age and Ageing.* Cambridge: Cambridge University Press (in press).

Staudinger, U. M. and Baltes, P. B. (1996) Interactive minds: a facilitative setting for wisdom-related performance? *Journal of Personality and Social Psychology,* 71(4), 746–62.

Staudinger, U. M., Lopez, D. F., Baltes, P. B. (1997) The psychometric location of wisdom-related performance: intelligence, personality and more? *Personality and Social Psychology Bulletin,* 23, 2100–14.

Staudinger, U. M., Maciel, A. G., Smith, J. and Baltes, P. B. (1998) What predicts wisdom-related performance? A first look at personality, intelligence and facilitative experiential contexts. *European Journal of Personality,* 12, 1–17.

Staudinger, U. M., Marsiske, M. and Baltes, P. B. (1995) Resilience and reserve capacity in later adulthood: potentials and limits of development across the life span. In Cicchetti, D. and Cohen, D. (eds) *Developmental Psychopathology. Volume 2: Risk, Disorder and Adaptation.* New York: Wiley, 801–47.

Staudinger, U. M., Smith, J. and Baltes, P. B. (1992) Wisdom-related knowledge in a life review task: age differences and the role of professional specialisation. *Psychology and Aging,* 7, 271–81.

Staudinger, U. M., Smith, J. and Baltes, P. B. (1994) *Manual for the assessment of wisdom-related knowledge* (Tech. Rep. 46). Berlin: Max Planck Institute for Human Development.

Sternberg, R. J. (1985) Implicit theories of intelligence, creativity and wisdom. *Journal of Personality and Social Psychology,* 49, 607–27.

Sternberg, R. J. (ed.) (1990) *Wisdom: Its Nature, Origins and Development.* New York: Cambridge University Press.

Sternberg, R. J. (1998) A balance theory of wisdom. *Review of General Psychology,* 2, 347–65.

Sternberg, R. J. (2000) Wisdom as a form of giftedness. *Gifted Child Quarterly,* 44(4), 252–60.

Sternberg, R. J. (2001) Why schools should teach for wisdom: the balance theory of wisdom in educational settings. *Educational Psychologist,* 36(4), 227–45.

Stewart, A. J. and Vandewater, E. A. (1998) The course of generativity. In McAdams, D. P. and de St Aubin, E. (eds), *Generativity and adult development: how and why we care for the next generation.* American Psychological Association, 75–100.

Stewart, A. J., Ostrove, J. M. and Helson, R. (2001) Middle aging in women: patterns of personality change from the 30s to the 50s. *Journal of Adult Development,* 8(1), 23–37.

Stewart, A. J., Franz, C. and Layton, L. (1988) The changing self: using personal documents to study lives. *Journal of Personality,* 56, 41–74.

Stokes, G. (1996) Challenging behaviour in dementia: a psychological approach. In Woods, R. T. (ed.) *Handbook of the Clinical Psychology of Ageing.* Chichester: Wiley, 601–28.

Strawbridge, W. J., Shema, S. J., Balfour J. L., Higby, H. R. and Kaplan, G. A. (1998b) Antecedents of frailty over three decades in an older cohort. *Journal of Gerontology: Social Sciences,* 53B, S9–S16.

Strawbridge, W. J., Shema, S. J., Cohen, R. D., Roberts, R. E. and Kaplan, G. A. (1998a) Religiosity buffers effects of some stresses on depression but exacerbates others. *Journal of Gerontology: Social Sciences*, 53B, S118–S126.

Sugarman, L. (2001) *Life-Span Development: Frameworks, Accounts and Strategies* (2nd edn). Hove, East Sussex: Psychology Press.

Sutton, L. (2004) Cultures of care in severe depression and dementia. In Hepple, J. and Sutton, L. (eds) *Cognitive Analytic Therapy in Later Life. A New Perspective on Old Age*. London: Brunner-Routledge (in press).

Tangri, S. S. (1972) Determinants of occupational role-innovation among college women. *Journal of Social Issues*, 28, 177–200.

Tangri, S. S. and Jenkins, S. (1993) The University of Michigan Class of 1967: the women's life pathos study. In Hulbert, K. D. and Schuster, D. T. (eds) *Women's Lives Through Time*. San Francisco: Jossey-Bass, 259–81.

Taranto, M. A. (1989) Facets of wisdom: a theoretical synthesis. *International Journal of Aging and Human Development*, 29, 1–21.

Taylor, C. (2002) *Varieties of Religion Today. William James Revisited*. Cambridge, MA: Harvard University Press.

Taylor, R. J., Chatters, L. M., Jayakody, R. and Levin, J. S. (1996) Black and white differences in religious participation: a multi-sample comparison. *Journal for the Scientific Study of Religion*, 35, 403–10.

Tedeschi, R. G. and Calhoun, L. G. (1995) *Trauma and Transformation: Growing in the Aftermath of Suffering*. Thousand Oaks, CA: Sage.

Thomae, H. (ed.) (1976) *Patterns of Aging: Findings from the Bonn Longitudinal Study of Aging*. Basel: Karger.

Thomae, H. (1987) Conceptualizations of responses to stress. *European Journal of Personality*, 1, 171–92.

Thomas, L. E. (1994) Reflections on death by spiritually mature elders. Omega. *Journal of Death and Dying*, 29, 177–85.

Thompson, P. (1992) 'I don't feel old': subjective ageing and the search for meaning in later life. *Ageing and Society*, 12, 23–48.

Thompson, P., Itzin, C. and Abdenstern, M. (1990) *'I Don't Feel Old': The Experience of Later Life*. Oxford: Oxford University Press.

Thornton, S. and Brotchie, J. (1987) Reminiscence: a critical review of the empirical literature. *British Journal of Clinical Psychology*, 26, 93–111.

Tilak, S. (1989) *Religion and Aging in the Indian Tradition*. Albany, NY: State University of New York Press.

Tobin, S. S. (1989) The effects of institutionalization. In Markides, K. S. and Cooper, C. L. (eds) *Aging, Stress and Health*. Chichester: Wiley, 139–63.

Tobin, S. S. (1991) *Personhood in Advanced Old Age. Implications for Practice*. New York: Springer.

Tobin, S. S. (1999) *Preservation of the Self in the Oldest Years: With Implications for Practice*. New York: Springer.

Tornstam, L. (1994) Gerotranscendence: a theoretical and empirical exploration. In Thomas, L. E., Eisenhandler, S. A. (eds) *Aging and the Religious Dimension*. Westport, CT: Greenwood, 203–25.

Tornstam, L. (1996a) Gerotranscendence – a theory about maturing in old age. *Journal of Aging and Identity*, 1, 37–50.

Tornstam, L. (1996b) Caring for elderly – introducing the theory of gerotranscendence as a supplementary frame of reference for the care of elderly. *Scandinavian Journal of Caring Sciences*, 10, 144–50.

Tornstam, L. (1997) Gerotranscendence in a broad cross-sectional perspective. *Journal of Aging and Identity*, 2, 17–36.

Tornstam, L. (1999a) Later-life transcendence: a new developmental perspective on aging. In Thomas, L. E. and Eisenhandler, S. A. (eds) *Religion, Belief and Spirituality in Late Life*. New York: Springer, 178–201.

Tornstam, L. (1999b) Gerotranscendence and the functions of reminiscence.

Journal of Aging and Identity, 4, 155–66.

Townsend, P. (1962) *The Last Refuge: A Survey of Residential Institutions and Homes for the Aged in England and Wales*. London: Routledge and Kegan Paul.

Townsend, P. (1981) The structured dependency of the elderly: the creation of social policy in the twentieth century. *Ageing and Society*, 1, 5–28.

Treharne, C. (1990) Attitudes towards the care of elderly people: are they getting better? *Journal of Advanced Nursing*, 15(7), 771–81

Troll, L. E. and Skaff, M. M. (1997) Perceived continuity of self in very old age. *Psychology and Aging*, 12, 162–9.

Tuckman, J. and Lorge, I. (1953) Attitudes of the aged toward the older work: for institutionalised and non-institutionalised adults. *Journal of Gerontology*, 7, 559–64.

Umberson, D., Wortman C. B. and Kessler, R. C. (1991) Widowhood and depression: explaining long-term gender differences in vulnerability. *Journal of Health and Social Behavior*, 33, 10–24.

Vaillant, G. (1993) *The Wisdom of the Ego*. Harvard University Press.

Vaillant, G. E. and Milofsky, E. (1980) Natural history of male psychological health: IX. Empirical evidence for Erikson's model of the life cycle. *American Journal of Psychiatry*, 137(11), 1348–60.

Van de Water, D. and McAdams, D. (1989) Generativity and Erikson's 'belief in the species', *Journal of Research in Personality*, 23, 435–49.

Vladeck, B. C. (1980) *Unloving Care. The Nursing Home Tragedy*. New York: Basic Books.

Wadsworth, M. E. J. (1991) *The Imprint of Time*. Oxford: Oxford University Press.

Walker, A. (1999) Public policy and theories of aging: constructing and reconstructing old age. In Bengtson, V. L. and Schaie, K. W. (eds) *Handbook of Theories of Aging*. New York: Springer, 361–78.

Walker, J. and Sofaer, B. (1998) Predictors of psychological distress in chronic pain patients. *Journal of Advanced Nursing*, 27, 320–6.

Waterman, A. S. and Archer, S. L. (1990) A life span perspective on identity formation: developments in form, function and process. In Baltes, P. B., Featherman, D. L. and Lerner, R. M. (eds) *Life-span Development and Behavior*. Vol. 10. Hillsdale, NJ: Lawrence Erlbaum, 29–57.

Webster, J. D. (1993) Construction and validation of the Reminiscence Functions Scale. *Journal of Gerontology: Psychological Sciences*, 48, P256–P262.

Webster, J. D. (1997) The Reminiscence Functions Scale: a replication. *International Journal of Aging and Human Development*, 44, 137–48.

Webster, J. D. (1998) Attachment styles, reminiscence function and happiness in young and elderly adults. *Journal of Aging Studies*, 12, 315–30.

Webster, J. D. (1999) World views and narrative gerontology: situating reminiscence behaviour within a lifespan perspective. *Journal of Aging Studies*, 13, 29–42.

Webster, J. D. (2001) The future of the past: continuing challenges for reminiscence research. In Kenyon, G., Clark, P. and De Vries, B. (eds) *Narrative Gerontology: Theory, Research and Practice*. New York: Springer, 159–85.

Webster, J. D. (2002) Reminiscence functions in adulthood: age, race and family dynamics correlates. In Webster, J. D. and Haight, B. K. (eds) *Critical Advances in Reminiscence Work: From Theory to Application*. New York: Springer, 140–52.

Webster, J. D. (2003) An exploratory analysis of a self-assessed wisdom scale. *Journal of Adult Development*, 10, 13–22.

Webster, J. D. and Cappeliez, P. (1993) Reminiscence and autobiographical memory: complementary contexts for cognitive aging research. *Developmental Review*, 13, 54–91.

Weinberger, L. E. and Millham, J. (1974) A multidimensional, multiple method analysis of attitudes towards the elderly. *Journal of Gerontology*, 30, 343–8.

Wiese, B. S., Freund, A. M. and Baltes, P. B. (2002) Subjective career success and emotional well-being: longitudinal predictive power of selection, optimization and compensation. *Journal of Vocational Behavior*, 60, 321–35.

Williams, R. (1990) *A Protestant Legacy. Attitudes to Death and Illness among Older Aberdonians*. Oxford: Clarendon Press.

Williams, R., Briggs, R. and Coleman, P. (1995) Carer-rated personality changes associated with senile dementia. *International Journal of Geriatric Psychiatry*, 10, 231–6.

Wilson, P. H. (1999) Memory, personhood and faith. In Jewell, A. (ed.) *Spirituality and Ageing*. London: Jessica Kingsley, 106–14.

Wink, P. (1999) Life review and acceptance in older adulthood. Paper presented at the 3rd Reminiscence and Life Review Conference, New York.

Wink, P. and Dillon, M. (2002) Spiritual development across the adult life course: findings from a longitudinal study. *Journal of Adult Development*, 9, 79–94.

Wink, P. and Helson, R. (1993) Personality change in women and their partners. *Journal of Personality and Social Psychology*, 65, 597–605.

Wink, P. and Helson, R. (1997) Practical and transcendent wisdom: their nature and some longitudinal findings. *Journal of Adult Development*, 4, 1–15.

Wink, P. and Schiff, B. (2002) To review or not to review? The role of personality and life events in life review and adaptation to older age. In Webster, J. D. and Haight, B. K. (eds) *Critical Advances in Reminiscence Work: From Theory to Applications*. New York: Springer, 44–60.

Winnicott, D. W. (1965) *The Maturational Processes and the Facilitating Environment*. London: Hogarth Press.

Wong, P. T. P. and Fry, P. S. (1998) *The Human Quest for Meaning. A Handbook of Psychological Research and Clinical Applications*. Mahwah, NJ: Lawrence Erlbaum.

Wong, P. T. P. and Watt, L. M. (1991) What types of reminiscence are associated with successful aging? *Psychology and Aging*, 6, 272–9.

Woods, B. and McKiernan, F. (1995) Evaluating the impact of reminiscence on older people with dementia. In Haight, B. K. and Webster, J. D. (eds) *The Art and Science of Reminiscing: Theory, Research, Methods and Application*. Washington, DC: Taylor & Francis, 233–42.

Woods, R. T. (1996) Psychological 'therapies' in dementia. In Woods, R. T. (ed.) *Handbook of the Clinical Psychology of Ageing*. Chichester: Wiley, 575–600.

Woods, R. T. (2001) Discovering the person with Alzheimer's disease: cognitive, emotional and behavioural aspects. *Aging and Mental Health*, 5 (Supp. 1), S7–S16.

Woods, R. T. (2005) Dementia. In Johnson, M., Bengtson, V. L., Coleman, P. G. and Kirkwood, T. (eds) *Cambridge Handbook of Age and Ageing*. Cambridge: Cambridge University Press (in press).

Wrosch, C., Heckhausen, J. and Lachman, M. E. (2000) Primary and secondary control strategies for managing health and financial stress across adulthood. *Psychology and Aging*, 15(3), 387–99.

Wullschleger, K. S., Lund, D. A., Caserta, M. S. and Wright, S. D. (1996) Anxiety about aging: a neglected dimension of caregivers' experiences. *Journal of Gerontological Social Work*, 26, 3–18.

Yardley, L. (ed.) (1997): *Material Discourses of Health and Illness*. London: Routledge.

Zeiss, A. M., Lewinsohn, P. M., Rohde, P. and Seeley, J. R. (1996) Relationship of physical disease and functional impairment to depression in older people. *Psychology and Aging*, 11, 572–81.

Zinnbauer, B. J., Pargament, K. I. and Scott, A. B. (1999) The emerging meanings of religiousness and spirituality: problems and prospects. *Journal of Personality*, 67, 889–919.

Index

LaVergne, TN USA
26 January 2011

214101LV00002B/14/P